Transformative Justice

Transitional justice mechanisms employed in post-conflict and post-authoritarian contexts have largely focused upon individual violations of a narrow set of civil and political rights, as well as the provision of legal and quasi-legal remedies, such as truth commissions, amnesties and prosecutions. In contrast, this book highlights the significance of structural violence in producing and reproducing rights violations. The book further argues that, in order to remedy structural violations of human rights, there is a need to utilise a different toolkit from that typically employed in transitional justice contexts. The book sets out and applies a definition of transformative justice as expanding upon, and providing an alternative to, transitional justice. Focusing on a comparative study of social movements, nongovernmental organisations and trade unions working on land and housing rights in South Africa, and their network relationships, the book argues that networks of this kind make an important contribution to processes advancing transformative justice. Providing an opportunity for affected communities to articulate their concerns over socioeconomic rights issues, such networks provide a vital means by which existing structures and practices may be contested.

Matthew Evans is a Teaching Fellow in Law, Politics and Sociology at the School of Law, Politics and Sociology, University of Sussex, Brighton, UK, and Visiting Researcher in Political Studies at the School of Social Sciences, University of the Witwatersrand, Johannesburg, South Africa.

Transitional Justice
Series Editor: Kieran McEvoy
Queen's University Belfast

For information about the series and details of previous and forthcoming titles, see www.routledge.com/Transitional-Justice/book-series/TRANJ

Transformative Justice

Remedying Human Rights Violations Beyond Transition

Matthew Evans

Routledge
Taylor & Francis Group
LONDON AND NEW YORK

First published 2018
by Routledge

2 Park Square, Milton Park, Abingdon, Oxfordshire OX14 4RN
52 Vanderbilt Avenue, New York, NY 10017

Routledge is an imprint of the Taylor & Francis Group, an informa business

First issued in paperback 2019

British Library Cataloguing-in-Publication Data
A catalogue record for this book is available from the British Library

Library of Congress Cataloging-in-Publication Data
Names: Evans, Matthew, (Political scientist), author.
Title: Transformative justice : remedying human rights violations beyond transition/Matthew Evans.
Description: New York : Routledge, 2018. | Series: Transitional justice | Includes bibliographical references and index.
Identifiers: LCCN 2018012135 | ISBN 9780815375623 (hardback)
Subjects: LCSH: Transitional justice—South Africa. | Political crimes and offenses—South Africa. | Human rights—South Africa.
Classification: LCC KTL4415 .E93 2018 | DDC 323.0968—dc23
LC record available at https://lccn.loc.gov/2018012135

ISBN: 978-0-8153-7562-3 (hbk)
ISBN: 978-0-367-89548-8 (pbk)

Typeset in Galliard
by Apex CoVantage, LLC

Contents

Tables and figures

Table

Figures

Preface

This book is the culmination of several years of research and writing, starting in earnest in 2010, with the most substantial periods of data collection taking place between 2010 and 2015. The book has its roots in curiosity regarding the role of and potential for land reform in effecting socioeconomic change in post-apartheid South Africa, which was first fostered in 2009. This curiosity has led to a series of related research projects over a period of years, steadily mutating from a concern primarily with land reform and the realisation of socioeconomic rights (particularly the right to housing) in South Africa to various adjacent, overlapping and broader issues. Whilst the research process has been both lengthy and rigorous, this book is not – and cannot be – the definitive end point in addressing the issues with which it is concerned. Rather, this book forms part of a conversation and serves to significantly move this conversation on. Primarily this is in relation to the theorisation and application of transformative justice. However, the book also intervenes in conversations about human rights more broadly, especially in relation to socioeconomic rights and the composition of advocacy networks. The book makes a significant contribution to these conversations, and aims to be of use to scholars and practitioners in putting forward theoretical, methodological and applied developments. Nevertheless, the questions raised in the book, and the answers proposed, are – like all research – contingent and temporary. Just as this book responds to and synthesises earlier literature, and newly collected data, the book is in itself a provocation and invitation for the development of new research, new questions and new answers building on and responding to those presented here. The book makes an attempt to reconcile (or perhaps transcend) the multiple, potentially competing, purposes and priorities of scholarly research engaged with actually existing social, economic and political problems and dilemmas. In making this attempt, the book is, no doubt, imperfect. The book is not an activist manifesto, a practitioner handbook or a wholly theoretical treatise. It is nevertheless hoped that elements of the book will be of use to activists, practitioners and theorists – as well as to those occupying the intersections of these categories. The intended purposes and audiences of a book such as this one are unavoidably contradictory. The hope remains that, despite the necessary limitations, these multiple purposes are achieved to some degree and that the multiple intended audiences are able to make use of (at least elements of) the book.

Acknowledgements

There are numerous people without whom this book would not have been possible. Necessarily, this list of acknowledgements will be incomplete. Nevertheless, specific thanks must go to a number of individuals and organisations. First and foremost, the practitioners, activists and scholars who gave up their time to participate in the research must be thanked. These are too numerous to list, but those who were interviewed and gave their permission to be identified are named in the citations of their contributions when they appear in the book.

Research and writing took place across a period of years whilst based at a number of institutions in various capacities. Thanks must go to these institutions: the Centre for Applied Human Rights at the University of York, the Institute for Poverty, Land and Agrarian Studies (PLAAS) at the University of the Western Cape (especially to Ruth Hall), the Department of Private Law at the University of Cape Town (UCT), the Department of Political Studies at the University of the Witwatersrand (Wits) and the School of Law, Politics and Sociology at the University of Sussex. The International Labour Research and Information Group also warrant particular acknowledgement for having hosted the internship which initially gave rise to the first germs of this research project. In this regard (and for subsequent assistance) Leonard Gentle and Koni Benson deserve particular acknowledgement.

Individual thanks must also go to Paul Gready, Jon Ensor, Rob Aitken and Hanri Mostert for research supervision and mentorship at York and UCT. Lars Waldorf and Paula Meth played critical roles in the development of this book from tentative research project to completed monograph and deserve particular thanks for this. Joel Quirk should be thanked for hosting the postdoctoral fellowship at Wits during which much of this research was developed, for mentorship during this time and for facilitating subsequent attachment to Wits as a visiting researcher, and the University Research Committee at Wits deserve thanks for funding the postdoctoral fellowship. The Sir Richard Stapley Educational Trust must also be thanked for contributing to some of the costs of carrying out the research whilst at York and the Worldwide Universities Network must be thanked for facilitating the Researcher Mobility Programme which allowed research in South Africa to take place whilst visiting UCT.

Additional thanks should go to Colin Perrin, Kieran McEvoy, Harriet Cross, Anashri Pillay, Rebecca Pointer, Steven Robins, Fiona Ross, Sophie Oldfield, Dale McKinley, Ahmed Veriava, Julian Brown, Shireen Hassim, Eric Worby, Alexander Beresford, Andrew Bowman, Dimitris Kitis, David Wilkins, Michelle Hay, Antonio Ciaglia, Stacey Sommerdyk, Anne Heffernan, Yusuf Has, Samantha Hargreaves, Lucy Harding, Kenneth Veitch, Neil Dooley, Lindsay Stirton, Susan Millns, Claire Annesley and Andrew Sanders. In various ways too numerous to document these each supported the research for, and the development of, this book either directly or indirectly.

A version of Chapter 2 has previously been published as Matthew Evans (2016), "Structural violence, socioeconomic rights and transformative justice", *Journal of Human Rights*, 15(1), 1–20. Elements of this book and related research have also been presented at a number of conferences. The organisers and participants in these deserve thanks for contributing to the development of the research which appears in this book, particularly *Land Divided: Land and South African Society in 2013, in Comparative Perspective* (University of Cape Town, Cape Town, 24–27 March 2013), *Gender, Neoliberalism and Financial Crisis Conference* (University of York, York, 27 September 2013), *"South Africa's Democracy at 20: Diagnosis and Prognosis", South African Association of Political Studies National Biennial Conference* (University of South Africa, Pretoria, 10–12 September 2014), *"Contours of Violence: Manifestations, Interventions and Social Justice", 22nd Annual South African Sociological Association Congress* (University of Johannesburg, Johannesburg, 28 June–1 July 2015), *"The State and Study of Africa", 58th Annual Meeting of the African Studies Association* (Sheraton San Diego Hotel and Marina, San Diego, 19–21 November 2015), *"Exploring Peace", The International Studies Association's 57th Annual Convention* (Hilton Atlanta Hotel, Atlanta, 16–19 March 2016) and *Activist Scholarship in Human Rights: New Challenges* (School of Advanced Study, University of London, London, 28 June 2017).

Ethical oversight and approval for conducting interviews was provided at various stages by the University of York's Department of Politics ethics committee (approved on 17 May 2010), its successor, the Economics, Law, Management, Politics and Sociology ethics sub-committee (approved on 30 May 2012) and by the University of the Witwatersrand's Human Research Ethics Committee (approved on 21 November 2014). Further discussion of ethical considerations is provided in the main body of the book.

Abbreviations

AbM	Abahlali baseMjondolo
AEC	Anti-Eviction Campaign, Western Cape Anti-Eviction Campaign
AFL-CIO	American Federation of Labor and Congress of Industrial Organizations
AIDC	Alternative Information Development Centre
ANC	African National Congress
APF	Anti-Privatisation Forum
CALS	Centre for Applied Legal Studies
COSATU	Congress of South African Trade Unions
COURC	Community Organising Urban Resource Centre
DA	Democratic Alliance
DAG	Development Action Group
DLF	Democratic Left Front
FAWU	Food and Allied Workers' Union
FEDUP	Federation of the Urban Poor
ICBL	International Campaign to Ban Landmines
ICESCR	International Covenant on Economic, Social and Cultural Rights
ICRC	Inner City Resource Centre
ILRIG	International Labour Research and Information Group
IRIN	Integrated Regional Information Networks
ISIS	Informal Settlements In Struggle
ISN	Informal Settlements Network
LPM	Landless People's Movement
LRC	Legal Resources Centre
MST	Movimento dos Trabalhadores Sem Terra, Landless Workers' Movement
NEDLAC	National Economic Development and Labour Council
NGO	Nongovernmental Organisation
NUMSA	National Union of Metalworkers of South Africa
PLAAS	Institute for Poverty, Land and Agrarian Studies
PT	Partido dos Trabalhadores, Workers' Party
SACP	South African Communist Party

SAFTU	South African Federation of Trade Unions
SAMWU	South African Municipal Workers' Union
SANCO	South African National Civic Organisation
SDI	Shack/Slum Dwellers International
SERI	Socio-Economic Rights Institute
SPP	Surplus People's Project
TRC	Truth and Reconciliation Commission
UCT	University of Cape Town
UDF	United Democratic Front
UDHR	Universal Declaration of Human Rights
UN	United Nations
WEF	World Economic Forum
Wits	University of the Witwatersrand
WSF	World Social Forum

Chapter 1

Introduction

Introduction

This book aims to contribute towards advancing the agenda of transformative justice. Specifically, it explores the role of networks in advancing transformative justice. Focusing on a case study of a landless people's and housing rights network in South Africa, the book explores the differing organisational forms of nongovernmental organisations (NGOs), trade unions and social movements, their strategies and their relationships with each other. The first aim of the book is to contribute to ongoing debates in human rights and related fields of scholarship and practice regarding the broad dilemma of how networks working on human rights issues should be composed. That is to say, to discuss which actors should cooperate, and in what ways, in order to best promote and protect particular human rights. The second aim of the book is to develop and operationalise the concept of transformative justice. In particular, on the basis of the analysis of network actors and relationships put forward, the book explores the prospects and possibilities of transformative justice as a practical reality, rather than as a theoretical aspiration.

This chapter introduces the case study and background to the book, highlighting the rationale for the research and the research design, and synthesises the analytical framework for overcoming tensions and strengthening networks through political responsibility. It also introduces the concept of transformative justice, which is developed and applied throughout the book.

In this chapter, background and context to the study are provided first. In particular, transitional justice in South Africa is discussed and the notion of transformative justice is introduced. Next, the chapter highlights the relevance of NGOs, trade unions and social movements to human rights and the importance of land and housing issues in post-apartheid South Africa. Following this, the chapter discusses the theory and practice of networks, coalitions and related forms of collective action, including in relation to political responsibilities and setting out how this interacts with the notion of transformative justice put forward in the book. The chapter goes on to set out the aims and objectives of the study and the overall structure of the book.

Background and context

Transitional justice mechanisms such as truth commissions, trials and amnesties covering gross violations of civil and political rights have been put in place in a variety of post-conflict and post-authoritarian contexts. However, these have largely failed to address violations of socioeconomic rights or structural violence (see, e.g., Waldorf 2012; Gready et al. 2010). The emerging concept of transformative justice is oriented around addressing these issues (Gready et al. 2010; Gready 2011a). This is important, as profound socioeconomic inequalities continue to affect South Africa (and other post-conflict and post-authoritarian societies), and addressing these issues is often seen as equally important as, or prioritised over, redress for victims of gross violations of civil and political rights by affected communities (Waldorf 2012; Robins 2013; Duthie 2008; Mani 2008). Moreover, these issues are important in themselves and in relation to their impact on the (re)emergence of societal conflicts, including direct interpersonal violence (Daly 2002; Pasipanodya 2008).

Transformative justice is a relatively young concept and is under-theorised. This study synthesises and applies a concept of transformative justice which develops the existing literature in the area (e.g., Gready and Robins 2014; Daly 2002). Key to this concept is that transformative justice is separate from transitional justice. Whilst the two may overlap at times, with transitional justice mechanisms contributing to transformative outcomes, this book develops the idea that transformative justice requires a separate toolkit from and a different focus than that of transitional justice. In proposing areas upon which transformative justice should focus and in discussing elements of a possible transformative justice toolkit, the book highlights the importance of processes – as well as outcomes – to the pursuit of transformative justice. This has implications for how future research on transformative justice might be carried out and regarding the phenomena with which future research on transformative justice might be concerned. This also has implications for practice, with regard to the ways in which transformative justice can actually be pursued.

The book is situated in the context of the mainstream human rights discourse's increasing focus upon economic and social rights following the end of the Cold War – particularly in recent years – and in the context of ongoing debates about how human rights NGOs and other actors should promote and protect these rights. Furthermore, perhaps in part due to the increasing attention being paid to economic and social rights, the linguistic and methodological framework of human rights is increasingly being adapted to a broader field of application. In recent years, there has been an increase in the adoption of a human rights–based approach and human rights framing by NGOs working on issues such as development and by actors including NGOs and trade unions working to promote and protect labour rights (see, e.g., Uvin 2004; Alston and Robinson 2005; Alston 2005; Kolben 2010). Moreover, a variety of issues and activism surrounding them may be analysed from a human rights point of view regardless of whether the actors concerned explicitly frame their practice in terms of human rights (Keck and Sikkink 1998: 18; Miller 2012). This is the case for many of the issues and actors explored in this book. Indeed, in order for transformative justice to be meaningfully defined and pursued, it is necessary to look beyond the constraints which the mainstream framing of human rights and the predominant focus of transitional justice mechanisms provide (Stammers 2009: 8; Gready et al. 2010).

Transitional justice and transformative justice in South Africa

Since the end of apartheid and the beginning of democracy in 1994, a number of transitional justice mechanisms have been employed in South Africa. Principally, these include the Truth and Reconciliation Commission (TRC) as well as both an amnesty process and some recommended prosecutions for apartheid-era political crimes (International Center for Transitional Justice n.d.). The South African model of transitional justice – particularly the TRC – has been held up as a successful and praiseworthy example and has been used as the basis for similar models in other post-conflict and post-authoritarian contexts (Tarrow 2005: 183–192; Robins 2008: 2). However, broadening the focus from truth commissions and trials to issues of societal transformation provides a lens through which the South African model may be seen as less successful (Gibson 2006). Steven Robins, for instance, posits that the whilst there have been "considerable gains" in the realisation of civil and political rights in post-apartheid South Africa, concurrent gains with regard to economic and social rights have not been evident (Robins 2005: 2).

Chapter 2 in particular sets out the ways in which the realisation of socioeconomic rights in South Africa is affected by structural violence. Here it is worth emphasising that structural violence contributes to, compounds and exists alongside persistent direct and interpersonal violence. On the one hand, the conflict between the apartheid state and armed liberation movements has come to an end. This might suggest that there is at least negative peace (as in an end to direct violence) in South Africa.[1] On the other hand, South Africa continues to be a violent society. High rates of criminal violence persist, as does a high level of sexual, gender-based and domestic violence (see, e.g., Moffett 2006; Kynoch 2005). Indeed, before considering the possibilities for positive peace in South Africa, it is worth asking whether there is even negative peace.

Organised, overtly political violence, at least, has largely come to an end since the transition to democracy. Nevertheless, there are political aspects to contemporary manifestations of violence. On the one hand, strikes and protests are frequently characterised as violent, whereas on the other, responses to these have themselves often been violent (most notably in the case of the Marikana massacre) (see, e.g., von Holdt 2013). Furthermore, in recent years, there have been several eruptions of what is usually described as xenophobic violence in South Africa (see, e.g., South African History Online 2015).

Paul Gready notes that "violence in South Africa was localised, privatised and depoliticised, rather than brought to an end" (Gready 2011b: 11). If there is indeed at least a negative peace in South Africa, it appears to be a violent peace (von Holdt 2013; see also Mitchell 2011). In part, this suggests one reason for considering negative peace to be inadequate. The ongoing presence and impact of structural violence is another. South Africa is tremendously unequal. By some measures, it is the most unequal country in the world (see, e.g., Ackroyd 2014; Bhorat 2015). Moreover, many of the social and economic injustices perpetuated during the apartheid era continue to have an ongoing effect. Negative peace is not enough (see, e.g., Sharp 2012). Furthermore, it is argued here that in order to move towards positive peace in South Africa, transformative justice is necessary. This is because the transitional justice mechanisms which were put in place in South Africa following apartheid have not addressed, and largely were not intended to address, widespread and ongoing structural violence. Whilst there have been a variety of policies put in place with a view to addressing social and economic transformation in the post-apartheid era, it is worthwhile considering these – and the broader political environment – in terms of their contribution to transformative justice. Moreover, the actors engaged in contesting the post-apartheid settlement and promoting alternatives warrant exploration.

At best, transformative justice in post-apartheid South Africa is an ongoing project. The sharp contrast between much of the perceived success of the South African model of transitional justice and the lack of broader societal transformation since 1994 provides a potentially illuminating context in which to study the actions of trade unions, social movements and NGOs. These kinds of actors have worked individually and in networks on promoting and protecting human rights beyond the narrow focus of transitional justice mechanisms. In relation to the case study network, the human rights issues which these actors address have their roots in the same set of (apartheid-era and earlier) injustices which transitional justice mechanisms also seek to remedy. Chapter 2 discusses the conceptual framework of transformative justice in more detail.

Land and housing

Land is a particularly important area of contestation with regard to socioeconomic inequalities and structural violence. According to Tafadzwa Pasipanodya "the demand for equitable redistribution of land motivated people to wage war" in a variety of countries (including South Africa) yet has largely failed to be addressed as a "source of unrest" in these countries post-conflict (Pasipanodya 2008: 390). Land ownership, access and use acts as a nexus in which a variety of – at times competing – human rights claims intersect. There are a number of established and legally protected human rights which can be seen as articulating a right to land. For example, there is a right to property (which may include land) articulated in the Universal Declaration of Human Rights.[2] The right to food (which is also protected by United Nations [UN] mechanisms)[3] may be seen as providing a gateway to a right to land, as this right may be realised through access to agricultural land. Similarly, the right to housing – again protected by international mechanisms (e.g. ICESCR Article 11) – can be seen as a gateway right through which existing structures of land ownership and access may be challenged on human rights grounds.

Land and housing (and human rights issues related to these) are very much intertwined. Post-apartheid housing policies have been criticised both for failing to provide enough housing and on the grounds that housing that has been provided is not adequate (see, e.g., Govender, Barnes and Pieper 2011: 335–342; Goebel 2007: 291–293; Bond and Tait 1997; Tissington 2013; Blake 2015). Whilst some support exists for the government's claims to have made significant progress in terms of the number of houses built (Goebel 2007: 291–293; see also Gilbert 2004: 18–19), it is also the case that the extent of these achievements, as well as identified shortcomings in housing quality, are partly shaped by the approach to land reform which has so far been taken post-apartheid. Moreover, even the scale of achievement in housing provision has been criticised given the extent of the existing housing deficit (see, e.g., Bond and Tait 1997: 27; Robins 2008: 167; Legassick 2010; Community Law Centre and SERI 2013). Chapter 2 explores South Africa's current, largely market-oriented, approach to land reform and the relationship this has to structural violence and the realisation of socioeconomic rights (including the right to housing) in greater detail. Here it is worth noting that, since the end of apartheid, the structures shaping land inequality are largely unchanged and that in order for housing to be provided on well-located land (and to avoid reinforcing existing ghettoisation and apartheid-influenced spatial segregation) a different approach to land reform would be necessary (see, e.g., Bond and Tait 1997: 27; Goebel 2007: 292; Ndabambi 2010). In post-apartheid South Africa, the unjust conditions which historically limited the realisation of the right to housing remain largely untransformed (Huchzermeyer 2003; Bond and Tait 1997).

Landlessness and human rights issues related to landlessness (such as the realisation of the right to housing) impact upon the praxis of trade unions, NGOs and social movements in a range of different contexts. Actors working on a variety of different issues and from a range of different perspectives are affected by landlessness. For instance, this includes groups which explicitly adopt human rights framings when working on issues to do with evictions, housing, tenure or food as well as those that adopt alternative linguistic and discursive frameworks such as development, anti-poverty, social justice or political emancipation framings. Land inequalities and landlessness are particularly relevant to the study of transformative justice (Gready et al. 2010). This is particularly the case given the necessary focus of transformative justice on structural violence and upon the socioeconomic inequalities which transitional justice mechanisms do not address. Moreover, addressing access to land and land inequalities remain key issues in many post-conflict and post-authoritarian contexts beyond South Africa (see, e.g., Pasipanodya 2008: 390).

In South Africa, social movements of landless people and shack dwellers have emerged in the post-apartheid period in sharp opposition to the African National

Congress (ANC) and, indeed, (often) to participation in electoral politics (see, e.g., War on Want n.d.). The fact that collective action by landless people in South Africa has taken place outside of the formal political sphere and is not well supported by a major political party contrasts with the experiences of landless peoples' movements in other contexts. In Brazil, for example, the Landless Workers' Movement (MST) is known to have had a close relationship with the (ruling from 2003 to 2016) Workers' Party (PT) (Hochstedler 2004: 10–11; Vergara-Camus 2009: 179). Whilst authoritarian rule in South Africa ended long enough ago for many aspects of transition to democracy to take place, as noted earlier, the effects of apartheid are still clear to see with wider societal transformation yet to occur. South Africa, therefore, occupies a space in which the effects of authoritarian rule as well as the effects of post-transition policies can be explored in relation to their influence on contemporary politics. In relation to landlessness, this means that South Africa is useful as a case study, as it is possible to compare and contrast the actions of social movements, NGOs and trade unions in the present with that of the earlier stages of post-apartheid transition, and indeed these actors' approaches and relationships during the (still comparatively recent) apartheid period. This, in turn, invites further comparison with and lessons to be drawn for other post-conflict and post-authoritarian contexts where the potential for transformative justice might be considered.

Advocacy networks

This book focuses on a case study of a South African landless people's and housing rights network. In their highly influential book *Activists beyond Borders: Advocacy Networks in International Politics*, Margaret Keck and Kathryn Sikkink argue that up to the late 1960s, networks did not appear to be major actors in fields such as human rights, labour and environmental campaigning but that by the early 1990s, a large number of transnational networks could be seen to be operating in these areas (Keck and Sikkink 1998: ix, 10–11).[4] Keck and Sikkink explain the increase in number and the contemporary pervasiveness of this kind of transnational collective action with reference to late twentieth century developments in communication technologies such as fax and email and the influence these have had on precipitating growth and effectiveness in transnational collective action (Keck and Sikkink 1998: 18–22). The end of the Cold War also precipitated new opportunities for transnational action which had previously been difficult to coordinate across cultures separated by Eastern or Western ideological influence (Keck and Sikkink 1998: 18–22). Furthermore, it has been argued that the rise of neoliberal globalisation in recent decades has both encouraged the formation of transnational networks by creating a new space for the emergence of a "global civil society" and has necessitated transnational collective mobilisation as a counter-hegemonic bloc (Baillie Smith and Jenkins 2011; Larmer, Dwyer and Zeilig 2009: 42–44).

Keck and Sikkink identify the groups they focus upon as "networks" (1998: 4), whereas other authors also refer to "coalitions" or "alliances" (see, e.g., Khagram,

Riker and Sikkink 2002: 6–10; Tarrow 2005: 163–165; Hubert 2004; Larmer, Dwyer and Zeilig 2009; Nelson and Dorsey 2008: 125–164). These are contrasted with transnational social movements, which imply a unity of purpose and organisational form which is not present in a network (or coalition) of separate actors (Khagram, Riker and Sikkink 2002: 6–10). That is to say, transnational social movements are characterised by joint mobilisation of members, and it is not easy to distinguish between the movement as a whole and its constituent actors (Khagram, Riker and Sikkink 2002: 6–10). In the case study, this book focuses upon collective action more closely definable as networks and coalitions than as movements. For the purposes of this book, networks and coalitions will for the most part be considered as analogous. This is as it seeks to explore collective action taken by different actors working together. Both networks and coalitions undertake this kind of action (whereas movements may more readily be analysed as single actors), and the distinction between a less formal network and a more formal coalition is often contested and hard to define (Tarrow 2005: 168; Keck and Sikkink 1998: 4; Khagram, Riker and Sikkink 2002: 9).[5] In any case, Keck and Sikkink suggest that there has been an increasing trend for collective action to be defined as taking the form of a network by the participants themselves (1998: 4). With this self-definition comes an associated set of expectations about the kind of actions the network takes and about the form of engagement between participants. In part, through reference to the case study of a domestic South African land and housing rights network, this book seeks to question and interrogate these expectations.

Action taken by networks

Keck and Sikkink identify four main fields of action utilised by networks. These are "information politics", "symbolic politics", "leverage politics" and "accountability politics" (1998: 16). Information politics is the generation and distribution of useful information (Keck and Sikkink 1998: 16, 18–22).[6] Symbolic politics is the use of stories and symbols in order to communicate the reality of a situation to disparate audiences (Keck and Sikkink 1998: 16, 22–23).[7] Leverage politics is the use of powerful actors to add influence to the causes of weaker members of a network (Keck and Sikkink 1998: 16, 23–24).[8] Accountability politics is mobilisation around holding a powerful actor to prior commitments (Keck and Sikkink 1998: 16, 24–25). This would include much of the naming and shaming activity human rights networks undertake in holding states to their own laws and rhetoric and to international treaties they have agreed to abide by (Gready 2004: 21).[9]

Keck and Sikkink identify the "boomerang pattern" as a method of advocacy made possible through networks (1998: 12–13).[10] The analysis of this mode of action has been further developed into the "spiral model" in an attempt to explain the process by which norms may be implemented through several stages of network action fitting the boomerang pattern (Risse and Sikkink 1999: 18–20; Risse and Ropp 2013: 5–9). These processes would not be possible if campaigning organisations were not acting collectively (Keck and Sikkink 1998: 12). Moreover, transnational action is required for these processes to take place. This is discussed throughout the book (particularly in Chapter 3) in relation to implications for domestic networks such as the case study.

Sally Engle Merry's concept of translation and vernacularisation in human rights advocacy has also been applied to network action (Merry 2006; Levitt and Merry 2009). This idea can be linked to the notion of symbolic power, and to the idea of strategic "venue shopping" (Keck and Sikkink 1998: 18). In this context, translation refers to the process by which actors within a network transform information about a cause provided by network partners in a different geographical or cultural location into information that can be understood, accepted and acted upon in their own (or a third) geographical or cultural location. The process by which information and norms originating in other contexts are linguistically and symbolically transformed and internalised by local actors is vernacularisation (Merry 2006). The diversity of actors within networks allows for this process to take place. This adds value in two ways. First, advocacy for a cause may be improved by actors within a network accepting its normative principles, whether in their original or vernacular forms. Second, linguistic and symbolic translation of information and principles may open up new arenas for action which would have been closed if a network had not been in place or translation had not occurred. This can be seen in the opportunities for "venue shopping" transnational collective action provides. For example, the framing – or rather, the translation – of environmental concerns into human rights issues provides the possibility of tapping into new constituencies of support and the possibility of achieving change through alternative sites of power to those that might otherwise have been pursued (Keck and Sikkink 1998: 18).

Structure, composition, capacity and resources

A network must be structured in a manner appropriate to the achievement of its aims. Moreover, to be successful, networks must be considered legitimate and credible actors in their structure and composition. Legitimacy is, of course, a concept subject to a variety of definitions dependent on context and perspective (see, e.g., Baillie Smith and Jenkins 2011; Hudson 2001). For example, where the International Campaign to Ban Landmines (ICBL) gained credibility with international institutions due to the legitimacy attached to states participating in the campaign, the World Social Forum's (WSF's) legitimacy as a grassroots network has been questioned precisely because of the closeness of the Brazilian state to its organisation (Hubert 2004; Larmer, Dwyer and Zeilig 2009: 45). The perception that a network lacks legitimacy can lead to the weakening of the network due to a breakdown in trust between participants. Networks must be legitimate in the eyes of a variety of constituents with different, and at times contradictory, emphases placed on which constituents should be prioritised depending on the aims of the network and the action it is taking at any given time (Hudson 2001: 331–332).

Another aspect influencing the strength of networks, which may appear on the surface to be obvious, is the question of a network's capacity and resources. There are several facets to this. A network's resources can be social, economic or cultural (Baillie Smith and Jenkins 2011: 172). Anything members depend upon in order to participate in the network can be considered to be a resource (Yanacopulos 2005: 97). Most fundamentally, members of a network must have the capacity to communicate and share information with each other and the financial and human resources to carry out collective action. Networks are, therefore, strengthened by their members' ability to access communication technologies such as email and by members' ability to travel internationally (Baillie Smith and Jenkins 2011: 164, 172). This is not a trivial point. Though access to communication technologies and travel has increased in recent decades, it is by no means ubiquitous or equal. In particular, grassroots groups from the global South are likely to lack the same access to these kinds of resources as Northern actors such as professionalised international NGOs (Baillie Smith and Jenkins 2011: 166–168). For instance, it is likely that a network seeking to gain access to and influence international economic and political bodies such as the United Nations, European Union, the World Bank or the World Trade Organisation will require individuals or organisations with specialist knowledge as members (Baillie Smith and Jenkins 2011: 170–171; Hudson 2001: 343–346; Tarrow 2005: 173). It is necessary for network members approaching these kinds of actors to be able to speak the accepted language of the institutions (Baillie Smith and Jenkins 2011: 170–173; Mackie 2001: 188). This applies both in the sense that there may be a need to understand and use specialist technical language and to instances such as the need to speak English (or another working language of the particular institution) in many contexts (Baillie Smith and Jenkins 2011: 170–173). Knowledge and information in these contexts are key resources for networks (Yanacopulos 2005: 97). The more equitable and regular information exchange is within a network, the more politically responsible it is likely to be (Jordan and Van Tuijl 2000: 2055). The greater access a network has to relevant knowledge and the greater its capacity to dispense information, the stronger it is likely to be.

Networks also rely upon the access to and mobilisation of a variety of other resources in order to remain strong. Moreover, the imperative to be able to carry out networked action influences other aspects of the network such as the way in which it is structured and the question of which of the participants' aims are taken up by the network as a whole. For example, in addition to the more obvious resources such as funding for network members, it can also be seen that perceived legitimacy is a resource (Yanacopulos 2005: 97). This is as the capacity to act in particular ways relies upon the gaining of access to particular arenas and on the legitimacy of the network to act in these arenas. As legitimacy in one arena (such as lobbying the World Bank) may preclude the participation of other actors (such as Southern grassroots movements) in a network, there are clear implications for the structure and composition of networks stemming from the network's use of resources such as legitimacy in particular arenas (Hudson 2001: 343). In order to strengthen a network, it is necessary to manage differences within the network over the use of resources. This means that politically responsible networks must agree upon how perceived legitimacy will be utilised and to what ends (Jordan and Van Tuijl 2000; Hudson 2001). Political responsibility is discussed in more detail ahead, where the analytical framework applied in this book is set out, synthesising political responsibilities with transformative justice (see Table 1.1). Before this, it is necessary to set out further context regarding the positioning of NGOs, trade unions and social movements in apartheid era and post-apartheid South Africa.

Positioning of NGOs, trade unions and social movements in South Africa

During the apartheid period, social movements emerged in opposition to the apartheid system. Many of these were aligned with the United Democratic Front (UDF) and forged close links to the African National Congress (ANC), which since the end of apartheid has been the ruling party in South Africa. During the apartheid period, social movements affiliated with the UDF shared many of the same aims as the ANC in striving towards principles such as those set out in the Freedom Charter (Gibson 2006: 18–23). However, the failure of the post-apartheid ANC government to fully implement these principles has led to contemporary social movements (plus NGOs and trade unions) operating across a broader spectrum of support for and opposition to the ANC and the wider post-apartheid state. It has been argued that these actors (especially social movements) have filled a vacuum in political opposition in post-apartheid South Africa since the late 1990s (Ballard et al. 2006: 15). There remain some social movements which engage the state and the ANC to some extent, and some which have been entirely co-opted, whereas others display outright opposition (Gibson 2006). A similar state of affairs exists regarding trade unions. The activities of trade unions, often in alliance with the ANC and anti-apartheid social movements, were central to the anti-apartheid struggle and the eventual transition to democracy (SAinfo n.d.). Indeed, since the end of apartheid, the Congress of South African Trade Unions (COSATU), the main trade union confederation in South Africa, has been partnered in government with the ANC and South African Communist Party (SACP) in the Tripartite Alliance (Congress of South African Trade Unions n.d.). However, COSATU has been critical of many of the ANC's policies in government, and a number of non-COSATU affiliated unions have emerged occupying a range of positions in relation to engagement with the state, such as the farm workers' union Sikhula Sonke, which has taken part in election boycott campaigns (Robins 2005: 9–11; SAinfo n.d.; Women on Farms Project n.d.; Naidoo 2009).[11]

NGOs occupy an important position in the politics of post-apartheid South Africa. With many NGOs having operated during the apartheid era working towards various specific ends and being based on a variety of ideological positions, the same is true in the post-apartheid era. As a result of the different ends being pursued and their varying political positions, there is a precarious relationship between NGOs and social movements, which themselves hold a range of different aims and political positions (Robins 2008: 21–25). This is complicated further by these actors' relationships with trade unions and with the post-apartheid state.

The state is a fact that must be engaged with one way or another. Whilst it has been argued that the South African state apparatuses increasingly overlap with the party structures of the ANC (see, e.g., Pithouse 2016), neither the state nor the party are monolithic. Multiple levels of government (not dominated by the ANC in all areas) and multiple tendencies within the ANC (as well as the presence of opposition parties) lead to different kinds of approaches to and relationships with the state (see, e.g., Beresford 2016; Ashman, Levenson and Ngwane 2017). The dynamics of relationships between NGOs, social movements, trade unions and the state vary considerably and (as discussed in later chapters) can potentially offer opportunities as well as threats to and limitations of land and housing rights advocacy (and, by extension, transformative justice) in South Africa (see, particularly, Chapter 3 and Chapter 4). This may also lead to lessons for other contexts.

Moreover, in South Africa and elsewhere, NGOs often act as intermediaries between local or community-based activism and the formal political sphere at a national level as well as providing links to international spheres of influence through funding streams and participation in transnational networks (Keck and Sikkink 1998: 9). It is, therefore, important to explore the ways in which the action of NGOs in promoting and protecting human rights in contemporary South Africa is affected by their approaches to partnerships with other actors and positions within transnational or domestic networks. This in turn can help to illuminate broader dynamics with regard to the roles of networks and the promotion of transformative justice beyond South Africa.

Aims and objectives of the book

This research centres on a case study of the South African landless people's and housing rights network. Focusing particularly on this case study, the book aims to analyse the paradox of transitional justice mechanisms largely failing to address structural issues and socioeconomic rights. Moreover, the book develops and applies the notion of transformative justice with a view to generating original insights and recommendations regarding the extent to which this can be linked to practice-oriented outcomes and experiences. Whilst the book explores a South African case study in detail, this is used to provide insight applicable to a variety of contexts. A key aim of the book, therefore, is to address the question: can transformative justice be advanced through networks of trade unions, social movements and NGOs in the global South? This necessitates the exploration of a number of related themes and areas of focus (set out ahead), as well as the formulation and addressing of subsidiary questions, which the subsequent chapters seek to answer.

Themes

The book explores the – at times diverging – approaches NGOs, trade unions and social movements have to network action protecting and promoting human rights. The study aims to provide useful recommendations for NGOs, trade unions and social movements working in networks so that they might improve the practice of promoting and protecting human rights – particularly economic and social rights – through engagement with and learning from each other. In particular, the research presented focuses on the relationships between NGOs, social movements and trade unions in networks; the strategies of NGOs, social movements and trade unions with regard to promoting and protecting human rights; and the concept of transformative justice, particularly in relation to the contribution of networks to transformative justice in theory and practice.

Focus

Importantly for this study, a variety of different actors including NGOs, trade unions and social movements take action both independently and in networks working on issues relating to landlessness in South Africa. Analysis of these networks is useful for this research both in terms of gaining an understanding of the relationships between and approaches of the social movements, trade unions and NGOs being researched and in terms of exploring how these relationships relate to the wider project of promoting human rights through broad social transformation in post-authoritarian societies. This represents an under-researched area, as most studies of networks working on human rights and social justice issues have focused upon North-South partnerships, particularly partnerships between NGOs.

In order to begin to resolve some of the tensions identified in the existing literature as existing within networks, studies such as this one are necessary. This is especially the case if reproductions of what Neil Stammers calls the distortions in mainstream human rights discourse (privileging individual over collective rights and privileging civil and political rights over economic, social and cultural rights) are to be avoided in future scholarship on networks (Stammers 2009: 8). The gaps in the existing literature invite the question of whether there could be value added to advocacy on issues such as human rights – especially economic and social rights – by expanding network participation to include groups such as labour organisations and trade unions (see, e.g., Evans 2015). In particular, there is the suggestion in the emerging literature on transformative justice that these kinds of networks, and action around a broader range of rights issues such as poverty and land inequalities, are in need of study (Gready et al. 2010).

Similarly, in order to establish whether there could be value added in broadening network participation, attention must be paid to the reasoning given for networks mobilising on issues such as human rights containing particular kinds of actor. Attention must also be paid to the reasons for networks containing labour organisations and trade unions apparently only (or at least largely) working on particular issues, which do not cross over with human rights networks (see, e.g., Kidder 2002; Hawkins 2002; Thomas 2002). This (and further) research is, therefore, necessary to bridge these gaps and overcome tensions so that a discussion of the potential for new forms of engagement between diverse actors in networks and coalitions may be explored. The case study for this book focuses on a network made up of diverse actors, including NGOs, social movements and trade unions. This focus begins to address and counterbalance the NGO-centric approach of much of the literature.

Furthermore, one tension identified in existing studies on networks is the potential disparity of influence between actors such as Southern social movements and Northern NGOs participating in a network (Baillie Smith and Jenkins 2011; Hudson 2001). In order to move towards resolving some of the tensions this kind of disparity may precipitate, it is necessary to examine not only the ways in which network participants engage with each other but also the overall aims of the network – in terms of both desired outcomes and process. It is necessary to analyse the political responsibilities of network actors, including those which are not Northern NGOs and to thereby develop the political responsibilities framework beyond its existing focus (see ahead, especially Table 1.1). The need for further exploration of South-South network partnerships and networks which are not strongly transnational is also highlighted by this.

Southern network relationships may contain potential not evident in the North-South (and NGO-centred) networks already explored by the literature and may overcome some of the tensions which appear to be inherent in North-South partnerships. As well as the added value which might be gained through further investigation of South-South networks, there is a question over the extent to which the analytical frameworks applied to transnational networks may be applied to domestic networks. The case study for this research is a network with few transnational connections. Focusing on this allows for the testing of the idea that there could be significant overlap between the ways that transnational networks and domestic networks can be categorised, analysed and understood (see, e.g., Keck and Sikkink 1998: 9–10, 30; Tarrow 2005: 164).

Specifically, this research develops and applies the political responsibilities framework, which the existing literature applies to North-South transnational NGO partnerships, to a Southern domestic network made up of social movements and trade unions as well as NGOs. By comparing the reality of the case study network with the ideal type campaigns involving different degrees of political responsibility, it is possible to gain an understanding of how relationships within and action taken by the network might be improved. In particular, the political responsibilities framework is synthesised with the key elements of transformative justice (which are set out in Chapter 2) in order to provide an analytical tool geared especially around thinking through the possible roles and contributions of networks in pursuing transformative justice.

Political responsibility

There is a focus in the book upon adapting and applying the framework of "political responsibility" to the case study network (Jordan and Van Tuijl 2000; Hudson 2001). Political responsibility in networks may be defined as "a commitment to embrace not only goals in a campaign but to conduct the campaign with democratic principles foremost in the process" (Jordan and Van Tuijl 2000: 2053). There are seven aspects to political responsibility in networks, which Jordan and Van Tuijl use to propose a typology of network relationships based upon the level of political responsibility achieved. The aspects of political responsibility are "dividing political arenas", "agenda setting and strategy building", "raising and allocating financial resources", "information flow", "information frequency and format", "information translation into useful forms" and "the formalisation of relationships" (Jordan and Van Tuijl 2000: 2054).

The political responsibilities framework is useful for a number of reasons. In particular, the emergence of the political responsibilities framework from practitioners' analysis provides a clear link between the framework and attempts to address the lived reality of practitioner concerns surrounding network action (Jordan and Van Tuijl 2000; Hudson 2001). The political responsibilities framework presents a means by which potentially problematic dynamics in network relationships may be identified, evaluated and, consequently, mitigated (Jordan and Van Tuijl 2000). The concept "differs slightly from accountability in that accountability has formal obligations embedded within its definition", whereas in networks such as the case study "there are no formal mechanisms to enforce obligations. Thus, to discuss accountability within these networks would be to suggest something that is not yet existent" (Jordan and Van Tuijl 2000: 2053).

This feeds into the analysis of transformative justice processes in the case study network put forward in the book. The book develops the framework, including greater focus on how conflict between network actors might be resolved in a politically responsible manner. Moreover, as Jordan and Van Tuijl's political responsibility framework could be applied to any network, pursuing any aims, the book specifically develops and synthesises this analysis with that of transformative justice. This is so that the case study network may be evaluated in terms of its contribution to processes of transformative justice rather than simply in terms of the political responsibilities of network actors in relation to their aims. The purpose is to assess the network actors' aims, the processes by which these are pursued, the degree of political responsibility in the network relationships and the extent to which these are consistent with or contribute towards transformative justice.

Table 1.1 expresses the possible tensions within networks and the areas which contribute to the strengthening of networks in a matrix. The populated fields indicate how these tensions might be overcome and networks strengthened in each area through highly politically responsible action as described by Jordan and Van Tuijl (2000) and by Hudson (2001). This expresses the analytical framework which is applied to the case study network in the book. In seeking to understand the case study network with regard to tensions, weaknesses and exploration of how these might be overcome (and recommendations for improved practice produced), the presence or absence of the politically responsible action articulated in Table 1.1 is assessed. The populated fields in Table 1.1 express the ideal type benchmark of politically responsible action in each area identified. The analytical framework this provides is referred back to in subsequent chapters and is applied to the case study network throughout the book. Politically responsible action is sought out and assessed, and its absence is explored in relation to how this might be overcome.

Table 1.1 Overcoming tensions and strengthening networks through political responsibility

	Focus	*Aims*	*Structure*	*Capacity and resources*
Hierarchy	Division of political arenas on the basis of recognised expertise	High degree of cooperation between network actors	Formalised or otherwise transparent relationships	Financial resources divorced from decision making
Legitimacy	Campaigning areas decided through equitable exchange of information	Network members' objectives in line and action taken by members in their own political arena	Activities of network members openly discussed and agreed	Imbalances of resources within the network recognised and greater costs borne by those with greater capacity to meet them
Politics and ideology	Strategies continuously reviewed	Transparent goals agreed by network partners	Shared decision making and members' agendas discussed by network	Risk managed according to capacity and resilience of most at risk network member

Research design

For this book, a greater understanding of the ways in which NGOs, trade unions and social movements work on human rights issues, and the ways in which NGOs, trade unions and social movements engage (or fail to engage) with each other is pursued through a variety of approaches. This especially focused upon consideration of the extent to which these actors might contribute to transformative justice. Within the case study, the research is predominantly based upon a series of in-depth interviews with NGO, trade union and social movement actors (activists, leaders and staff members) with regards to their approaches to promoting and protecting human rights and their approaches to partnerships and engagement with each other in taking action on land and housing rights. In addition to interviews, analysis of materials (not always published) produced by (and about) groups and organisations within the case study network was also carried out.

The research put forward in this book is not intended to attempt value-neutrality. This would be neither possible nor desirable (see, e.g., Gouldner 1962; Becker 1967). The book is a piece of human rights research, and within this is intended to advance the agenda of transformative justice. It is through the lens of an applied human rights–based approach and an awareness of the transformative justice research agenda that the data were collected, analysed and presented.

Case study research

Whilst this book presents a case study, case study research is not in itself a methodological choice as such. The actual methods of data collection, the kinds of data collected and the means by which data are analysed are not determined by the decision to carry out a case study (Thomas 2011). A case study is "not so much . . . a methodological choice as a choice of what is to be studied" (Flyvbjerg 2011: 301).

There are two key aspects of "what is to be studied" in a case study (Thomas 2011: 513). Using Gary Thomas's (2011: 513) definition, there is a "*subject* of the case study" and an "*object* of the case study" (emphases in original). The subject of the case study comprises what Thomas, borrowing from Michel Wieviorka's (1992: 159) definition of a "case", calls a "practical, historical unity" (Thomas 2011: 513). This is a specific, identifiable, time-bound "instance of a class of phenomena" such as "persons, events, decisions, periods, projects, policies, institutions, or other systems" (Thomas 2011: 513). The object of the case study is the "analytical or theoretical frame" which the "class of phenomena" provides. The study is conducted within the object and the case (subject) "illuminates and explicates" the object (Thomas 2011: 513). In this book, human rights advocacy networks are the "object" and the South African landless people's and housing rights network is the "subject".

The purpose of case study research is not to examine a representative sample of a wider group. It is not suggested that the results of a case study will be generalisable to all possible alternative cases. Rather, the case study sheds critical light upon the object within which it takes place (Thomas 2011: 514). Critical light is shed upon the phenomena of networks through exploring the South African landless people's and housing rights network as an example of a network. The assumptions and theoretical elements which make up the analytical frame in which the case study occurs may be questioned, reinforced, refined, expanded, or added to in light of the findings of a case study. To be clear, the subject of the case study – the South African landless people's and housing rights network – is chosen not due to any claims with regard to its representativeness or the generalisability of results but is selected precisely due to its status as an "interesting or unusual or revealing example" (Thomas 2011: 514).

Limits of case study research

A number of limits to case study research have been identified, with these impacting upon the utility of case studies to research (and this research in particular) to varying degrees. First, it has already been mentioned that case study research is not concerned with collecting data on representative cases and drawing conclusions which may be generalised across all possible alternative cases. The apparent inability to generalise from a case study has led to the approach being criticised as unable to provide reliable information by those following what Bent Flyvbjerg calls the "conventional wisdom" approach to case studies (Flyvbjerg 2006: 219–220). Further to this, "conventional" criticisms of case study research have suggested that case studies should be used only in preliminary investigations prior to wider comparative research. It has been suggested that a case study may generate a hypothesis but may not be used in theory building as hypothesis testing must occur in a broader study (Flyvbjerg 2006: 219–220). Following Flyvbjerg, each of these criticisms of case study research may be rejected. The "conventional wisdom" on case studies is "grossly misleading" (Flyvbjerg 2006: 220).[12]

The case study in this book

As previously mentioned, in this book, the case study is the network of actors (focusing on NGOs, trade unions and social movements) working on promoting and protecting the human rights (particularly the economic, social and cultural rights relating to land and housing) of landless people in post-apartheid South Africa. This network is a system which is geographically and time-bound as a "practical, historical unity" in contemporary, post-apartheid South Africa. The South African landless people's rights network is the "subject" of the case study in this research project. Networks (more specifically, advocacy networks or activist networks) are a "class of phenomena" (Thomas 2011; see also Keck and Sikkink 1998). The South African landless people's and housing rights network is an instance of this class of phenomena. Networks are the "object" of the case study in this research project.

This book does not compare multiple cases of the phenomena being studied (networks). There is, nevertheless, a comparative element. The case study provides a "nested study" (Thomas 2011: 517). Comparison is made between multiple "nested elements" within the case (Thomas 2011: 517; emphasis removed). That is to say that comparison is drawn between different actors (i.e. different NGOs, trade unions and social movement organisations) which participate in the South African landless people's rights network. Each network participant is an element "nested" within the network as a whole and "[t]he elements are nested only in the sense that they form an integral part of a broader picture" (Thomas 2011: 517). Studying the participants in the network provides interest as these elements make up and shed light upon the workings of the network as a whole, which is the subject of the case study. The network itself is significant as a subject of research in its own right, not merely as it contains the participants being studied. If the network itself was significant only due to containing the participating actors, each actor studied would constitute a separate case study; the elements would not be considered nested (Thomas 2011: 517).

Case selection and purpose

Cases may be selected for a variety of reasons and in order to fulfil a variety of purposes. In this book, the case (subject) has been selected due to its status as a "key case" (Thomas 2011: 514). This means that the case (the South African landless people's rights network) holds "inherent interest" (Thomas 2011: 514).[13] As alluded to previously, this case study has in no way been selected due to any claims with regard to its typicality or representativeness. Indeed, following Thomas's analysis, value is not added to research through cases being selected due to their presumed representativeness. In his words, "the notion of typicality may give an unwarranted impression to any reader that the significance of the analysis rests in the representativeness of the subject. It does not" (Thomas 2011: 514).

The purpose of the case study in this research is exploratory and heuristic as opposed to evaluative or descriptive. Carrying out the case study contributes to theory building rather than theory testing (Thomas 2011: 515–518). The aim of the study is to explore the South African landless people's rights network, mapping network participants and drawing comparisons between the approaches of the network's various nested elements. Through this exploration, based on the heuristic exploration of each nested element of the case, practice-oriented theory is developed and applied in relation to the network. This provides knowledge which is valuable in its application to the nested elements of the case (specific NGOs, trade unions and social movement organisations), the case study subject itself (the South African landless people's rights network) and, more broadly, reflects and sheds further intellectual light upon the object of the case study (human rights activist and advocacy networks).

Research strategy

Substantive research on particular NGOs, trade unions and social movements was carried out through an interaction with a number of groups and organisations over several periods of fieldwork in South Africa between 2010 and 2015. This aspect of the research included carrying out informal scoping of the network and formal interviews with key informants. The aim of this is to compare and contrast the various approaches of different NGOs, trade unions and social movements with a view to synthesising recommendations for modifications and improvements to their approaches. Keeping a focus on networks and the agenda of advancing transformative justice, the aim was to generate data on NGOs', social movements' and trade unions' understandings of – and approaches to protecting and promoting – human rights.

Interviews conducted in person and via telephone as well as both published and unpublished documents produced by actors in the case study network were analysed as data for the study. This included identifying links and relationships between different network actors and identifying common themes (and departures from these) in explanations of the nature and purpose of network relationships and actors' approaches to network action.

Research tools and methods

The data collected was qualitative and was analysed in an interpretative manner. As mentioned earlier, data were primarily collected through interviews. These are largely individual semi-structured interviews, though some group interviews were carried out. In addition to conducting face-to-face interviews in the field some telephone interviews also took place. Where possible, and where permission was granted by interviewees, interviews were recorded prior to being transcribed and thematically coded.

Efforts were also made to ensure research participants gave informed consent for participation and that ethical research principles were maintained throughout. For example, serious consideration was given to the decision to name research participants in the study if they so wished. There are important ethical implications of refusing people the right to be named in research if they so wish. It is imperative in research to treat participants as "subjects not as the objects of research or as a means to an end" (Anthropology Southern Africa 2005: 142). This requires recognising, appreciating and facilitating the autonomy of research participants (see, e.g., Pittaway, Bartolomei and Hugman 2010; Human Rights Media Centre 2006). There is a danger of undermining participants' autonomy if their capacity to decide that they wish to be named is ignored and if their wishes are denied (Tilley and Woodthorpe 2011; Wiles et al. 2006). In keeping with the need to recognise and support the autonomy of research participants including with regard to their ownership of their own stories (see, e.g., Gready 2010; Giordano et al. 2007), this study followed the positions of James Giordano et al. (2007) and of Liz Tilley and Kate Woodthorpe (2011: 200) that "there is a strong case to be made for offering individuals and organizations the choice as to whether their identities are disclosed". Consequently, participants in the study are not anonymised as a matter of course in instances where this runs contrary to the informed, expressed wishes of those participants (Giordano et al. 2007).

Whilst accommodating participants' right to be named in research does not automatically compromise the anonymity of unnamed participants, in certain circumstances, for instance, where multiple participants from the same organisation are interviewed, it is possible that there could be a risk attached to revealing the identities of some participants and not others. It was decided that in the event that there were grounds to believe using specific information would place a research participant (or others) at risk, the information would not be used. In these circumstances, anonymity was prioritised over the desire of some participants to be named. With regard to both the anonymity of participants and the ethics of using direct quotations, it was decided that if it is deemed necessary by the participant or researcher, identifying data would be redacted from interview transcripts. Importantly, when instances of a participant giving consent for sensitive or identifying information to be used occurred but there was also reason to believe that using this information would place the participant or a third party at risk, the information was not used. These principles account for a variety of possible situations, including those where the anonymity of one group of participants may be compromised by revealing the identity of another. Many of these possible situations did not arise over the course of the study. However, some did. It is, therefore, particularly important to note that an assessment of risk took place and a plan for the ethical conduct of the research was in place prior to the collection of primary data.

As the research strategy of this book is to undertake a case study, and the aim is not to produce representative results or results which are generalisable to every possible alternative case, the sampling is not random. A purposive sample was carried out with a view to interviewing groups and/or individuals who are a part of a number of the nested elements of the case. Informants within social movement organisations, trade unions and NGOs were interviewed aiming to shed light on their organisations in relation to the network of actors working on landless people's rights in South Africa. Snowballing was pursued in order to identify and interview potential informants. As part of the purpose of the research is to map the participants in the network, snowballing is particularly useful. If, for instance, an interview with an informant from one participant organisation signposted a network relationship with a previously unknown partner, this could lead to further investigation into this partner and any potential informants and relevant data it may yield for the research project. The sampling was also to some degree based on convenience – the ability to access an informant being a key determinant of whether they were interviewed. Further discussion of the methodology, including regarding the gaps in the data and limitations of the approach taken, is provided in the conclusion section of the book.

With regard to the analytical tools employed in the research project, several aspects may be highlighted here. It has previously been mentioned that this research takes an interpretative approach and is heuristic. The data collected through the empirical aspects of the case study research (interviews and documents) were analysed in relation to themes which were emergent within the data as they were collected and initially evaluated, as well as in relation to findings from the existing literature and a reflexive synthesis of the existing literature and the themes emergent within and across the interviews and documents. Furthermore, methods adapted from social network analysis, including the production of sociograms, were applied.

Drawing upon social network analysis, the book maps the elements of the case study network which were observed. Whilst this research is not strictly a social network analysis, adapting social network analysis tools allows for the data collected on the relationships between different groups to be organised and represented clearly, including diagrammatically (Hanneman and Riddle 2005). This is particularly useful, as once it has been established what the currently existing network looks like (which is done in Chapter 3) it is possible to move on to questions which emerge from reflexive application of the evidence from existing literature and analysis of the empirical data collected with regard to why the network is structured as it is and whether it might be possible to change or improve the network. The use of sociograms in the book to map the case study network diagrammatically is discussed next.

Use of sociograms

In order to produce the sociograms which diagrammatically map the case study network (in Chapter 3), *NetDraw* computer software was used (Borgatti 2002). This produces images of networks based on relationship information which can be described in matrices. For the simple sociograms used in this book, it is necessary to input a matrix listing network actors in a column followed by a row of each actor to which they are linked (Hanneman and Riddle 2005; Borgatti 2002).

The diagrams of the network in this book are simple sociograms. This means they do not plot directionality or reciprocity of relationships and do not differentiate between different kinds of links between actors in the diagrams. In more complex sociograms (which are not used in this book), differentiation would be made (e.g., through adding directional arrowheads to lines linking network nodes) between reciprocated and unreciprocated relationships (Hanneman and Riddle 2005). It is also possible to differentiate between different kinds of relationship diagrammatically, for instance by using different coloured or shaped lines and arrows (Hanneman and Riddle 2005).

However, for the purposes of this book, it is not necessary to use sociograms to analyse in detail the different kinds of relationships or the extent to which they are reciprocated. Indeed, with regard to many of the relationships in the case study network, it would not make sense to discuss reciprocity, as the links described are not of the sort which can be one sided. Moreover, the purpose of using sociograms to depict the case study network is to present an overall map of links between the network actors rather than to disaggregate the data according to the variety of relationship. For the purposes of this book, it is useful to see the shape and extent of the network presented diagrammatically in broad terms whilst the detail and specific characteristics of relationships within the network can better be discussed textually.

Scope and contribution of the study

There is a large body of work in human rights scholarship exploring transnational collective action and networks in relation to transitional justice. The actions and influence of networks involved in precipitating the arrest of General Pinochet are particularly well documented (see, e.g., Roht-Arriaza 2005). In (relatively) more recent years especially, there has been a trend towards exploring the implications of transnational collective action and the application of models such as the boomerang pattern and spiral model in relation to transitional justice in post-war and post-authoritarian contexts such as Chile and Argentina (see, e.g., Lutz and Sikkink 2001; Sikkink and Walling 2006). These works largely focus upon trials and the impacts networks can have upon legal processes in transitional justice. These kinds of processes are by their nature narrowly centred on the law. Moreover, transitional justice instruments – such as the trials analysed by Kathryn Sikkink and Carrie Booth Walling (2006), as well as truth commissions – tend to deal with only a narrow set of human rights, focusing particularly on civil and political rights to do with bodily integrity (disappearances and torture for example) (see, e.g., Gready 2011a). There is a recognised gap in the literature with regard to the role of human rights networks in promoting economic, social and cultural rights. Furthermore, there is a particular lack of existing study exploring the role networks could take in more holistic forms of transformative (rather than transitional) justice.

This study makes an original contribution to theory by significantly developing the concept of transformative justice. The book proposes and applies a working definition of transformative justice (detailed more fully in Chapter 2) and makes the case for future research in this area to take account of the considerations proposed. In particular, it is argued that transformative justice should be considered separate to (though potentially at times overlapping with) transitional justice. Key features of a transformative justice approach are identified regarding the importance of processes (such as participation of affected communities) as well as outcomes. Moreover, it is proposed that transformative justice must be concerned with socioeconomic structures and wide-reaching societal changes.

Practical recommendations are also proposed. These relate to the ways in which actors engaged in or pursuing relationships in advocacy networks might strengthen these networks and overcome risks attached to network action. In particular, key practical contributions are made through the findings that ostensibly unconnected or even antagonistic actors may in fact be able to build useful links with one another (e.g., based on individual rather than organisational ties) in order to pursue mutually beneficial goals (these are explored in detail in Chapters 3 and 4). In the chapters that follow, the theoretical framework of transformative justice is developed and applied to South Africa and to the case study of land and housing activism in particular. Furthermore, the book explores the implications the analysis and findings put forward might have for analogous case studies, reflecting on the possibilities for a new agenda in research and practice. Chapters 5 and 6, especially, consider how this research can be developed and applied beyond the case study.

Structure of the book

Following this introduction, Chapter 2 ("Structural violence, socioeconomic rights and transformative justice") discusses the concepts of structural violence and transformative justice, particularly in relation to socioeconomic rights and their interaction with land and landlessness in South Africa. It puts forward a critique of the standard model of transitional justice and proposes a definition of transformative justice which is drawn upon in the subsequent analysis of the case study network. This chapter provides a critique of the scope of existing models of transitional justice and highlights the significance of structural violence in producing and reproducing violations of human rights, particularly of socioeconomic rights. Focusing on the case study of land and housing rights in post-apartheid South Africa, the chapter outlines a definition of transformative justice, relevant actors and relationships for such an agenda, and discusses the kinds of strategies that promise a more transformative approach.

Chapter 3 ("Network relationships, existing ties and opportunities") is the first chapter focused upon discussing empirical findings from the case study. The chapter is focused on the existing ties between network nodes in the case study network and the opportunities for developing new or stronger ties. The chapter analyses what kinds of ties exist between different network nodes. It first attempts to explain which of the various organisations and groups working on land reform and anti-eviction in the urban Western Cape (and urban Gauteng) are linked to each other and shows some of the wider national and international links these groups have. In particular, the chapter further explores the links between actors operating in Johannesburg and the Gauteng province and the links these have to actors in the Western Cape. Following this, it establishes that some groups engage in highly formalised partnerships with others, whereas some other relationships appear to be much more ad hoc, informal or based largely on irregular sharing of platforms and information sharing. The Housing Assembly, which links several community-based organisations and movements such as Informal Settlements In Struggle (ISIS) with the South African Municipal Workers' Union (SAMWU) in Cape Town and the International Labour Research and Information Group (ILRIG), for example holds formal meetings and produces jointly authored materials for lobbying the local government. On the other hand, the Western Cape Anti-Eviction Campaign (AEC) and Sikhula Sonke have both put their names to rhetorically supporting the same campaigns but do not maintain close or regular contact or coordinate action together. The chapter continues with an analysis of the opportunities that exist for new or more effective collaboration between actors within the network.

Chapter 4 ("Threats, limitations and political responsibilities in the network") covers the limitations of and threats to the existing and potential ties between network nodes. The chapter moves further away from the descriptive elements of the earlier chapters and consolidates the analysis put forward in Chapter 3. Specifically, the chapter balances the focus of Chapter 3 on opportunities with a critique. This covers the limitations of existing ties between network nodes and of the possibilities for building new or stronger relationships between nodes viewed through the lens of political responsibilities. Ultimately, a synthesis of the analyses put forward in Chapters 3, 4 and 5 are used as the main basis for the conclusions and recommendations presented in the book.

Chapter 5 ("Transformative justice processes, policies and practice") builds on Chapters 3 and 4, asking, based on the case study, whether and to what extent networks can contribute to transformative justice processes, policies and practice. It considers the conditions for effective network relationships with regard to the effective pursuit of transformative justice in South Africa and discusses how these lessons might apply to other contexts. In particular, the chapter highlights the importance of financial and non-financial resources to effective network action.

The sixth and final chapter is the conclusion of the book. This links the case study back to a number of broader themes explored in the study. The conclusion presents recommendations about how networks of NGOs, trade unions and social movements – specifically those explored in the case study, but also those in other contexts which share similar characteristics – may usefully analyse their existing and potential relationships with other actors in order to be as effective as possible. Within this chapter, there are conclusions drawn and recommendations made about the kinds of decision-making processes which appear to have been most appropriate for the development of effective relationships and for advancing transformative justice in the case study network. The conclusion also features a significant discussion of power. Conclusions are drawn with regard to the instances within the case study network where existing power dynamics between (and within) network nodes hinder effective action. Similarly, conclusions are drawn about when existing power dynamics may be challenged or altered in order to better facilitate networked action. Following on from this, conclusions are made with regard to whether actors in the case study network live up to their political responsibilities. Recommendations are then made regarding the extent to which the political responsibility framework can be applied to nodes within the case study network in order to promote more effective collective action. Key to all of the conclusions and recommendations put forward in this section is recognition of the limitations of different actors' capacities to act due to constraints on access to power and other resources.

Notes

1 See Galtung (1969) for a discussion (and influential definitions) of positive and negative conceptions of peace.

2 United Nations (1948) *Universal Declaration of Human Rights.* General Assembly Resolution 217A (III), 1948, UN Doc A/810 at 71 (hereafter, UDHR), Article 17.

3 United Nations (1966) *International Covenant on Economic, Social and Cultural Rights.* General Assembly resolution 2200A (XXI) of 16 December 1966, Entered into Force 3 January 1976 (hereafter, ICESCR), Article 11.

4 This does not, however, suggest that this kind of action originated in the twentieth century (see, e.g., Keck and Sikkink 1998: 41–51; Sikkink and Smith 2002: 25; David 2007; Nimtz 2002).

5 For example, Tarrow's (2005: 163–164) definition of a coalition is by his own admission intended to be a narrowing down of certain kinds of action which would come under Keck and Sikkink's (1998: 4) broader definition of a network.

6 The International Campaign to Ban Landmines' (ICBL's) use of television documentaries, videos and travelling photograph exhibitions communicating the

impact of landmines, plus newspaper reports of their position in relation to high-profile international conferences, is one example of a network utilising information politics (Hubert 2004: 86–87, 96–97).

7 This has several aspects. For example, the decision to hold the World Social Forum (WSF) at the same time as the World Economic Forum (WEF) is a form of symbolic politics. Attention is drawn to the alternative narrative of the WSF (as contributing to global democracy through promoting ideas such as participatory budgeting) through its symbolic association with and opposition to the parallel WEF (Teivainen 2002; Falk 2004: 44). Alternatively, instances such as the Indian women's rights group Vikalp drawing on traditional myths and dance in order to promote lesbian rights can be seen as utilising symbolic politics (Rajaram and Zararia 2009: 473–476).

8 For instance, the ICBL's use of sympathetic states to influence international opinion was leverage politics (Hubert 2004: 83–99).

9 Keck and Sikkink cite the example of the network of actors mobilising around holding the Soviet Union to its human rights commitments under the Helsinki Accords to illustrate this (1998: 24).

10 In this pattern, organisations which are unable to directly influence a powerful actor such as their own state ("State A") "activate" their network so that organisations within the network in another state ("State B") put pressure on State B and/or third-party organisations in order to influence the actions of State A (Keck and Sikkink 1998: 12–13). This pattern of action makes use of information politics, as organisations in State A share information with network partners in State B, and leverage politics, as pressure from State B and/or third-party organisations adds influence to the organisation in State A's cause. Depending on the specific campaign and the way in which information is distributed throughout the network, both symbolic politics and accountability politics could also be utilised in this mode of action.

11 Furthermore, following a split from COSATU by the National Union of Metalworkers of South Africa (NUMSA) in 2014, a new federation – the South African Federation of Trade Unions (SAFTU) – was formed in 2017 by NUMSA and a number of its allies. SAFTU is now the second largest union federation in South Africa (see, e.g., Webster 2017; see also McKinley 2015).

12 According to Flyvbjerg (2006: 221), the conventional approach misunderstands case study research in five main ways:

> *Misunderstanding 1:* General, theoretical (context-independent) knowledge is more valuable than concrete, practical (context-dependent) knowledge.
> *Misunderstanding 2:* One cannot generalize on the basis of an individual case; therefore, the case study cannot contribute to scientific development.
> *Misunderstanding 3:* The case study is most useful for generating hypotheses; that is, in the first stage of a total research process, whereas other methods are more suitable for hypotheses testing and theory building.
> *Misunderstanding 4:* The case study contains a bias toward verification, that is, a tendency to confirm the researcher's preconceived notions.
> *Misunderstanding 5:* It is often difficult to summarize and develop general propositions and theories on the basis of specific case studies.

Addressing these misunderstandings, Flyvbjerg concludes that these five conventional rules should be altered as follows:

> [1] *Predictive theories and universals cannot be found in the study of human affairs. Concrete, context-dependent knowledge is, therefore, more valuable than the vain search for predictive theories and universals*. . . [2] *One can often generalize on the basis of a single case, and the case study may be central to scientific*

> *development via generalization as supplement or alternative to other methods. But formal generalization is overvalued as a source of scientific development, whereas "the force of example" is underestimated . . .* [3] *The case study is useful for both generating and testing of hypotheses but is not limited to these research activities alone . . .* [4] *The case study contains no greater bias toward verification of the researcher's preconceived notions than other methods of inquiry. On the contrary, experience indicates that the case study contains a greater bias toward falsification of preconceived notions than toward verification . . .* [5] *It is correct that summarizing case studies is often difficult, especially as concerns case process. It is less correct as regards case outcomes. The problems in summarizing case studies, however, are due more often to the properties of the reality studied than to the case study as a research method. Often it is not desirable to summarize and generalize case studies. Good studies should be read as narratives in their entirety.*
>
> (Flyvbjerg 2006: 224–241; emphasis in original)

13 A "key case" differs to that of an "outlier case", which provides interest and sheds light upon the case study's object due to its observable difference to or deviation from what might otherwise be expected. Key cases also differ from those selected as "local knowledge" cases, which rely upon the researcher's pre-existing knowledge of and placement within "one's own place of work, one's placement, or even one's home" in order to provide "intimate knowledge and ample opportunity for informed, in-depth analysis" of the case (Thomas 2011: 514).

References

Ackroyd, Bianca. (2014) Report Declares SA as World's Most Unequal Country. *eNews Channel Africa*, 30 October. www.enca.com/south-africa/extreme-inequality-continues-bring-sadown-says-oxfam-report [accessed March 6, 2016].

Alston, Philip (ed.). (2005) *Labour Rights as Human Rights* (Oxford: Oxford University Press).

Alston, Philip and Robinson, Mary (eds.). (2005) *Human Rights and Development: Towards Mutual Reinforcement* (Oxford: Oxford University Press).

Anthropology Southern Africa. (2005) Ethical Guidelines and Principles of Conduct for Anthropologists. *Anthropology Southern Africa*, 28(3/4), 142–143.

Ashman, Sam, Levenson, Zachary and Ngwane, Trevor. (2017) South Africa's ANC: The Beginning of the End? *Catalyst*, 1(2), 75–106.

Baillie Smith, Matt and Jenkins, Katy. (2011) Disconnections and Exclusions: Professionalization, Cosmopolitanism and (Global?) Civil Society. *Global Networks*, 11(2), 160–179.

Ballard, Richard, Habib, Adam, Valodia, Imraan and Zuern, Elke. (2006) Introduction: From Anti-Apartheid to Post-Apartheid Social Movements. In *Voices of Protest: Social Movements in Post-Apartheid South Africa*, edited by Richard Ballard, Adam Habib and Imraan Valodia (Scottsville: University of KwaZulu-Natal Press), 1–22.

Becker, Howard S. (1967) Whose Side Are We On? *Social Problems*, 14(3), 239–247.

Beresford, Alexander. (2016) *South Africa's Political Crisis: Unfinished Liberation and Fractured Class Struggles* (Basingstoke: Palgrave Macmillan).

Bhorat, Haroon. (2015) FactCheck: Is South Africa the Most Unequal Society in the World? *The Conversation*, 30 September. https://theconversation.com/factcheck-is-south-africa-the-mostunequal-society-in-the-world-48334 [accessed March 6, 2016].

Blake, Michael. (2015) Personal interview, Johannesburg, South Africa, 10 April.
Bond, Patrick and Tait, Angela. (1997) The Failure of Housing Policy in Post-Apartheid South Africa. *Urban Forum*, 8(1), 19–41.
Borgatti, Steve P. (2002) *NetDraw Network Visualization* (Harvard: Analytic Technologies).
Community Law Centre and SERI. (2013) *Executive Summary – "Jumping the Queue", Waiting Lists and Other Myths: Perceptions and Practice around Housing Demand and Allocation in South Africa* (Johannesburg: SERI).
Congress of South African Trade Unions. (n.d.) Tripartite Alliance. www.cosatu.org.za/show.php?ID=2051 [accessed August 31, 2011].
Daly, Erin. (2002) Transformative Justice: Charting a Path to Reconciliation. *International Legal Perspectives*, 12(1/2), 73–183.
David, Huw T. (2007) Transnational Advocacy in the Eighteenth Century: Transatlantic Activism and the Anti-Slavery Movement. *Global Networks*, 7(3), 367–382.
Duthie, Roger. (2008) Toward a Development-Sensitive Approach to Transitional Justice. *International Journal of Transitional Justice*, 2(3), 292–309.
Evans, Matthew. (2015) Trade Unions as Human Rights Organizations. *Journal of Human Rights Practice*, 7(3), 466–483.
Falk, Richard. (2004) Human Rights and Global Civil Society: On the Law of Unintended Effects. In *Fighting for Human Rights*, edited by Paul Gready (London: Routledge), 33–53.
Flyvbjerg, Bent. (2006) Five Misunderstandings about Case-Study Research. *Qualitative Inquiry*, 12(2), 219–220.
Flyvbjerg, Bent. (2011) Case Study. In *The Sage Handbook of Qualitative Research*, 4th Edition, edited by Norman K. Denzin and Yvonna S. Lincoln (Thousand Oaks: Sage), 301–316.
Galtung, Johan. (1969) Violence, Peace, and Peace Research. *Journal of Peace Research*, 6(3), 167–191.
Gibson, Nigel C. (2006) Introduction – Calling Everything into Question: Broken Promises, Social Movements and Emergent Intellectual Currents in Post-Apartheid South Africa. In *Challenging Hegemony: Social Movements and the Quest for a New Humanism in Post-Apartheid South Africa*, edited by Nigel C. Gibson (Trenton: Africa World Press), 1–28.
Gilbert, Alan. (2004) Helping the Poor through Housing Subsidies: Lessons from Chile, Colombia and South Africa. *Habitat International*, 28(1), 13–40.
Giordano, James, O'Reilly, Michelle, Taylor, Helen and Dogra, Nisha. (2007) Confidentiality and Autonomy: The Challenge(s) of Offering Research Participants a Choice of Disclosing Their Identity. *Qualitative Health Research*, 17(2), 264–275.
Goebel, Allison. (2007) Sustainable Urban Development? Low-Cost Housing Challenges in South Africa. *Habitat International*, 31(3/4), 291–293.
Gouldner, Alvin W. (1962) Anti-Minotaur: The Myth of a Value-Free Sociology. *Social Problems*, 9(3), 199–213.
Govender, Thashlin, Barnes, Jo M. and Pieper, Clarissa H. (2011) Housing Conditions, Sanitation Status and Associated Health Risks in Selected Subsidized Low-Cost Housing Settlements in Cape Town, South Africa. *Habitat International*, 35(2), 335–342.
Gready, Paul. (2004) Introduction. In *Fighting for Human Rights*, edited by Paul Gready (London: Routledge), 1–32.

Gready, Paul. (2010) Introduction: "Responsibility to the Story". *Journal of Human Rights Practice*, 2(2), 177–190.

Gready, Paul. (2011a) Transformative Justice. (Unpublished paper presented at "Transformative Justice: Global Perspectives", Worldwide Universities Network International Conference, University of Leeds, Leeds, 12 May).

Gready, Paul. (2011b) *The Era of Transitional Justice: The Aftermath of the Truth and Reconciliation Commission in South Africa and Beyond* (Abingdon: Routledge).

Gready, Paul, Boesten, Jelke, Crawford, Gordon and Wilding, Polly. (2010) *Transformative Justice: A Concept Note*. Draft Concept Note Developed by the Worldwide Universities Network Transformative Justice Group, October.

Gready, Paul and Robins, Simon. (2014) From Transitional to Transformative Justice: A New Agenda for Practice. *International Journal of Transitional Justice*, 8(3), 339–361.

Hanneman, Robert A. and Riddle, Mark. (2005) *Introduction to Social Network Methods* (Riverside: University of California, Riverside).

Hawkins, Darren. (2002) Human Rights in US Foreign Policy. In *Restructuring World Politics: Transnational Social Movements, Networks, and Norms*, edited by Sanjeev Khagram, James V. Riker and Kathryn Sikkink (Minneapolis: University of Minnesota Press), 71–95.

Hochstedler, Kathryn. (2004) *Civil Society in Lula's Brazil*. Working Paper 57, Centre for Brazilian Studies, University of Oxford (Oxford: University of Oxford).

Hubert, Don. (2004) "New" Humanitarian Advocacy? Civil Society and the Landmines Ban. In *Fighting for Human Rights*, edited by Paul Gready (London: Routledge), 78–103.

Huchzermeyer, Marie. (2003) A Legacy of Control? The Capital Subsidy for Housing, and Informal Settlement Intervention in South Africa. *International Journal of Urban and Regional Research*, 27(3), 591–612.

Hudson, Alan. (2001) NGOs' Transnational Advocacy Networks: From "Legitimacy" to "Political Responsibility"? *Global Networks*, 1(4), 331–352.

Human Rights Media Centre. (2006) *The Story Is Yours, the Choice Is Yours: Media Ethics for Storytellers* (Cape Town: Human Rights Media Centre).

International Center for Transitional Justice. (n.d.) South Africa. http://ictj.org/our-work/regions-and-countries/south-africa [accessed August 31, 2011].

Jordan, Lisa and Van Tuijl, Peter. (2000) Political Responsibility in Transnational NGO Advocacy. *World Development*, 28(12), 2051–2065.

Keck, Margaret E. and Sikkink, Kathryn. (1998) *Activists beyond Borders: Advocacy Networks in International Politics* (Ithaca: Cornell University Press).

Khagram, Sanjeev, Riker, James V. and Sikkink, Kathryn. (2002) From Santiago to Seattle: Transnational Advocacy Groups Restructuring World Politics. In *Restructuring World Politics: Transnational Social Movements, Networks, and Norms*, edited by Sanjeev Khagram, James V. Riker and Kathryn Sikkink (Minneapolis: University of Minnesota Press), 3–23.

Kidder, Thalia G. (2002) Networks in Transnational Labor Organizing. In *Restructuring World Politics: Transnational Social Movements, Networks, and Norms*, edited by Sanjeev Khagram, James V. Riker and Kathryn Sikkink (Minneapolis: University of Minnesota Press), 269–298.

Kolben, Kevin. (2010) Labor Rights as Human Rights? *Virginia Journal of International Law*, 50(2), 449–484.

Kynoch, Gary. (2005) Crime, Conflict and Politics in Transition-Era South Africa. *African Affairs*, 104(416), 493–514.
Larmer, Miles, Dwyer, Peter and Zeilig, Leo. (2009) Southern African Social Movements at the 2007 Nairobi World Social Forum. *Global Networks*, 9(1), 41–62.
Legassick, Martin. (2010) Personal interview, Cape Town, South Africa, 4 August.
Levitt, Peggy and Merry, Sally. (2009) Vernacularization on the Ground: Local Uses of Global Women's Rights in Peru, China, India and the United States. *Global Networks*, 9(4), 441–461.
Lutz, Ellen and Sikkink, Kathryn. (2001) The Justice Cascade: The Evolution and Impact of Foreign Human Rights Trials in Latin America. *Chicago Journal of International Law*, 2(1), 1–33.
Mackie, Vera. (2001) The Language of Globalization, Transnationality and Feminism. *International Feminist Journal of Politics*, 3(2), 180–206.
Mani, Rama. (2008) Dilemmas of Expanding Transitional Justice, or Forging the Nexus between Transitional Justice and Development. *International Journal of Transitional Justice*, 2(3), 253–265.
McKinley, Dale T. (2015) Labor-Community Alliances in South Africa: Reclaiming (Some of) the Past, Inventing the Future? *The South Atlantic Quarterly*, 114(2), 457–466.
Merry, Sally Engle. (2006) Transnational Human Rights and Local Activism: Mapping the Middle. *American Anthropologist*, 108(1), 38–51.
Miller, Hannah. (2012) A Change in Charity Law for England and Wales: Examining War on Want's Foremost Adoption of the New Human Rights Charitable Purpose. *International Journal of Human Rights*, 16(7), 1003–1022.
Mitchell, Audra. (2011) *Lost in Transformation: Violent Peace and Peaceful Conflict in Northern Ireland* (Basingstoke: Palgrave Macmillan).
Moffett, Helen. (2006) "These Women, They Force Us to Rape Them": Rape as Narrative of Social Control in Post-Apartheid South Africa. *Journal of Southern African Studies*, 32(1), 129–144.
Naidoo, Yugendree. (2009) Farm Workers Announce Election Boycott. *West Cape News*, 7 April. http://westcapenews.com/?p=599 [accessed August 31, 2011].
Ndabambi, Luthando. (2010) Personal interview, Cape Town, South Africa, 12 August.
Nelson, Paul J. and Dorsey, Ellen. (2008) *New Rights Advocacy: Changing Strategies of Development and Human Rights NGOs* (Washington: Georgetown University Press).
Nimtz, August. (2002) Marx and Engels: The Prototypical Transnational Actors. In *Restructuring World Politics: Transnational Social Movements, Networks, and Norms*, edited by Sanjeev Khagram, James V. Riker and Kathryn Sikkink (Minneapolis: University of Minnesota Press), 245–268.
Pasipanodya, Tafadzwa. (2008) A Deeper Justice: Economic and Social Justice as Transitional Justice in Nepal. *International Journal of Transitional Justice*, 2(3), 378–397.
Pithouse, Richard. (2016) *Writing the Decline: On the Struggle for South Africa's Democracy* (Johannesburg: Jacana Media).
Pittaway, Eileen, Bartolomei, Linda and Hugman, Richard. (2010) "Stop Stealing Our Stories": The Ethics of Research with Vulnerable Groups. *Journal of Human Rights Practice*, 2(2), 229–251.
Rajaram, N. and Zararia, Vaishali. (2009) Translating Women's Human Rights in a Globalizing World: The Spiral Process in Reducing Gender Injustice in Baroda, India. *Global Networks*, 9(4), 462–484.

Risse, Thomas and Ropp, Stephen C. (2013) Introduction and Overview. In *The Persistent Power of Human Rights: From Commitment to Compliance*, edited by Thomas Risse, Stephen C. Ropp and Kathryn Sikkink (New York: Cambridge University Press), 3–25.

Risse, Thomas and Sikkink, Kathryn. (1999) The Socialization of Human Rights Norms into Domestic Practices: Introduction. In *The Power of Human Rights: International Norms and Domestic Change*, edited by Thomas Risse, Stephen C. Ropp and Kathryn Sikkink (Cambridge: Cambridge University Press), 1–38.

Robins Simon. (2013) *Families of the Missing: A Test for Contemporary Approaches to Transitional Justice* (Abingdon: Routledge).

Robins, Steven L. (2005) Introduction. In *Limits to Liberation after Apartheid*, edited by Steven L. Robins (Oxford: James Currey).

Robins, Steven L. (2008) *From Revolution to Rights in South Africa: Social Movements, NGOs and Popular Politics after Apartheid* (Woodbridge: James Currey).

Roht-Arriaza, Naomi. (2005) *The Pinochet Effect: Transnational Justice in the Age of Human Rights* (Philadelphia: University of Pennsylvania Press).

SAinfo. (n.d.) Trade Unions in South Africa. www.southafrica.info/business/economy/policies/tradeunions.htm [accessed August 31, 2011].

Sharp, Dustin N. (2012) Addressing Economic Violence in Times of Transition: Toward a Positive-Peace Paradigm for Transitional Justice. *Fordham International Law Journal*, 35(3), 780–814.

Sikkink, Kathryn and Smith, Jackie. (2002) Infrastructures for Change: Transnational Organizations, 1953–93. In *Restructuring World Politics: Transnational Social Movements, Networks, and Norms*, edited by Sanjeev Khagram, James V. Riker and Kathryn Sikkink (Minneapolis: University of Minnesota Press), 24–44.

Sikkink, Kathryn and Walling, Carrie Booth. (2006) Errors about Trials: The Emergence and Impact of the Justice Cascade. (Paper presented at the Princeton International Relations Faculty Colloquium, Princeton University, Princeton, NJ, 27 March).

South African History Online. (2015) Xenophobic Violence in Democratic South Africa. *South African History Online*, 17 April. www.sahistory.org.za/article/xenophobic-violencedemocratic-south-africa [accessed March 6, 2016].

Stammers, Neil. (2009) *Human Rights and Social Movements* (London: Pluto Press).

Tarrow, Sidney. (2005) *The New Transnational Activism* (New York: Cambridge University Press).

Teivainen, Teivo. (2002) The World Social Forum and Global Democratisation: Learning from Porto Alegre. *Third World Quarterly*, 23(4), 621–632.

Thomas, Daniel C. (2002) Human Rights Norms and Networks in Authoritarian Chile. In *Restructuring World Politics: Transnational Social Movements, Networks, and Norms*, edited by Sanjeev Khagram, James V. Riker and Kathryn Sikkink (Minneapolis: University of Minnesota Press), 47–70.

Thomas, Gary. (2011) A Typology for the Case Study in Social Science Following a Review of Definition, Discourse, and Structure. *Qualitative Inquiry*, 17(6), 511–521.

Tilley, Liz and Woodthorpe, Kate. (2011) Is It the End for Anonymity as We Know It? A Critical Examination of the Ethical Principle of Anonymity in the Context of 21st Century Demands on the Qualitative Researcher. *Qualitative Research*, 11(2), 197–212.

Tissington, Kate. (2013) *Minding the Gap: An Analysis of the Supply of and Demand for Low-Income Rental Accommodation in Inner City Johannesburg.* Research Report, November (Johannesburg: SERI).

United Nations. (1948) *Universal Declaration of Human Rights.* General Assembly Resolution 217A (III), 1948, UN Doc A/810 at 71.

United Nations. (1966) *International Covenant on Economic, Social and Cultural Rights.* General Assembly resolution 2200A (XXI) of 16 December 1966, Entered into Force 3 January 1976.

Uvin, Peter. (2004) *Human Rights and Development* (Bloomfield: Kumarian Press).

Vergara-Camus, Leandro. (2009) The Politics of the MST: Autonomous Rural Communities, the State, and Electoral Politics. *Latin American Perspectives*, 36(4), 178–191.

von Holdt, Karl. (2013) South Africa: The Transition to Violent Democracy. *Review of African Political Economy*, 40(138), 589–604.

Waldorf, Lars. (2012) Anticipating the Past: Transitional Justice and Socio-Economic Wrongs. *Social and Legal Studies*, 21(2), 171–186.

War on Want. (n.d.) No Land! No House! No Vote!. www.waronwant.org/component/content/article/16523 [accessed August 31, 2011].

Webster, Edward. (2017) South Africa Has a New Trade Union Federation: Can It Break the Mould? *The Conversation*, 25 April. https://theconversation.com/south-africa-has-a-new-trade-union-federation-can-it-break-the-mould-76609 [accessed May 11, 2017].

Wieviorka, Michel. (1992) Case Studies: History or Sociology? In *What Is a Case? Exploring the Foundations of Social Enquiry*, edited by Charles C. Ragin and Howard S. Becker (Cambridge: Cambridge University Press), 159–172.

Wiles, Rose, Charles, Vikki, Crow, Graham and Heath, Sue. (2006) Researching Researchers: Lessons for Research Ethics. *Qualitative Research*, 6(3), 283–299.

Women on Farms Project. (n.d.) Who Is Sikhula Sonke? www.wfp.org.za/sikhula-sonke/ [accessed August 31, 2011].

Yanacopulos, Helen. (2005) The Strategies That Bind: NGO Coalitions and Their Influence. *Global Networks*, 5(1), 93–110.

Chapter 2

Structural violence, socioeconomic rights and transformative justice

Introduction

This chapter provides a critique of the scope of existing models of transitional justice (i.e. truth commissions, amnesties and prosecutions). Transitional justice mechanisms have largely focused upon individual violations of a narrow set of civil and political rights and the provision of legal and quasi-legal remedies. In contrast, this chapter highlights the significance of structural violence in producing and reproducing violations of human rights, particularly of socioeconomic rights. There is a need to utilise a different toolkit, and a different understanding of human rights, from that typically employed in transitional justice in order to remedy structural violations of human rights (i.e. those which do not constitute direct interpersonal violence). In this context, the potential for transformative (rather than transitional) justice in post-apartheid South Africa and other post-authoritarian contexts is discussed with particular reference to land inequalities and related socioeconomic rights issues. The chapter outlines a definition of transformative justice, relevant actors and relationships for such an agenda, and discusses the kinds of strategies that promise a more transformative approach.

In exploring the relationships between structural violence, socioeconomic rights and transformative justice, this chapter takes a human rights perspective. Particular attention is paid in this chapter to the interaction between structural violence, landlessness and broader human rights issues in post-apartheid South Africa and to the potential for advancing transformative justice within post-apartheid South Africa. As noted in Chapter 1, this provides a useful empirical case study in which the possible application of transformative justice can be explored. This is an appropriate case study because since the end of apartheid in 1994, a number of transitional justice mechanisms have been employed in South Africa. As mentioned in Chapter 1, these include the TRC, an amnesty process and some recommended prosecutions (see, e.g., International Center for Transitional Justice n.d.-a). As noted in Chapter 1, the South African model of transitional justice has been held up as a successful and praiseworthy example and has been used as the basis for similar models in other contexts (Tarrow 2005: 183–192), whereas taking a broader focus on societal transformation provides a lens through which this model may be seen as less successful (see, e.g., Gibson

2006: 1–28). Whilst many aspects of transition to democracy have taken place in South Africa, the effects of apartheid are still persistent and wider societal transformation is yet to occur. In the context of South Africa, it is, therefore, possible to explore the effects of not only authoritarian rule but also post-transition policies. Discussion of the case study then informs the analysis put forward in the final section and the conclusion of the chapter.

Building a critique of existing models of transitional justice, this chapter first explores the relationship between structural violence and transitional justice. Shortcomings of existing models of transitional justice are highlighted. Next, the chapter outlines a definition of transformative justice and contrasts the approach of transitional justice to structural issues to the approach of transformative justice. This takes place with specific reference to land and related socioeconomic rights. Third, the particular focus upon post-apartheid South Africa is introduced. Land inequalities and responses to these are discussed in relation to the potential for transformative justice as an illustrative case study of how the concept might be applied. Finally, a discussion of relevant actors and relationships for transformative justice is provided and conclusions are drawn regarding gaps in the existing literature and need for practice-oriented research to explore the kinds of strategies that promise a more transformative approach.

Three key debates are highlighted in this chapter. There is a question over how transitional justice mechanisms can better take account of structural, socioeconomic issues and whether these mechanisms are appropriate or adequate for dealing with these issues (see, e.g., Mani 2008). A second debate surrounding how to resolve potentially competing rights claims of the landless and landowners is also discussed (see, e.g., James 2007). Third, there is a broader debate over what strategies and tools are appropriate and likely to be effective in both addressing structural violence in general and addressing inequalities in land specifically which is highlighted in the chapter (see, e.g., Duthie 2008).

The chapter concludes that existing models of transitional justice are not adequate for addressing structural violence and land inequalities or for ensuring the realisation of socioeconomic rights. Transformative justice may address these shortcomings. The case study of landlessness and related socioeconomic rights issues in South Africa is put forward in order to explore this potential. It is proposed that for transformative justice to be achieved, the involvement of a diverse range of actors is required. An exploration of the strategies of and relationships between social movements and trade unions as well as nongovernmental organisations in relation to transformative justice in general and land inequalities in particular is proposed.

Structural violence and shortcomings of transitional justice

The concept of structural violence provides a means of expressing the category of human rights violations which are produced and reproduced by landlessness and land inequalities. This section of the chapter outlines the shortcomings of existing models of transitional justice in addressing these. Following this, transformative justice is outlined as an approach which puts forward an understanding of the links between human rights violations within this category (see, e.g., Gready et al. 2010).

Structural violence

Structural violence refers to a condition in which violence occurs without being precipitated by the direct actions of specific individuals against other specific individuals. It may be defined, in contrast to direct or personal violence, as a condition akin to (perhaps even synonymous with) social injustice (Galtung 1969: 171). It may be conceived of as a form of violence because "violence is present when human beings are being influenced so that their actual somatic and mental realizations are below their potential realizations" (Galtung 1969: 168; emphasis removed). Structural violence has also been explained as being social arrangements which are "*structural* because they are embedded in the political and economic organization of our social world" and "*violent* because they cause injury to people" (Farmer et al. 2006: 1686; emphases in original). Though this definition of violence is broad, in the view of Johan Galtung (1969: 168), it is necessary in order for the idea of peace as the absence of violence to be validly maintained without "[h]ighly unacceptable social orders" being compatible with peace.

This broad definition of violence (to include forms of social injustice as structural violence) can be seen as a logical extension of more narrow conceptions of violence as direct, intended and personal (Galtung 1969: 168). Direct actions carried out by individuals or groups can affect the ability of human beings to realise their physical and mental potential. Structures which promote or maintain particular conditions also affect the ability of human beings to realise their physical and mental potential. For instance, a person's life expectancy may be reduced by an act of direct, intended personal violence or by the failure of a system to provide adequate care for those with treatable illnesses. Similarly, a person may be physically prevented from attending school by another individual or they may be prevented from accessing education due to resources being diverted away from education or towards providing education to a different group of people. Referring particularly to factors which limit access to health care and thus contribute to deaths from disease in Haiti, Paul Farmer (2004: 315) argues that

> Structural violence is structured and *stricturing*. It constricts the agency of its victims. It tightens a physical noose around their necks, and this garroting determines the way in which resources – food, medicine, even affection – are allocated and experienced. Socialization for scarcity is informed by a complex web of events and processes stretching far back in time and across continents.
> [emphasis in original]

Despite the differences in the process, under Galtung's definition (1969: 169), each of these instances would constitute examples of violence due to the outcome in each case being that someone's potential was not realised when it might otherwise have been. As Farmer puts it (2004: 317),

> Social inequalities are at the heart of structural violence. Racism of one form or another, gender inequality, and above all brute poverty in the face of affluence are linked to social plans and programs ranging from slavery to the current quest for unbridled growth. These conditions are the cause and result of displacements, wars both declared and undeclared, and the seething, submerged hatreds that make the irruption of *Schadenfreude* a shock to those who can afford to ignore, for the most part, the historical underpinnings of today's conflicts.

Critique of transitional justice

Structural violence has been identified as an important issue by scholars addressing a variety of related and overlapping fields, such as peacebuilding, transitional justice and human rights (Laplante 2008; Mani 2008; Muvingi 2009). This importance has been highlighted both in terms of addressing structural violence in itself and in terms of addressing structural violence as a root cause of, or contributing factor towards, direct and personal violence (see, e.g., Galtung 1969; Laplante 2008).

Transitional justice has been defined as comprising

> the full range of processes and mechanisms associated with a society's attempts to come to terms with a legacy of large-scale past abuses, in order to ensure accountability, serve justice and achieve reconciliation. These may include both judicial and non-judicial mechanisms, with differing levels of international involvement (or none at all) and individual prosecutions, reparations, truth-seeking, institutional reform, vetting and dismissals, or a combination thereof.
>
> (Annan 2004: 6)[1]

However, in the application of transitional justice processes, emphasis has largely been placed upon a relatively narrow set of tools (particularly truth commissions, amnesties and trials) addressing only "bodily integrity" human rights violations relating to direct, personal violence (Gready 2011). Indeed, such issues as social justice, poverty and land inequalities have tended to be overlooked by or considered outside the remit of transitional justice (Mani 2008: 254; de Greiff 2006: 205).[2] There have, though, been moves towards expanding the focus of transitional justice to consider the impact of socioeconomic structures and be "sensitive" to (if not always to directly address) these, which might otherwise be treated as entirely separate issues relating to development (Duthie 2008).

However, in the view of Mani (2008), expanding the focus of transitional justice to take account of social injustice presents a number of dilemmas, whilst also being necessary for transitional justice to maintain credibility.[3] Drawing on these dilemmas, this chapter focuses particularly on how transitional justice and transformative justice address the nexus of land inequalities and socioeconomic rights.

Recent moves towards transitional justice being used to address socioeconomic inequalities, and the consequent production of dilemmas such as those raised by Mani, have engendered a range of responses. Various means of reconciling transitional justice with addressing structural violence have been suggested. These include allowing further space for the airing of socioeconomic grievances in truth commissions and specifically addressing collective, societal injustices (such as land inequalities) through reparations (Pasipanodya 2008: 392–395). These kinds of suggestions have, nevertheless, focused upon addressing structural violence only inasmuch as existing transitional justice tools can be adapted to do so. This is a shortcoming of transitional justice processes.

Lars Waldorf (2012: 171–186), on the other hand, argues that, even through the limited means of truth commissions and reparations programmes, transitional justice should not attempt to directly address structural, socioeconomic inequalities. Waldorf (2012) highlights that a number of studies (e.g., Robins 2011a) have suggested that in post-conflict societies, victims (including those narrowly defined as suffering direct violence during the conflict) often prioritise addressing socioeconomic issues such as housing, education and basic economic subsistence over the civil and political rights issues usually focused upon by transitional justice (Waldorf 2012: 175). He accepts that "everyday injustices rooted in historical inequalities may be as important, if not more important, for many survivors than the extraordinary injustices" of severe violations of civil and political rights (Waldorf 2012: 175).

Bringing to mind Mani's dilemma over the difficulty in applying transitional justice measures to socioeconomic injustice (Mani 2008: 255), Waldorf questions whether transitional justice can adequately address socioeconomic issues in practice (2012: 176–177). Indeed, he suggests that transitional justice processes are not necessarily particularly successful even in carrying out narrow "bodily integrity" violations-oriented mandates (Waldorf 2012). For instance, truth commissions have been suggested as one of the transitional justice mechanisms which might most readily be adapted to address socioeconomic grievances (Pasipanodya 2008: 392–395). However, the political weakness attached to and the necessarily short lifespans of truth commissions mean their recommendations are easily (and frequently) ignored (Waldorf 2012: 176–177). This is echoed in Steven Robins's suggestion that on the one hand the South African Truth and Reconciliation Commission "became a number one export" whereas, on the other hand, since the end of apartheid "the gap has widened between this bright vision of a 'rights paradise' and the grim everyday social, economic and political realities experienced by the majority of South Africa's citizens" (Robins 2008: 2). Similarly, reparations programmes might be more readily adapted to addressing socioeconomic inequalities than other transitional justice mechanisms.

A lack of easy means of identifying potential beneficiaries for inclusion (or exclusion) in schemes, limited resources and time constraints make it difficult (following Waldorf's view, perhaps even impossible) though to adequately address socioeconomic grievances through reparations (Waldorf 2012: 177–179). The possibility of utilising reparations in order to address socioeconomic rights violations is further constrained by the fact there is little political will to implement reparations in transitional justice programmes, and that in practice reparations are rarely implemented (Waldorf 2012: 177).

The case can be made that "transitional justice is inherently short-term, legalistic and corrective" (Waldorf 2012: 179). This, however, merely describes rather than solves the problem at hand. It may well be the case that the standard toolkit of transitional justice is ill-suited to addressing structural violence and violations of socioeconomic rights. The standard toolkit of transitional justice in fact often seems ill-suited to addressing even the narrow set of "gross violations of civil and political rights" which Waldorf suggests should be its focus (2012: 179). According to Waldorf's analysis (2012: 175–179), transitional justice overpromises that reconciliation may be delivered, cannot address the socioeconomic inequalities prioritised by victims and regularly fails to deliver reparations or follow through on recommended institutional reforms. This does not leave much room for success. Even if other transitional justice mechanisms, for example, prosecutions for gross violations of civil and political rights, are wholly successful, there remains a question over how structural violence and socioeconomic grievances might be addressed in post-conflict and post-authoritarian societies.

Defining transformative justice

A common thread that runs through the emerging transformative justice discourse is that transformative justice seeks to broaden the focus of measures aimed at promoting post-conflict or post-authoritarian justice for human rights abuses beyond that of transitional justice. Crucial to this "transformative" agenda is a focus upon socioeconomic structures, the ways in which inequalities may produce structural violence and a focus upon how this structural violence may effectively be addressed (Gready et al. 2010). This focus is a key point of commonality between various different attempts to define transformative justice (see, e.g., Gready et al. 2010; Daly 2002; Lambourne 2011).

In proposing her model of transformative justice, Erin Daly (2002: 74) points out that the literature often conflates "transition" and "transformation" (see, e.g., Teitel 2000: 4–6). This conflation is problematic. Transition may be seen as a change "at the top" (Daly 2002: 74), based on "elite bargains" (Waldorf 2012: 179). Transformation may be seen as more wide-reaching change throughout society. According to Daly (2002: 74),

> [t]ransition suggests movement from one thing to another – from oppression to liberation, from oligarchy to democracy, from lawlessness to due

> process, from injustice to justice. Transformation, however, suggests that the thing that is moving from one place to another is itself changing as it proceeds through the transition; it can be thought of as radical change.

Importantly, Daly (2002: 80) suggests that in some cases, the pursuit of transformative justice would require "a central economic component". However, she largely concentrates on the idea that culture must be transformed in post-conflict and post-authoritarian societies in order to prevent a return to violence (Daly 2002: 73–74). In her view, the primary purpose of transformative justice is to facilitate the two "related aims of reconciliation and deterrence" (Daly 2002: 84). This is not entirely satisfactory. First, this definition of transformative justice places the aims of a transformative agenda as being very similar to those of transitional justice (see, e.g., Annan 2004). Second, there is a risk that, in setting up reconciliation as one of the primary aims of transformative justice, the agenda is being set up for failure.

As previously alluded to, there has been criticism of the ability of transitional justice processes to successfully promote reconciliation (Waldorf 2012: 175–179). In practice, the discourse of reconciliation in post-conflict societies may be an empty one (Waldorf 2009: 104–105). Promotion of reconciliation at the expense of accountability may undermine gains made through transitional justice (Huggins 2009: 336; see also Collins 2010). Furthermore, Daly's (2002) focus on "deterrence" as the second key aim of transformative justice appears to reinforce the focus of transitional justice on direct interpersonal violence and violations of civil and political rights. Maintaining this focus but recognising the potential importance of socioeconomic grievances leaves Daly's approach to transformative justice closer to the suggestion that there may be transformative potential within existing transitional justice mechanisms (see Skaar 2011) than to broader definitions of transformative justice (e.g., Gready et al. 2010). This peripheral or indirect impact may be the best that can be expected regarding the contribution of standard transitional justice mechanisms to transformative justice.

In recent years, several attempts have been made at defining transformative justice as more clearly broader than and separate to transitional justice. Wendy Lambourne has put forward wide-reaching suggestions that transformative justice should cover socioeconomic, political, psychosocial, symbolic and ecological aspects (Lambourne 2009, 2011). Lambourne acknowledges that this conception may be too broad, overreaching the practical possibilities of a model of justice (2009: 46), and has drawn criticism for this (Waldorf 2012: 180). Nevertheless, there are clear points of overlap between Lambourne's model for transformative justice and the narrower proposals of Gready et al. (2010) and, indeed, the (narrower still) proposals of Daly (2002).

It has been suggested that there can be transformative elements within transitional justice. The reform and effective use of legal institutions and the development of rights-based constitutional reforms as transitional justice programmes may strengthen wider democratic structures and means of political participation by building confidence in the rule of law and providing new forums in which societal inequalities and structural grievances may be aired (Skaar 2011). However, given the necessarily limited participation of affected communities, and the typically narrow definition of victimhood applied in truth commissions and similar processes, it is necessary for participation in transformative justice to be pursued primarily via a different toolkit. Whilst the transformative effects of certain transitional justice processes may not be their primary function and they may be unintended, it is still the case that these processes can contribute towards transforming socioeconomic structures (Skaar 2011). Nevertheless, a focus upon these structures in transformative justice requires new, specifically focused, tools. For instance, reparations could in some circumstances be transformative, but this cannot be relied upon (Brett and Malagon 2013; Uprimny Yepes 2009). However, in addition to the abovementioned criticism that reparations programmes are rarely implemented due to a lack of political will (see also Brett and Malagon 2013: 269–270), and the difficulty in identifying who should be included or excluded from reparations programmes, it is also the case that reparations do not in themselves address structural issues. This is particularly the case as in practice reparations programmes are typically concerned with restitution rather than transformation (Gready and Robins 2014: 347). Moreover, there is a danger that the addressing of socioeconomic issues becomes (unevenly) attached to reparations for particular victim groups rather than to a more inclusive, or longer term, claim for justice (Gready and Robins 2014: 347; Firchow 2013). If, as it is argued here, there is a need from a transformative justice perspective to address structural violence and socioeconomic conditions in post-conflict and post-authoritarian contexts, then it follows that these should be addressed as directly as possible. This is likely to require utilising longer term and less individualised economic tools than those typically employed in transitional justice reparations programmes.

Though pursuing transformative justice may include the addressing of structural violence through transitional justice mechanisms, transformative justice looks beyond these mechanisms and the "transitional" lens they provide. It must be defined separately. The intention of transformative justice is to address the structural, social and economic issues which are merely overlapping with and peripheral to the existing transitional justice toolkit (see, e.g., Gready et al. 2010). Figure 2.1 illustrates the relationship between transformative justice and transitional justice.

The diagram in Figure 2.1 is not intended to pin down or limit transitional justice or transformative justice to a complete set of necessary and sufficient components. Instead, the purpose is to indicate the main transitional justice mechanisms (particularly those already discussed in some capacity earlier) and their foci and to compare and contrast these with the focus of transformative justice in order to provide some clarity on the differences and overlaps between the two concepts. Necessarily, elucidation of mechanisms to promote transformative justice is vague. Relatively little analytical and political attention has yet been paid to concretising transformative justice processes. One purpose of this chapter (and

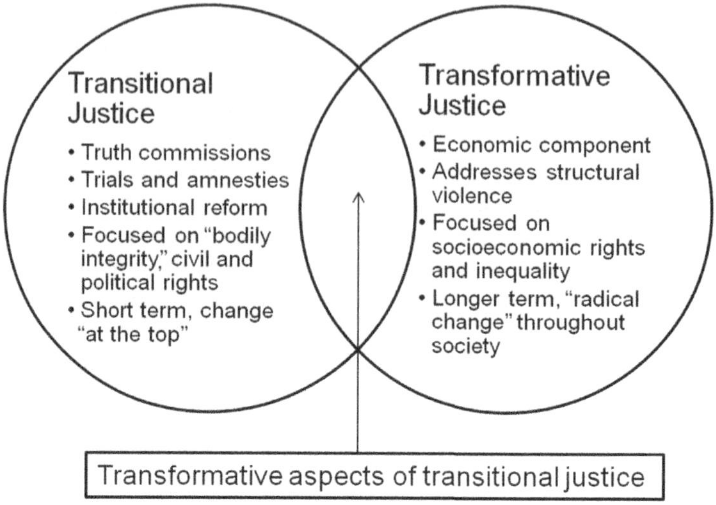

Figure 2.1 Relationship between transformative justice and transitional justice

the book as a whole) is to move towards defining action which could contribute to transformative justice.

Importantly, as indicated in Figure 2.1, it is argued here that transformative justice is not part of transitional justice. The question of how to pursue transformative justice outcomes is not merely a question of improving or expanding transitional justice. First, as indicated earlier, the established toolkit of transitional justice is not adequate for pursuing the socioeconomic and structural outcomes transformative justice necessitates (except, possibly, as peripheral or unintended consequences). Second, the processes by which transformative justice is pursued matter.

For transformative justice to be meaningfully defined, it is necessary to give significant consideration to action which falls outside of the inherently legalistic and elite-driven sphere of transitional justice. For post-conflict and post-authoritarian outcomes to address the needs of affected communities, it is necessary for them to be involved in the process of shaping these outcomes. This is principally for two reasons. First, participatory processes provide a means by which issues which concern affected communities (rather than outside elites) may be raised (Gaventa and Barrett 2010: 36). Participation of affected communities in shaping these processes also increases the likelihood of outcomes being considered legitimate, particularly in comparison to outcomes resulting from the imposition of an agenda by outside elites (see, e.g., Robins and Kumar Bhandari 2012; Robins 2013a). Moreover, a lack of meaningful participation by affected communities can lead to the institutionalisation of unequal, corrupt, socially exclusionary or otherwise negative processes, undermining positive outcomes in the long term (Uvin 2004: 137–138; Gaventa and Barrett 2010: 25–26). Meaningfully participatory processes can mitigate these risks by, for instance, validating the experiences, and agendas, of affected communities, including with regard to how these are expressed in the vernacular rather than necessarily in the language of elite terminology (Robins 2013b: 205–206, 209; Robins 2011b: 281–283).

Second, participatory processes can be an end in themselves (Robins 2013b: 210). Participatory processes provide a means by which the marginalised attain agency and are empowered to engage in addressing injustices which affect them (Robins 2013b: 15). John Gaventa and Gregory Barrett argue that the "knowledge and awareness" necessary to create and define an "empowered self-identity" is often "gained through a process of participation itself" (Gaventa and Barrett 2010: 27–28). This can be beneficial even if mobilisation and engagement in participatory processes do not lead to a positive outcome (such as government action). For instance, Simon Robins argues that regardless of the wider result of such mobilisation, meaningful participation in these processes "allows victims to meet others in the same position and to construct the meaning and identities that permit them to cope" (Robins 2011b: 286). Uvin (2004: 138), similarly, concludes that "process is as important if not more important than the product in most development work". The same principle can be applied to transformative justice.

It is also necessary, in order for transformative justice to remain meaningful, for the concept to be defined as different to more general ideas of social justice. This is for a number of reasons. Perhaps most important is the focus of transformative justice upon post-conflict and post-authoritarian contexts and the related need to recognise that transformative justice cannot do everything. There is a danger that if transformative justice attempted to address all social injustices, in all contexts, that the agenda would, on the one hand, be set up to fail and, on the other hand, that it would lose meaning. It is important that clarity is maintained regarding the areas of injustice which transformative justice might hope to address. There is still value added by applying the concept of transformative justice without over-claiming with regard to its potential impact in practice. Transformative justice, as conceived here, emerges particularly in the context of the need to address structural violence and socioeconomic rights issues which precipitate, and are produced and reproduced by, conflict and authoritarianism. These are not the only (social) injustices. However, the lens of transformative justice is particularly useful for illuminating these issues – and potential resolutions to them – whereas other lenses may be more clearly applicable to broader contexts of social injustice (see Gready and Robins 2014: 340). Necessary conditions for transformative justice can be seen as the inclusion of affected communities (not just elites) in shaping the agenda for policy and practice, a focus on addressing economic conditions, emphasis on long-term societal changes and attention to the historical and structural roots of contemporary injustices.

It is important to keep in mind that transformative justice, whilst separate, does emerge from the same point of departure as transitional justice. Both concepts are defined in relation to the same set of *in*justices. As discussed earlier, transitional justice cannot adequately address all of the socioeconomic injustices and structural violence present during periods of conflict or authoritarian rule. Nevertheless, the civil and political rights issues and interpersonal violence which are addressed by the standard toolkit of transitional justice are precipitated by the same conditions which also precipitate socioeconomic injustices and structural violence. That is to say conflict and authoritarian rule produce injustices. Transitional justice may address some – but not all – of these injustices. Transformative justice is a means of conceptualising how some of these other injustices may be addressed in post-conflict and post-authoritarian contexts.

With regard to the mechanisms which might be employed in order to promote transformative justice, there is a case to be made that existing tools designed for combating poverty, inequality or corruption, for instance, are appropriate. This could be the case. However, to ascertain whether these mechanisms genuinely contribute to transformation in any given case, there is a need to analyse and understand them in terms of the injustices they seek to address. The concept of transformative justice is useful as an analytical tool maintaining a focus upon the specific forms of socioeconomic injustice and structural violence which affect post-conflict and post-authoritarian societies. This allows tools aimed at addressing poverty or other socioeconomic rights issues to be evaluated in terms of the extent to which they resolve socioeconomic injustices which continue to be rooted in past conflict or authoritarianism. This contrasts with an analysis of these mechanisms from a standpoint (implicitly) assuming that such injustices are unrelated to other aspects of societal transition (or indeed transformation). An anti-poverty tool contributes to transformative justice (rather than a less specific kind of social justice) only if it combats (contemporary) poverty which has its root in a (past) context of injustice caused by conflict or authoritarian rule. The transformative justice conceptual framework might also be usefully applied to advocacy and policymaking. This could be either as an explicit framework for action (i.e. through practices or policies overtly described as intending to promote transformation from socioeconomic conditions rooted in past injustices) or as a means of assessing whether action (regardless of how it is framed) is effective in addressing the kinds of injustice mentioned earlier. As a conceptual framework, it is useful for linking together a broad set of issues (and potentially the tools used to address these) which might appear under another analytical lens to be separate to one another.

Applying concepts to the case study of South Africa

This section of the chapter utilises the concepts of structural violence and transformative justice discussed earlier to analyse the case study of land inequalities in South Africa. The aim here is to illustrate one possible application of the transformative justice concept to empirical realities. This section concentrates more on exploration of transformative justice in practice than on theorising the concept, which much of the rest of the chapter is concerned with.

There is a tension between protecting the rights of existing property owners and realising the right of those without property to own property without discrimination. An analytical lens on socioeconomic inequalities and structural violence may be useful in revealing resolutions to this tension. With this transformative justice lens, it is possible to judge whether existing structural conditions are just and whether they promote or inhibit positive transformation and the realisation of human rights in post-conflict and post-authoritarian societies.

The vast majority of people in South Africa are landless; around 85% of land remains under white ownership, though estimates vary (War on Want n.d.). Indeed, it has been estimated that by the end of apartheid in 1994, up to 87% of land in South Africa was owned by the white minority (IRIN 2008; Moyo 2004: 1–2; James 2007: 3). This was largely a result of colonialism and the subsequent implementation of laws such as the 1913 Native Lands Act and the policy of forced removals under apartheid (IRIN 2008; Moyo 2004: 1–2; James 2007: 3). In South Africa, addressing structural violence stemming from land inequalities can be seen as a key element in the promotion of transformation towards a more just society post-apartheid.

The redistribution and restitution of land and the reform of tenure was central to the ANC's programme prior to the end of apartheid. Despite land issues reducing in prominence in the ANC's priorities since the 1990s, a certain degree of rhetorical commitment to address land inequalities has remained since the ANC entered government. Some land reform has taken place, predominantly restitution to the formerly dispossessed (rather than wider redistribution), through market-based "willing buyer, willing seller" processes.[4] However, even the (arguably) modest commitments of the post-apartheid government to addressing land issues have not been realised. Consequently, the ANC has been subject to criticism over its land policies (Greenberg 2004; IRIN 2008; Kienast n.d.; Losier 2009; Ntsebeza and Hall 2007; South African Press Association 2006; Tilley 2002; Urban LandMark 2007: 13–16; War on Want n.d.).

One issue, which is particularly pertinent when analysing the degree to which structural violence can be reduced, is the suggestion that the current land reform process has focused too much on restitution rather than on redistribution or on addressing tenure reform (Walker 2008: 28–29; James 2007: 7–8). Chris Huggins (2009: 352) states that "there is a strong argument that any attempt to redress injustice over land rights must look not just at individual cases of dispossession but at the entire land tenure system". In South Africa, many of those who have benefited from land reform (through restitution) have not been the poorest or most marginalised groups (who might benefit from wider redistribution or tenure reform). Those black people who are in a position to have land restored to them are likely to have been part of the relatively small and comparatively well-off group of black people who owned land prior to losing it during minority rule (Gready 2010; James 2007: 7–8). In order to address the structural inequalities which remain present in South Africa, a wider reaching, transformative agenda is necessary.

As well as being protected by international mechanisms,[5] the right to property is also legally protected in the South African Constitution (Constitution of the Republic of South Africa 1996: Section 25). However, South African law and international instruments also protect rights (such as to food and to housing) which can be seen as articulating a right to land.[6]

Section 25 of the South African Constitution specifically provides for the possibility of property (including land) being expropriated for a public purpose including for the purpose of creating more equitable land distribution through land reform (Constitution of the Republic of South Africa 1996: Section 25). Use of this provision is one way in which transformative justice in relation to land could be pursued. Indeed, there is some support for using this provision amongst activists and scholars (see, e.g., Papayya 2008; Berrisford 2009; Pityana 2013).[7]

To privilege the rights of existing property owners without exception would necessarily limit the rights of the landless to access land, for example for food or for housing. It is also the case that land reform is likely to limit the rights of existing property owners to some degree. This is particularly the case with policies aiming to redistribute land. On the face of it, there might appear to be a dilemma from a human rights perspective. The degree to which either the rights of existing property owners or the rights of the landless may justifiably be limited in order to facilitate the realisation of the others' rights is not self-evident. However, keeping in mind the concept of structural violence and the aim of promoting transformative justice goes some way to resolve instances of prima facie competing rights claims over land. This is not to say that dilemmas or contradictions are wholly removed. Rather, keeping a focus on transformative justice (e.g. on the necessary conditions for transformative justice discussed earlier) and on structural violence provides criteria by which the justness or otherwise of prioritising one specific rights claim over another can be determined. Applying these criteria allows a choice to be made in practice in individual cases without privileging one right (such as to property or to housing) over another in principle or in all possible instances of apparently competing rights claims.

A question may be asked regarding whether existing structures of land distribution maintain a form of violence, and whether it is possible to move towards its negation (peace – broadly defined). Land distribution in South Africa maintains structural violence. For example, Huggins (2009: 352) highlights that South Africa's

> business-as-usual agrarian policy has meant that those black farmers who have claimed land and have attempted to start smallholder farm enterprises are struggling to succeed within a wider economic system geared for large-scale production.

The "socio-spatial exclusion" and the division between shack settlements of landless people and "citadelis[ed] and securitis[ed]" urban areas present in formally desegregated South African cities is another example of this (Gibson 2011:

25–27). The transformative justice analytical lens can be used as a means of evaluating existing structures and policies surrounding access to land and housing. Inasmuch as it can be seen that maintaining (or changing) existing conditions of access or ownership in favour of one competing rights claimant maintains or reproduces the structural violence inherent in the apartheid system, upholding that rights claim may be seen as unjust. Keeping this focus allows for competing rights claims to be distinguished according to those which are consistent with a transformative justice framework and those which are not.

The demand-driven, market-oriented (as opposed to egalitarian), approach to land reform (see James 2007: 57) can be seen as failing to address the (structural) violence inherent in existing land distribution in South Africa. Moreover, this approach has been pursued despite evidence suggesting that the distribution of land continues to be considered important by the South African population. James Gibson's (2009: 35–37) study of a representative sample population found that land ownership and redistribution was viewed as a "very important" social problem by 46 percent of respondents (and 50 percent of the black respondents) in 2004. Indeed, during the apartheid era, the ANC and its allies had advocated a more egalitarian approach to land reform. The Freedom Charter stated that "land [shall be] re-divided amongst those who work it, to banish famine and land hunger . . . All shall have the right to occupy land wherever they choose" (Congress of the People 1955). Moreover, the rhetoric of high-profile ANC members, such as Joe Slovo, prior to the negotiated settlement to end apartheid, indicated that land redistribution would be a central component of any transition to democracy. In 1986, Slovo (who was at the time General Secretary of the South African Communist Party and Chief of Staff of the ANC's armed wing, Umkhonto weSizwe), argued that "the redistribution of the land is the absolute imperative in our conditions" (Walker 2008: 51). The ANC's alliance partners in the SACP and COSATU have continued to call for a change in land reform policy (see, e.g., Nzimande 2007; Thomas 2007: 135; South African Press Association 2006). However, despite the recent re-emergence of pro-redistribution sentiment in pronouncements by leading ANC members (outlined further ahead), post-apartheid land policy has thus far followed the demand-driven paradigm.[8]

The strong legal protection of the right to property provided by the South African Constitution has been suggested as one of the key determinants, if not the most important factor, influencing the imposition of South Africa's demand-driven, market-led approach to land reform (Kahn 2007: 4–5). This means it may be possible for some more aggressive policies than "willing buyer, willing seller" to be challenged legally. It is important, however, to note that Section 25 of the South African Constitution does allow land to be expropriated without market-level compensation, though the market value must be taken into account (Constitution of the Republic of South Africa 1996: Section 25). Whilst constitutional protection of the right to property might legally hamper certain land reform policies, more radical policies than those so far pursued are nevertheless permissible.

Despite the suggestion that current policies are ineffective and result in the maintenance of existing land inequalities, the ANC has maintained that addressing land inequalities is a continuing priority. In February 2012, Gwede Mantashe (then ANC General Secretary) commented that to "remove the land question from the centre of the ANC's agenda, [would] be betraying what was the immediate challenge after the formation of the African National Congress" (South African Press Association 2012). Even more recently, (then) President Jacob Zuma suggested that the abovementioned clauses in the South African Constitution allowing for the possibility of land to be expropriated will be used (Zuma 2013), and the ANC's National Executive Committee and party president Cyril Ramaphosa have endorsed moves towards pursuing expropriation, including the possibility of expropriation without compensation and amending the constitution to reflect this (see, e.g., Merton 2017). Given this – at least rhetorical – commitment, the presence of the tension between demand-driven and egalitarian development paradigms is once again evident. At least in terms of providing a means for describing and analysing the problem at hand and for forming priorities for policy and practice, the framework of transformative justice may be of use in forging just resolutions to these tensions. Actors relevant to the pursuit of transformative justice as well as the roles of their relationships and strategies are explored ahead.

Relevant actors and relationships for a transformative approach

Keeping a focus on the pursuit of transformative justice, particular actors, their relationships and their strategies in relation to addressing land inequalities are especially worthy of exploration. This is important, particularly, because of the need in transformative justice to facilitate the meaningful participation of affected communities in shaping policy and practice. This requires taking account of the praxis of actors – such as social movements, NGOs and trade unions – which are made up of and articulate the concerns of those affected by the injustices transformative justice seeks to address. The historic and contemporary importance of social movements, trade unions and NGOs to the praxis of human rights and social justice in South Africa is important for exploration of land, socioeconomic rights and the pursuit of transformative justice (see, e.g., Gibson 2006: 1–27; Ballard et al. 2006: 15). In particular, the positioning of NGOs, trade unions and social movements in relation to each other and in relation to the state is relevant to this issue.

As noted earlier, one of the shortcomings of transitional justice processes has been a tendency for change to occur through elite bargains and the transfer of power at the top (Daly 2002: 74; Waldorf 2012: 179). The centrality of elite bargains might go some way to explaining why post-apartheid land policies have not been heavily geared around redistribution or otherwise addressing the structural violence inherent in the existing distribution of land. In order for the shortcomings of transitional justice to be overcome and a transformative approach pursued, there need to be attempts to move away from elite bargains. If a move away from elite bargains is not in itself possible, there is at least a need to interrogate and pursue strategies which allow for such bargains to be contested, influenced and altered by affected communities. Social movements and community-based organisations articulate concerns of those affected by issues such as land inequalities (Twalo 2012; Greenberg 2004; Ballard et al. 2006). Social movement praxis is, therefore, important for understanding how a transformative justice agenda might be promoted.

As noted earlier, post-apartheid, COSATU has at times been critical of many of the ANC government's policies.[9] Moreover, independent and non-COSATU affiliated unions have also emerged. Some of these take a more critical position than COSATU in relation to engagement with the ANC and the state. For example, the farm workers' union Sikhula Sonke has taken part in election boycott campaigns of the sort carried out by landless people's social movements heavily critical of the ANC (Robins 2005: 9–11; SAinfo n.d.; Women on Farms Project n.d.; Naidoo 2009). Whilst the (often) different membership constituencies of social movements organised around land and related issues and trade unions (and organisations' political affiliations) can cause tensions, there can be value added by trade unions to action on land issues (Louw 2012). For instance, trade unions often have greater resources than grassroots social movements, which can lead to more effective action if these resources are made available for land rights campaigning purposes. Furthermore, in instances where land issues overlap with the recognised industrial mandate of trade unions (e.g., regarding farm workers' housing) then the established arenas for negotiation with employers and government might be used to advance transformative justice aims in relation to land (Jacobs 2012; Mbana 2012; Sikhula Sonke Official 2012).

NGOs are important political actors in post-apartheid South Africa. Post-apartheid "social movements and NGOs have mobilised locally in order to leverage access to state resources such as land, housing and health care" (Robins 2008: 5). Moreover, as noted in Chapter 1, NGOs can act as intermediaries between grassroots activism and more formal politics nationally and internationally, not least through funding streams and through opening up access to transnational networks (Keck and Sikkink 1998: 9). As Robins puts it (2008: 5), NGOs and social movements acting in partnership deploy "both local rights-based strategies and globally connected modes of collective mobilisation in marginalised communities". It is, therefore, important to explore the ways in which these relationships and the strategies of these actors might be used to promote transformative justice. Maintaining a critical lens on the realisation of socioeconomic rights, the addressing of structural violence and the pursuit of transformative justice provides a means by which the strategies of these actors might be evaluated.

Conclusion

There are several major themes which emerge consistently in debates over structural violence, socioeconomic rights and transformative justice. There are also gaps evident in the foci of existing studies, which warrant exploration through further research. The first key theme is that structural, socioeconomic inequalities impact upon post-conflict and post-authoritarian societies significantly. This is both as sources of tension which can lead to unrest and conflict and as social justice issues which must be addressed to facilitate development.

Another theme present in the debates covered by this chapter, and responding to the first theme mentioned previously, surrounds the concern that structural, socioeconomic issues are not being widely or effectively addressed. There is the suggestion that there is potential for the widely applied transitional justice mechanisms to address these issues to a greater extent but that this has (for the most part at least) not happened (see, e.g., Pasipanodya 2008).

Moreover, there is the suggestion that transitional justice on its own cannot adequately resolve structural, socioeconomic issues (Mani 2008; Waldorf 2012). Focusing specifically on addressing land and related inequalities in South Africa, a tension is highlighted between the legal rights of existing landowners and the legal and moral rights of landless people. It is suggested that post-apartheid policies have largely failed to address structural inequalities in land in South Africa (see, e.g., Greenberg 2004; James 2007; Walker 2008).

On the basis of these themes, a number of conclusions are drawn, which are laid out more fully ahead. It is concluded that existing models of transitional justice are not adequate for addressing structural violence and land inequalities or for ensuring the realisation of socioeconomic rights. Following on from this conclusion, it is proposed that exploration of the strategies of and relationships between social movements, trade unions and NGOs in relation to transformative justice in general, and land inequalities in particular, is necessary.

Keeping in mind the focus in wider literature on the impact of structural violence on post-conflict societies and the potential for this to impact upon continuing and future conflicts, there is a gap within the literature on land in South Africa. This relates to the detail of how actors such as NGOs, trade unions and social movements might effectively promote alternatives to the current paradigm. It is argued earlier that these actors are important to promoting a more transformative approach. NGOs, trade unions and social movements engage in a variety of action and interact with each other in various formal and informal networks. There is a need to investigate these relationships further, applying an analytical lens turned to the effectiveness of, and potential for, new approaches to addressing land and related socioeconomic rights issues.

Related to the previous conclusion is the following. Whilst there is some literature on the need for transformative justice to be pursued using a different toolkit from that associated with transitional justice (Mani 2008; Skaar 2011; Gready et al. 2010), there is not a great deal written about what tools could be used effectively to promote a transformative agenda addressing structural, socioeconomic inequalities such as land distribution in South Africa. There is, therefore, a particular need for research in contexts such as South Africa to be carried out exploring the practical possibilities for furthering transformative justice and addressing structural issues such as land inequalities. This chapter has attempted to highlight the shortcomings of transitional justice in relation to these areas and has put forward a broad definition of transformative justice. Moreover, some proposals have been made with regard to the need to engage with the praxis of social movements, trade unions and NGOs in order to gain insight into how a transformative agenda might be pursued. Indeed, following this line of thinking, the practical application of transformative justice to a possible case study – landlessness and related socio-economic rights issues in South Africa – has been explored. This chapter, however, does not propose answers to all the questions it raises. The key conclusions here are taken forward as areas to be explored by scholars and practitioners, including in the rest of this book. In particular, there is a need for a conception of transformative justice to be applied in order to overcome some of the shortcomings of transitional justice and regarding the need to explore the strategies of diverse actors and networks in promoting this agenda. The aim in highlighting these themes is to develop them further and through the rest of the book (as well as future research and practice) to come to more detailed conclusions regarding the content of effective strategies in promoting transformative justice.

Notes

1 See also the similar definition put forward by the International Center for Transitional Justice (n.d.-b).

2 Cath Collins's concept of "post-transitional justice", though questioning the established transitional justice framework to some extent, likewise places emphasis on addressing political violence committed by state actors rather than structural or socioeconomic human rights issues (Collins 2010: 7–25).

3 Four dilemmas are put forward by Mani (2008: 255–261). The most relevant of these to the discussion in this chapter is the concern that the targeted measures associated with transitional justice (truth commissions, trials and institutional reform) are difficult to apply to the wide-reaching effects of structural violence and social injustice (Mani 2008: 255).

4 Since 1994, a number of land reform policies have been put in place. These cover three broad categories: restitution, redistribution and tenure reform (James 2007: 3–5). The initial target of these policies was to redistribute 30% of white-owned agricultural land into black ownership by 2014 (Walker 2008: 20; World Bank 1993). This was to be achieved through a market-based "willing buyer, willing seller" approach (World Bank 1993). By 2008, however, the date by which this target was expected to be achieved was moved back to 2025 (Republic of South Africa, Department of Land Affairs and Department of Agriculture 2008: 35). These targets are not as far-reaching as many would have liked. James Gibson highlights that in surveys of a representative sample population, 85% of the black respondents indicated agreement with the statement that "Most land in South Africa was taken unfairly by white settlers, and they therefore have no right to the land today" and 68% of black respondents agreed that "land must be returned to blacks in South Africa, no matter what the consequences are for the current owners and for political stability in the country" (Gibson 2009: 31–32).

5 See, for example, UDHR, Article 17 (United Nations 1948); International Convention on the Elimination of All Forms of Racial Discrimination, Article 5 (United Nations 1965).

6 Protected in Article 11 of the ICESCR (United Nations 1966) and Sections 26 and 27 of the South African Constitution (Constitution of the Republic of South Africa 1996: Sections 26–27).

7 Also, personal interviews with Legassick (2010); Brown-Luthango (2010); Ndabambi (2010); Poni (2010); Smit (2010); and Hall (2010).

8 Various explanations for this have been posited, including limited success of more radical policies in other contexts and the importance of pressure enacted by business groups and international financial institutions (James 2007: 10–11; Walker 2008: 51–52, 63–64). Concerns have also been raised that policies such as expropriation of land might bring results in line with the "terrifying exemplar" of Zimbabwe (Gibson 2009: 18). However, it is worth noting that despite the widely held view that "Zimbabwe seems to be totally imploding" (Gibson 2009: 213), with regard to redistribution of land, the reality may be more complex, and perhaps less disastrous, than this implies (see, e.g., Scoones et al. 2011).

9 Indeed, the largest COSATU union, NUMSA, recently withdrew support for the ANC (and SACP), and has announced plans to create a new political party. By the time the bulk of the research for this book was completed, NUMSA's future in the COSATU federation remained uncertain (see Letsoalo and Mataboge 2013; South African Press Association 2014a, 2014b; see also McKinley 2015). Subsequently, NUMSA and its allies have announced the formation of SAFTU – a new trade union federation challenging COSATU (see Webster 2017).

References

Annan, Kofi. (2004) *The Rule of Law and Transitional Justice in Conflict and Post-Conflict Societies.* Report of the Secretary-General, United Nations Security Council, 23 August, UN Doc S/2004/616.

Ballard, Richard, Habib, Adam, Valodia, Imraan and Zuern, Elke. (2006) Introduction: From Anti-Apartheid to Post-Apartheid Social Movements. In *Voices of Protest: Social Movements in Post-Apartheid South Africa*, edited by Richard Ballard, Adam Habib and Imraan Valodia (Scottsville: University of KwaZulu-Natal Press), 1–22.

Berrisford, Stephen. (2009) Land Expropriation Key Tool in Urban Transformation. *Urban LandMark*, October. www.urbanlandmark.org.za/newsletter/issue/0405/01.php [accessed September 6, 2010].

Brett, Roddy and Malagon, Lina. (2013) Overcoming the Original Sin of the "Original Condition": How Reparations May Contribute to Emancipatory Peacebuilding. *Human Rights Review*, 14(3), 257–271.

Brown-Luthango, Mercy. (2010) Personal interview, Cape Town, South Africa, 10 August.

Collins, Cath. (2010) *Post-Transitional Justice: Human Rights Trials in Chile and El Salvador* (University Park: Pennsylvania State University Press).

Congress of the People. (1955) *The Freedom Charter*, adopted 26 June, Kliptown.

Constitution of the Republic of South Africa. (1996) Act No. 108 of 1996. [*Date of Promulgation* 18 December 1996, *Date of Commencement* 4 February 1997].

Daly, Erin. (2002) Transformative Justice: Charting a Path to Reconciliation. *International Legal Perspectives*, 12(1/2), 73–183.

De Greiff, Pablo (ed.). (2006) *The Handbook of Reparations* (New York: Oxford University Press).

Duthie, Roger. (2008) Toward a Development-Sensitive Approach to Transitional Justice. *International Journal of Transitional Justice*, 2(3), 292–309.
Farmer, Paul E. (2004) An Anthropology of Structural Violence. *Current Anthropology*, 45(3), 305–325.
Farmer, Paul E., Nizeye, Bruce, Stulac, Sara and Keshavjee, Salmaan. (2006) Structural Violence and Clinical Medicine. *PLoS Medicine*, 3(10), 1686–1691.
Firchow, Pamina. (2013) Must Our Communities Bleed to Receive Social Services? Development Projects and Collective Reparations Schemes in Colombia. *Journal of Peacebuilding and Development*, 8(3), 50–63.
Hall, Ruth. (2010) Personal interview, Cape Town, South Africa, 13 August.
Galtung, Johan. (1969) Violence, Peace, and Peace Research. *Journal of Peace Research*, 6(3), 167–191.
Gaventa, John and Barrett, Gregory. (2010) *So What Difference Does It Make? Mapping the Outcomes of Citizen Engagement*. IDS Working Paper 347, Institute of Development Studies, University of Sussex (Brighton: Institute of Development Studies).
Gibson, James L. (2009) *Overcoming Historical Injustices: Land Reconciliation in South Africa* (Cambridge: Cambridge University Press).
Gibson, Nigel C. (2006) Introduction – Calling Everything into Question: Broken Promises, Social Movements and Emergent Intellectual Currents in Post-Apartheid South Africa. In *Challenging Hegemony: Social Movements and the Quest for a New Humanism in Post-Apartheid South Africa*, edited by Nigel C. Gibson (Trenton: Africa World Press), 1–53.
Gibson, Nigel C. (2011) *Fanonian Practices in South Africa: From Steve Biko to Abahlali baseMjondolo* (New York: Palgrave Macmillan).
Gready, Paul. (2010) Land Scarcity, Land Grabs, Land Reform, Land Rights. (Lecture, University of York, York, 25 February).
Gready, Paul. (2011) Transformative Justice. (Unpublished paper presented at "Transformative Justice: Global Perspectives", Worldwide Universities Network International Conference, University of Leeds, Leeds, 12 May).
Gready, Paul, Boesten, Jelke, Crawford, Gordon and Wilding, Polly. (2010) Transformative Justice: A Concept Note. Draft Concept Note Developed by the Worldwide Universities Network Transformative Justice Group, October.
Gready, Paul and Robins, Simon. (2014) From Transitional to Transformative Justice: A New Agenda for Practice. *International Journal of Transitional Justice*, 8(3), 339–361.
Greenberg, Stephen. (2004) *The Landless People's Movement and the Failure of Post-Apartheid Land Reform* (Durban: University of KwaZulu-Natal).
Huggins, Chris. (2009) Linking Broad Constellations of Ideas: Transitional Justice, Land Tenure Reform, and Development. In *Transitional Justice and Development: Making Connections*, edited by Pablo de Greiff and Roger Duthie (New York: Social Science Research Council), 332–374.
Integrated Regional Information Networks (IRIN). (2008) South Africa: Land Redistribution Back on the Front Burner, 23 October. www.unhcr.org/refworld/docid/4901bec0c.html [accessed September 1, 2010].
International Center for Transitional Justice. (n.d.-a) South Africa. http://ictj.org/our-work/regions-and-countries/south-africa [accessed August 31, 2011].
International Center for Transitional Justice. (n.d.-b) What Is Transitional Justice? http://ictj.org/about/transitional-justice [accessed September 15, 2014].
Jacobs, Mario. (2012) Personal interview, Cape Town, South Africa, 30 July.

James, Deborah. (2007) *Gaining Ground? "Rights" and "Property" in South African Land Reform* (Abingdon: Routledge).

Kahn, Naefa. (2007) Land and Agrarian Reform in South Africa. *Policy: Issues & Actors*, 20(12), 1–38.

Keck, Margaret E. and Sikkink, Kathryn. (1998) *Activists beyond Borders: Advocacy Networks in International Politics* (Ithaca: Cornell University Press).

Kienast, Gerhard. (n.d.) Abahlali baseMjondolo: How Poor People's Struggle for Land and Housing Became a Struggle for Democracy. http://suedafrika.habitants.de/?p=15 [accessed September 1, 2010].

Lambourne, Wendy. (2009) Transitional Justice and Peacebuilding after Mass Violence. *International Journal of Transitional Justice*, 3(1), 28–48.

Lambourne, Wendy. (2011) Transformative Justice and Peacebuilding: A Psychological Perspective. (Unpublished paper presented at "Transformative Justice: Global Perspectives", Worldwide Universities Network International Conference, University of Leeds, Leeds, 12 May).

Laplante, Lisa J. (2008) Transitional Justice and Peace Building: Diagnosing and Addressing the Socioeconomic Roots of Violence through a Human Rights Framework. *International Journal of Transitional Justice*, 2(3), 331–355.

Legassick, Martin. (2010) Personal interview, Cape Town, South Africa, 4 August.

Letsoalo, Matuma and Mataboge, Mmanaledi. (2013) Gatvol Numsa Cuts Ties with ANC. *Mail and Guardian*, 20 December. http://mg.co.za/article/2013-12-20-00-gatvol-numsa-turns-off-anc-tap [accessed June 5, 2014].

Losier, Toussaint. (2009) The Struggle for Land & Housing in Post-Apartheid South Africa. *The San Francisco Bay Area Independent Media Center*, 12 January. www.indybay.org/newsitems/2009/01/12/18562116.php [accessed September 1, 2010].

Louw, Mike. (2012) Personal interview, Cape Town, South Africa, 6 July.

Mani, Rama. (2008) Dilemmas of Expanding Transitional Justice, or Forging the Nexus between Transitional Justice and Development. *International Journal of Transitional Justice*, 2(3), 253–265.

Mbana, Howard. (2012) Telephone interview, 16 July.

Merton, Marianne. (2017) #ANCdecides2017: Land Expropriation without Compensation Makes Grand Entrance. *Daily Maverick*, 21 December. www.dailymaverick.co.za/article/2017-12-21-ancdecides2017-land-expropriation-without-compensation-makes-grand-entrance/ [accessed January 28, 2018].

McKinley, Dale T. (2015) Labor-Community Alliances in South Africa: Reclaiming (Some of) the Past, Inventing the Future? *The South Atlantic Quarterly*, 114(2), 457–466.

Moyo, Sam. (2004) *The Politics of Land Distribution and Race Relations in Southern Africa*. Identities, Conflict and Cohesion (2000–2005) Programme Paper No. 10 (Geneva: United Nations Research Institute for Social Development).

Muvingi, Ismael. (2009) Sitting on Powder Kegs: Socioeconomic Rights in Transitional Societies. *International Journal of Transitional Justice*, 3(2), 163–182.

Naidoo, Yugendree. (2009) Farm Workers Announce Election Boycott. *West Cape News*, 7 April. http://westcapenews.com/?p=599 [accessed August 31, 2011].

Ndabambi, Luthando. (2010) Personal interview, Cape Town, South Africa, 12 August.

Ntsebeza, Lungisile and Hall, Ruth (eds.). (2007) *The Land Question in South Africa: The Challenge of Transformation and Redistribution* (Cape Town: Human Sciences Research Council Press).

Nzimande, Blade. (2007) Build Working Class Power in the Whole of Society: SACP May Day 2007 Message. (Address to SACP May Day Rally, Secunda, Mpumalanga, 1 May). www.sacp.org.za/main.php?include=docs/sp/2007/sp0501.html [accessed September 1, 2010].

Papayya, Mary. (2008) The Poor Need Proper Homes. *The Sowetan*, 1 September. www.abahlali.org/node/3984 [accessed September 1, 2010].

Pasipanodya, Tafadzwa. (2008) A Deeper Justice: Economic and Social Justice as Transitional Justice in Nepal. *International Journal of Transitional Justice*, 2(3), 378–397.

Pityana, Sipho. (2013) The Constitution, the Land Question, Citizenship and Redress. (Unpublished paper presented at Land Divided: Land and South African Society in 2013, in Comparative Perspective, University of Cape Town, Cape Town, 24 March).

Poni, Mzonke. (2010) Personal interview, Cape Town, South Africa, 12 August.

Republic of South Africa, Department of Land Affairs and Department of Agriculture. (2008) *The Land and Agrarian Reform Project (LARP): The Concept Document*, February (Pretoria: Department of Agriculture).

Robins, Simon. (2011a) Untransformative Justice: The Limits of Civil Society and the Rights Discourse in Post-Conflict Nepal. (Unpublished paper presented at "Transformative Justice: Global Perspectives", Worldwide Universities Network International Conference, University of Leeds, Leeds, 12 May).

Robins, Simon. (2011b) *Addressing the Needs of the Families of the Missing: A Test of Contemporary Approaches to Transitional Justice.* PhD thesis. Post-War Reconstruction and Development Unit, Department of Politics, University of York, York, June.

Robins, Simon. (2013a) An Empirical Approach to Post-Conflict Legitimacy: Victims' Needs and the Everyday. *Journal of Intervention and Statebuilding*, 7(1), 45–64.

Robins, Simon. (2013b) *Families of the Missing: A Test for Contemporary Approaches to Transitional Justice* (Abingdon: Routledge).

Robins, Simon and Kumar Bhandari, Ram. (2012) *From Victims to Actors: Mobilising Victims to Drive Transitional Justice Process.* Research Report, June (Kathmandu: National Network of Families of Disappeared and Missing Nepal).

Robins, Steven L. (2005) Introduction. In *Limits to Liberation after Apartheid*, edited by Steven L. Robins (Oxford: James Currey), 1–21.

Robins, Steven L. (2008) *From Revolution to Rights in South Africa: Social Movements, NGOs and Popular Politics after Apartheid* (Woodbridge: James Currey).

SAinfo. (n.d.) Trade Unions in South Africa. www.southafrica.info/business/economy/policies/tradeunions.htm [accessed August 31, 2011].

Scoones, Ian, Marongwe, Nelson, Mavedzenge, Blasio, Murimbarimba, Felix, Mahenehene, Jacob and Sukume, Chrispen. (2011) Zimbabwe's Land Reform: Challenging the Myths. *Journal of Peasant Studies*, 38(5), 967–993.

Sikhula Sonke Official. (2012) Personal interview, Stellenbosch, South Africa, 17 July.

Skaar, Elin. (2011) Transformative Aspects of Formal TJ Initiatives: Opportunities and limitations. (Unpublished paper presented at "Transformative Justice: Global Perspectives", Worldwide Universities Network International Conference, University of Leeds, Leeds, 12 May).

Smit, Warren. (2010) Personal interview, Cape Town, South Africa, 13 August.

South African Press Association. (2006) Speed Up Land Reform: Cosatu. *Fin24*, 9 February. www.fin24.com/Economy/Speed-up-land-reform-Cosatu-20060209 [accessed September 1, 2010].

South African Press Association. (2012) No Abandoning Land Reform. *Independent Online*, 21 February. www.iol.co.za/business/business-news/no-abandoning-land-reform-1.1239139 [accessed March 4, 2012].

South African Press Association. (2014a) Numsa asks Cosatu Not to Kick It Out. *Mail and Guardian*, 10 March. http://mg.co.za/article/2014-03-10-numsa-asks-cosatu-not-to-kick-it-out [accessed June 5, 2014].

South African Press Association. (2014b) Numsa's New Party Could Run in 2016. *Mail and Guardian*, 15 May. http://mg.co.za/article/2014-05-15-numsa-sa-workers-want-a-new-party [accessed June 5, 2014].

Tarrow, Sidney. (2005) *The New Transnational Activism* (New York: Cambridge University Press).

Teitel, Ruti G. (2000) *Transitional Justice* (New York: Oxford University Press).

Thomas, David P. (2007) The South African Communist Party (SACP) in the Post-Apartheid Period. *Review of African Political Economy*, 34(111), 123–138.

Tilley, Susan. (2002) *An Examination of Market-Assisted Agrarian Reform in South Africa* (Cape Town: International Labour Research and Information Group).

Twalo, Mncedisi. (2012) Personal interview, Cape Town, South Africa, 4 July.

United Nations. (1948) *Universal Declaration of Human Rights*. General Assembly Resolution 217A (III), UN Doc A/810 at 71.

United Nations. (1965) *International Convention on the Elimination of All Forms of Racial Discrimination*. General Assembly Resolution 2106 (XX) of 21 December 1965, Entered into Force 4 January 1969.

United Nations. (1966) *International Covenant on Economic, Social and Cultural Rights*. General Assembly Resolution 2200A (XXI) of 16 December 1966, Entered into Force 3 January 1976.

Uprimny Yepes, Rodrigo. (2009) Transformative Reparations of Massive Gross Human Rights Violations: Between Corrective and Distributive Justice. *Netherlands Quarterly of Human Rights*, 27(4), 625–647.

Urban LandMark. (2007) *Do Informal Land Markets Work for Poor People? An Assessment of Three Metropolitan Cities in South Africa*. Literature Review (Tshwane: Urban LandMark).

Uvin, Peter. (2004) *Human Rights and Development* (Bloomfield: Kumarian Press).

Waldorf, Lars. (2009) Revisiting *Hotel Rwanda*: Genocide Ideology, Reconciliation, and Rescuers. *Journal of Genocide Research*, 11(1), 101–125.

Waldorf, Lars. (2012) Anticipating the Past: Transitional Justice and Socio-Economic Wrongs. *Social and Legal Studies*, 21(2), 171–186.

Walker, Cherryl. (2008) *Landmarked: Land Claims and Land Restitution in South Africa* (Johannesburg: Jacana Media).

War on Want. (n.d.) Landless in South Africa. www.waronwant.org/overseas-work/food-justice/landless-in-south-africa [accessed September 1, 2010].

Webster, Edward. (2017) South Africa Has a New Trade Union Federation: Can It Break the Mould? *The Conversation*, 25 April. https://theconversation.com/south-africa-has-a-new-trade-union-federation-can-it-break-the-mould-76609 [accessed May 11, 2017].

Women on Farms Project. (n.d.) Who Is Sikhula Sonke? www.wfp.org.za/sikhula-sonke/ [accessed August 31, 2011].
World Bank. (1993) Options for Land Reform and Rural Restructuring in South Africa. (Report presented at the Conference on Land Distribution Options, Land and Agricultural Policy Centre, Johannesburg, 12–15 October).
Zuma, Jacob. (2013) State of the Nation Address by Jacob G Zuma, President of the RSA on the Occasion of the Joint Sitting of Parliament, 14 February. http://anc.org.za/show.php?id=10074 [accessed March 10, 2013].

Chapter 3

Network relationships, existing ties and opportunities

Introduction

Taking a particular focus on South Africa, the previous two chapters posited that networks, including those containing social movements and trade unions (as well as NGOs) are important for addressing landlessness, and related structural violence, and to the pursuit of transformative justice. The purpose of this chapter is to build on this. Specifically, the chapter maps the relationships between actors within the case study network and discusses the nature of existing ties and opportunities for more effective collaboration in the network.

The case study focuses on social movements, NGOs and trade unions taking action on anti-eviction and land reform–related issues in South Africa, particularly the urban Western Cape and urban Gauteng. This chapter first describes the main groups and organisations within this category and maps their relationships to one another as well as some of their wider national and international links. After this, the chapter builds on the analysis of the existing ties between network nodes by exploring the opportunities that exist for new or more effective collaboration between actors within the network within the urban Western Cape and urban Gauteng. There is also a discussion of threats to effective collaboration between actors. This is based largely on the data collected from interviews with staff members and activists within groups and organisations. In particular, the analysis focuses upon interviewees' comments about what their aims are in entering into relationships with other groups and the ways in which these relationships are approached. In addition to interview data, the exploration of opportunities for more effective collaboration between network actors is informed and guided by findings from existing literature and informal discussion with scholars and practitioners.

In addition to mapping out the three main clusters of actors within the network and their wider national and international ties, this chapter presents this diagrammatically. Here, the three main clusters of actors within the network – those associated with the Housing Assembly, the Poor People's Alliance and Shack/Slum Dwellers International (SDI) – are introduced. Moreover, on the basis of an analysis of the relationships mapped out early on in the chapter, the focus of discussion to be put forward in the later parts of this chapter and in subsequent chapters is narrowed. The key findings put forward in the first part of this chapter are as follows. First, the case study network is not a transnational advocacy network in a meaningful sense. Consequently, it is concluded that it is necessary to pay particular attention, in applying to domestic networks the frameworks identified in the literature as appropriate to the analysis of transnational networks, to expanding or developing these in areas where existing frameworks are inappropriate or inadequate. Second, it is concluded that there is more potential for a transformative justice agenda to be developed through further exploration of the Housing Assembly and Poor People's Alliance clusters within the network rather than through exploration of other points of focus within the network. This is due to the existing overlaps between the two clusters and due to the apparent degree to which these may be built upon in contrast with the interaction between and scope for development of relationships with other clusters within the network.

The purpose of later sections of this chapter is to analyse the kinds of ties which exist between the case study network nodes in more detail. This narrows the focus of the earlier part of the chapter. The discussion is focused upon the existing ties and opportunities for more effective collaboration between the cluster of actors within the network associated with the Poor People's Alliance and the cluster of actors within the network associated with the Housing Assembly. This is because, as the first part of the chapter establishes, these two clusters already overlap to some degree. Conversely, the cluster of actors associated with SDI largely works within its own structures. There is not much scope for further or more effective collaboration between SDI-associated network nodes and those associated with either the Housing Assembly or the Poor People's Alliance. The opportunities that do exist for more effective collaboration between network actors are discussed further ahead. In this section of the chapter, the reasons behind the relationships which already exist between network actors are explored first. Second, the opportunities for improving or developing links between network actors and the threats to this are discussed.

Four areas of opportunity for and threats to effective collaboration are identified. These are, first, those which emanate from the specific characteristics of trade unions and their role in the network. Second, issues surrounding the capacity of and resources available to social movements and community-based organisations. Third, opportunities and threats which emerge from the influence of individual personalities on organisations and on the network, plus the influence of the politics and internal governance of organisations. Fourth, the issues which arise out of apparently shared rhetorical commitments across different actors within the network. Ultimately, conclusions are drawn with regard to the double-edged nature of opportunities which may also become threats and vice versa, with regard to the importance of resource access and allocation to pursuing more effective network action and with regard to the role of shared motivation between disparate actors in building effective collaboration.

The case study network

Primarily on the basis of empirical data collected during fieldwork, this part of the chapter puts forward a picture of the case study network as experienced and described by those involved. These network relationships are described and set out in diagrams. As mentioned previously, there are three principal clusters of actors which are referred to throughout this chapter and the rest of the book. These are the groups and organisations within or strongly linked to the Poor People's Alliance, the groups and organisations which make up the Housing Assembly and the groups and organisations closely tied to SDI. There are some areas of crossover between these three clusters, which is detailed further ahead. However, it is useful to understand that there are a number of focal points and power centres within the network.

The Poor People's Alliance is made up of grassroots, community-based social movement organisations. These are the AEC, Abahlali baseMjondolo (AbM), the Rural Network and the Landless People's Movement (LPM) (Poor People's Alliance n.d.). In the Western Cape (where the first part of this case study took place), the AEC and Abahlali baseMjondolo operate but the LPM and Rural Network do not (Poor People's Alliance n.d.). The groups which make up the Poor People's Alliance engage in a variety of action including community mobilisation, contentious protest actions and legal activism relating to opposing evictions, promoting housing rights and the rights of landless people. There are several further national ties emanating from this cluster of actors. The AEC, Abahlali baseMjondolo and (inasmuch as they continue to function) LPM work with the Socio-Economic Rights Institute (SERI). SERI is an NGO based in Johannesburg. SERI provides support of a predominantly legal kind to community-based and social movement organisations focusing in particular on urban and peri-urban contexts, including the abovementioned groups working on anti-eviction and housing issues.[1] SERI is also linked to some other organisations which come under the case study network.

The Housing Assembly is a forum for collaboration between a large number of actors in Cape Town. Principally, these are ILRIG (an NGO providing education, training and support to social movements and trade unions), the municipal workers' trade union SAMWU and a number of social movement organisations and community-based organisations (Blake 2012).[2] These include ISIS, a community-based organisation based in the Zille-raine Heights informal settlement, as well as other social movement organisations, some of which have links to the Poor People's Alliance (Blake 2012; Blake 2015; Heunis and Hoedemaker 2012).[3] The Housing Assembly also contains individuals who are not members or representatives of organised structures (Blake 2012).

SDI operates across South Africa and internationally. Affiliated federations of slum dwellers and shack dwellers have relationships with SDI and local partner NGOs in a large number of countries across the global South (SDI Programme Officer 2012; SDI 2012). SDI works in partnership with organisations and groups which fit into its structure in close relationships. In South Africa, this cluster of actors is made up of the SDI secretariat, an affiliate local NGO and a federation of shack dwellers and slum dwellers. In South Africa, SDI's affiliated local NGO is the Community Organising Urban Resource Centre (COURC). The federation of slum dwellers and shack dwellers is made up of the Federation of the Urban Poor (FEDUP) and the Informal Settlements Network (ISN). ISN joins up community-based organisations and groups in informal settlements across South Africa (SDI Programme Officer 2012; van Rensburg 2015; ISN Gauteng Provincial Leadership 2015). The work of SDI focuses on promoting savings schemes and microcredit for affected communities to acquire housing and on negotiating with all levels of government, plus international actors, in order to advocate for slum dwellers, shack dwellers and the urban poor (SDI Programme Officer 2012; see also van Rensburg 2015; ISN Gauteng Provincial Leadership 2015). In South Africa, the uTshani Fund finances the housing projects initiated through SDI affiliates' savings schemes (van Rensburg 2015; ISN Gauteng Provincial Leadership 2015).

In addition to affiliates of ISN and FEDUP being linked to the SDI secretariat and local NGO in South Africa, SDI also has relationships with some actors outside of its own structures (SDI Programme Officer 2012; SDI 2012; van Rensburg 2015). For instance, SDI in South Africa has a relationship with the Gauteng-based development NGO Planact (SDI Programme Officer 2012; van Rensburg 2015). SDI also has ties to government at all levels throughout South Africa and international links to UN bodies (SDI Programme Officer 2012; SDI 2012; South African SDI Alliance 2013; van Rensburg 2015). On the basis of research participant responses, outside of its own structures, SDI appears to focus its relationship-building largely on direct ties to policymakers through either local or national government or UN structures and upon ties with academic institutions and planners such as through the relationship SDI has with the University of Cape Town's planning department (SDI Programme Officer 2012; van Rensburg 2015; see also SDI 2012; South African SDI Alliance 2013). Due to the lack of crossover between this cluster of actors and the rest of the case study network, the SDI cluster is not focused upon in this book to the same extent as the other two identified clusters. The Housing Assembly and the Poor People's Alliance especially share a large number of ties, whereas the SDI cluster does not have a great many, or strong, links to groups outside its own structures.[4]

Interpreting data on network relationships

Before the sociograms of the network are presented, it is worthwhile to highlight some of the sources of data about relationships within the network and some of the factors which influence the ways in which this data is interpreted. Data from both interviews and written (published and unpublished) documents were used in order to map the case study network. The data are interpreted in light of the evidence and analysis put forward in existing literature. In particular, the potential pitfalls associated with research on social movements and the overlap between activism and scholarship in this area are brought to the forefront here (see Evans 2017). The main pitfalls are the danger of uncritically accepting the claims made by social movements and their academic advocates, the contrary danger of dismissing social movement praxis altogether and the risk of debates and disagreements between academics and commentators overshadowing engagement with the issues around which social movements mobilise (see Evans 2017).[5] These come to the forefront particularly in consideration of the extent to which social movement organisations and other groups live up to their (or their supporters') claims regarding democratic, participatory governance and politically consistent and principled engagement with other groups and organisations (see, e.g., Mdlalose 2014; Pointer 2004).

Mapping the network diagrammatically

Representing the case study network diagrammatically in sociograms made using *NetDraw* serves to highlight the direct and indirect local, national and international ties between different actors (Borgatti 2002). It is possible to acquire a sense of the extent of relations within and between the abovementioned clusters of actors within the network. A full list of acronyms and abbreviations used is also provided at the beginning of the book. Moreover, further details of the methodology used to create the sociograms in this chapter are provided in the introduction to the book.

Figure 3.1 maps the case study network as a basic sociogram. This shows all of the major relationships between actors described in the literature and in interviews with research participants.[6] The diagram does not describe every single relationship each actor has with any other organisation or group. Rather, this diagram focuses upon the relationships which are of most relevance to action taken on housing and land rights. Moreover, it is likely that further relationships which are not described in the literature or in research participants' interview responses exist. Nevertheless, the diagram provides an indication of the shape of the network and the extent of the overlap between the various clusters which act as hubs for ties between numerous network nodes.

Figure 3.2 highlights the Housing Assembly, Poor People's Alliance and SDI clusters of actors within the network. It is clear to see in this diagram the extent to which there are points of overlap between the three clusters. The Housing Assembly and the Poor People's Alliance especially share a large number of ties. The implications of and potential surrounding the association between these two clusters is discussed in greater detail in the chapters that follow. The high degree of separation between the cluster of actors associated with SDI and the other clusters within the network is also made clear in Figure 3.2. The diagram includes a relationship between SDI and Abahlali baseMjondolo. This is alleged to exist by Heinrich Böhmke, who has claimed that Abahlali baseMjondolo has an affiliation with SDI (Böhmke 2010a). However, it is highly questionable as to whether this

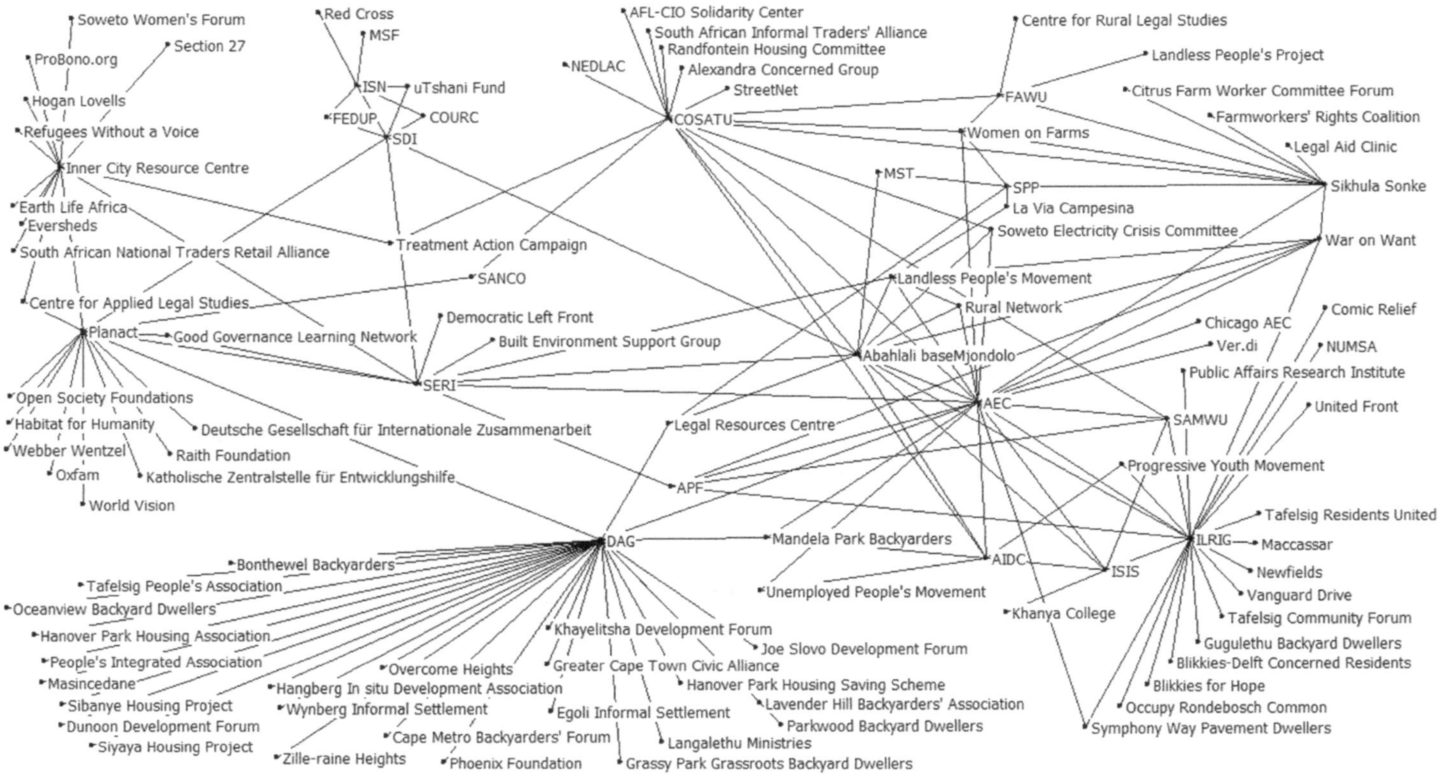

Figure 3.1 The case study network

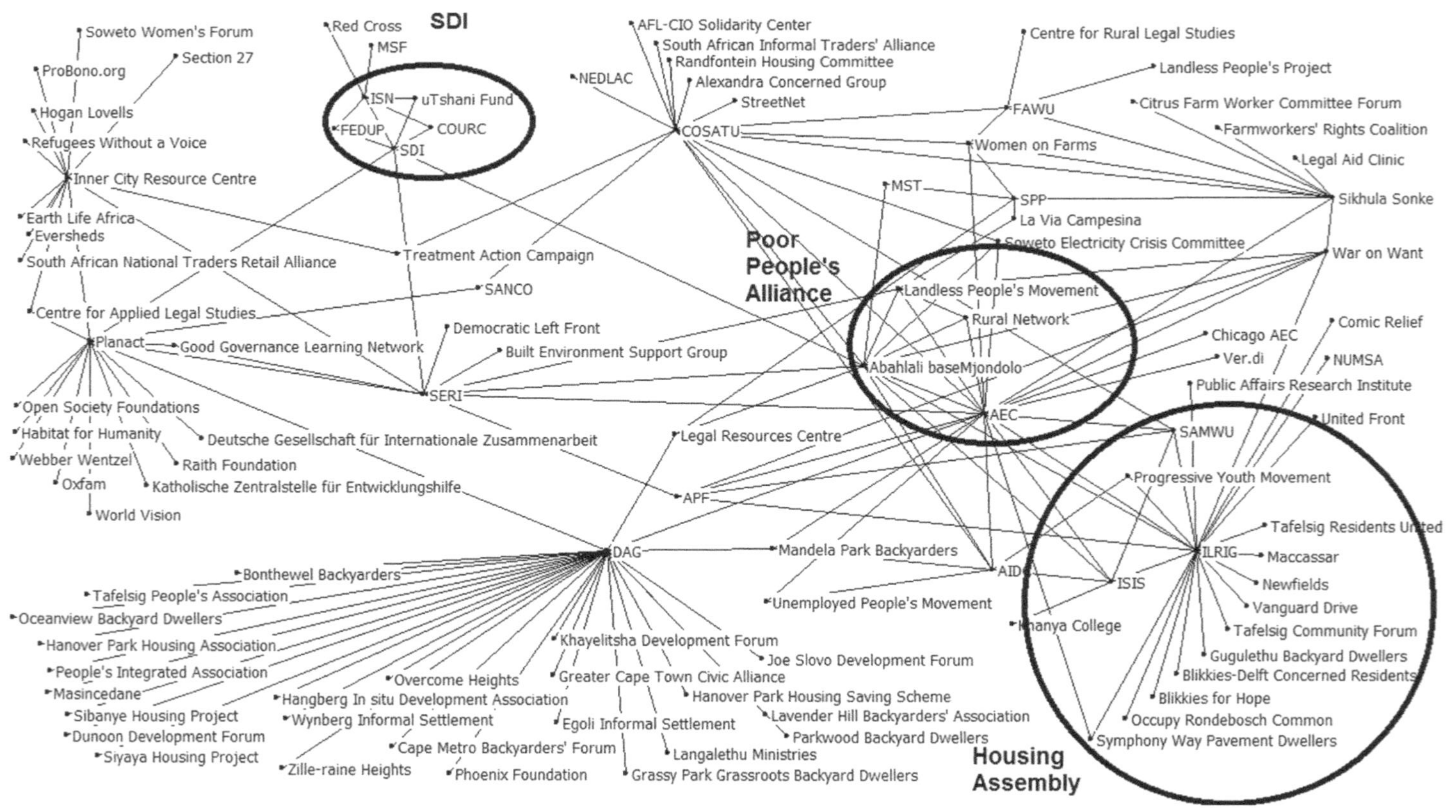

Figure 3.2 Housing Assembly, Poor People's Alliance and SDI clusters

relationship does in fact exist (in the form described by Böhmke at least) and, particularly in relation to this research, whether there is any relationship between the two groups in the Western Cape or urban Gauteng (see, e.g., Majavu 2012a; van Rensburg 2015; see also Evans 2017). Indeed, interviewees from SDI indicated that whilst there has been informal contact between SDI and Abahlali baseMjondolo, and the two groups have been present in the same meetings (such as with the Human Rights Commission), that there is not a close or formal relationship (van Rensburg 2015).[7] Even if the relationship described by Böhmke is genuine, this provides one of only three direct associations between the SDI cluster and the rest of the case study network found to exist in this research.

With regard to understanding the case study network usefully for this research, the diagrams in this chapter illustrate several key points but must also be contextualised. As mentioned earlier, it is likely that further relationships within the network not expressed in the diagrams exist. For instance, many of the nodes associated with ILRIG (but not shown as tied to other actors) in the Housing Assembly cluster of actors (detailed in Figure 3.2) are likely to have relationships with each other and possibly other actors. It is due to the limits of the data collection for this research that it is not possible to confirm this. Similarly, as the diagrams in this chapter take the form of basic sociograms, there is no differentiation made between different kinds of relationships between actors in the network. It may appear from Figures 3.1 and 3.2 that the Development Action Group (DAG) is the hub of a cluster of more actors and, therefore, of greater importance than some of the three main clusters that have been focused upon in this chapter. Whilst DAG does not work with any trade unions, it does have relationships with social movements and community-based organisations (Development Action Group 2012a; Development Action Group 2012b; Mchunu 2012). However, DAG's relationships with many of the community-based organisations, which act as nodes tied to DAG in the diagrams, are based on short-term collaboration linked to particular events and projects (Development Action Group 2012b; Mchunu 2012).[8] This contrasts with the more formalised and long-term relationship between the actors tied to SDI, the close collaboration between the groups which make up the Poor People's Alliance and the ongoing longer term collaboration between the Housing Assembly members.

It is also necessary to note that, in line with the focus of this research, the diagrams mapping the case study network in this chapter focus upon the groups and organisations active on land and housing rights in the urban Western Cape and urban Gauteng. As the relations between actors move away from this geographical and thematic focus, less data was collected, and less is expressed diagrammatically, about wider ties between different groups and organisations. Some broader relationships are expressed in the diagrams for illustrative purposes, emphasising the commonalities and indirect links between different nodes and clusters within the network, but the network map put forward in this chapter is not intended to be a definitive description of every relationship every actor has. The Democratic Left Front (DLF) for instance, is an organisation (described by some as a "pre-political party") which works with various trade unions and social movements (Böhmke 2012; Links 2011). The focus is not directly on land, housing or anti-eviction issues. However, as an interviewee from SERI explained that the organisation has taken part in events hosted by the DLF (but does not have a formal relationship with the organisation), the association is expressed in the diagrams (Tissington 2012a). Furthermore, an interviewee from the Alternative Information Development Centre (AIDC) indicated that he is a member of the DLF and individuals associated with the AEC are also members (Ashley 2012; Legassick 2010). These relationships are not detailed in the diagrams, as they are not organisation level and as they fall outside of the thematic focus of this research. Similarly, the diagrams depict a relationship between Khanya College and ISIS, as interviewees reported that Khanya College hosted a "Winter School" in which ISIS and other organisations participated (Heunis and Hoedemaker 2012). For this research, it is not, however, necessary to map all of Khanya College's ties to other community-based organisations.

In Figure 3.3, the international ties of the network are highlighted. It is worth re-emphasising that there are very few transnational ties in the network. Of the 107 nodes plotted on the diagram, just fourteen represent international actors.[9] Of these fourteen, interview responses and literature indicate that only four (MST, War on Want, Ver.di and the Chicago AEC group) are associated with groups which currently operate in the urban Western Cape. Interviewee responses and literature indicate that three of these (MST, the Chicago AEC group and Ver.di) are short-term or weak ties. Furthermore, including the international ties of groups which operate in urban Gauteng, the majority of these links are funding relationships, such as those between international foundations and the NGO Planact (see, e.g., Makwela and Simelane 2015). The relationship War on Want has with South African groups within the network is also as a funder, and one of the groups War on Want has a relationship with – the Anti-Privatisation Forum (APF) – has collapsed (Ashley 2012; Tissington 2012a; Twalo 2012; War on Want n.d.-a, n.d.-b, n.d.-c, n.d.-d, n.d.-e). Nevertheless, the association with War on Want is the strongest international tie plotted on the diagram. It would not, therefore, be accurate to describe the network as characterised by horizontal and reciprocal transnational relationships. In Keck and Sikkink's terms, the case study network is not a transnational advocacy network (Keck and Sikkink 1998: 8–9).

There are some other international ties which are not plotted on the diagram. In particular, SDI has links to UN agencies. However, due to the lack of crossover between this cluster of actors and the rest of the case study network, and because these international links were not highlighted by interviewees as especially important for activities related to this research, this is not focused upon in this book. There are also relationships with international actors through South Africa–based organisations with international links, such as the AFL-CIO Solidarity Center (linked to COSATU in the network), which is part of the US trade union federation AFL-CIO's international outreach work (Barrett 2015). However, again, these ties are not strongly linked to the rest of the network, nor were their activities found to be very significant in relation to the areas this research is concerned with.

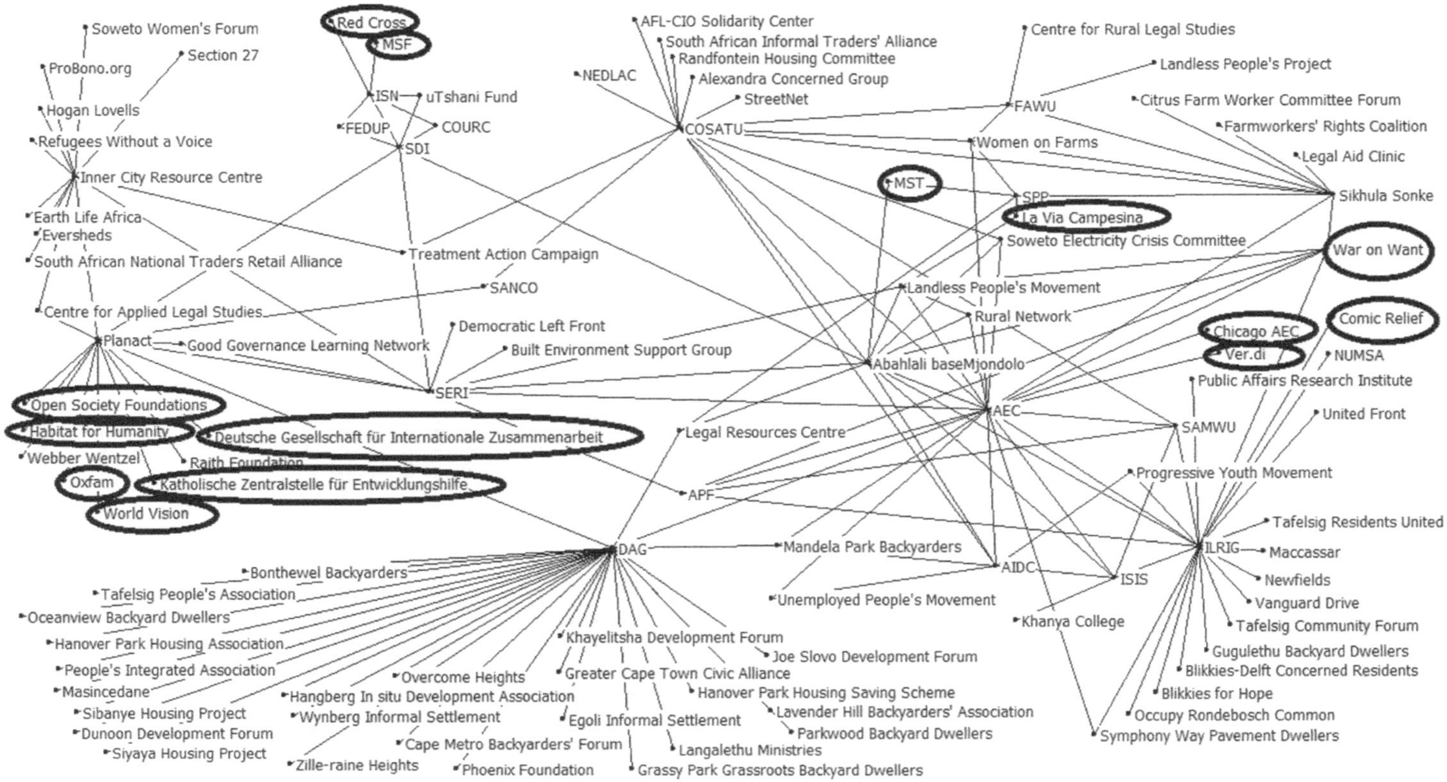

Figure 3.3 International ties of the case study network

Interrogating assumptions from the literature

The themes identified in the earlier chapters bring to light a number of assumptions which it is necessary to interrogate in regard to the case study network. There is some suggestion that domestic networks might be analysed in the same terms as and are likely to display similar features to transnational networks. There is a suggestion that NGOs (especially Northern NGOs) are the key actors in human rights networks and that human rights networks are (for the most part) analytically distinct from those addressing other issues such as labour networks. None of these assumptions are wholly confirmed by exploration of the case study network.

Boomerangs and spirals

The boomerang effect and the spiral process have been identified as key tools utilised by advocacy networks (see Keck and Sikkink 1998: 12–13; Risse and Sikkink 1999: 18–20; Risse and Ropp 2013: 5–9). Both these processes require significant transnational elements to the network. Significant transnational elements are not evident in the case study network. Moreover, neither process is evident in the case study network's repertoire of action. Severe limits on the capacity and resources of actors within the network (discussed in more detail in the next chapter) exclude the use of these tools from the realm of possibility. Additionally, the (few) transnational connections in the case study network are not in any significant way based upon the mobilisation of constituencies of support into the sort of action the boomerang effect and spiral process require.

In the case study network, there are relatively few NGOs. Far more numerous are social movements and community-based organisations. Indeed, the Poor People's Alliance, which is identified as a key cluster in the network, does not contain any actors other than social movements. Where NGOs are present in the network, they are not always key elements. On the one hand, ILRIG is an important hub node in the Housing Assembly and the NGO elements of the SDI-associated cluster are central to its structures. On the other hand, NGOs such as SERI and the Legal Resources Centre (LRC) are less integrated into the network – with long-term, strong ties – than other actors, and other NGOs, such as Planact, are not strongly connected to most of the network.[10] Moreover, international (especially Northern) NGOs are almost entirely absent from the network. Where there are connections to such actors, these have been described as funding relationships rather than as being based on participation in the network's core activities.

Framing, expertise and venue shopping

In the case study network, the various characteristics and positions of network nodes are utilised in the action taken by the network. For instance, the legal expertise of nodes such as SERI and the LRC are at times utilised by social movements within the network, whereas at others, the industrial relations mandate of the trade unions in the network is utilised (see, e.g., Jacobs 2012; Tissington 2012a; Mbana 2012). Whilst actors within the network make use of their relationships with one another to leverage resources (in the form of expertise as well as financial resources for instance), which is in line with descriptions of transnational networked action in the literature, wider strategies surrounding the mobilisation of disparate transnational constituencies of support and harnessing pressure from states or powerful international actors remain absent.

There is some evidence that actors in the case study network do make use of venue shopping to some extent (see Keck and Sikkink 1998). Translation of issues into a variety of different frames is also evident (see Merry 2006). For instance, some of the actors in the case study network are explicitly rights based in their framing of the issues they work on, whereas most are not. However, strategies which are utilised by the network include framing land and housing rights issues in terms of labour and industrial relations, political emancipation and, in some cases, in terms of rights (including legally defined rights) (see, e.g., Tissington 2012a; Twalo 2012; Jacobs 2012; Blake 2012).[11] The network as a whole does not frame the issues of land and housing rights in a consistent or uniform manner. Rather, the elements within the network put forward their own analyses and understandings which, where there is a degree of compatibility, facilitate the forging of relationships. Moreover, as mentioned earlier, actors in the network engage in venue shopping, for instance, framing anti-eviction action in terms of legally codified rights when pursuing court cases and in terms of political emancipation and ongoing resistance to the effects of apartheid in other arenas (Twalo 2012; Tissington 2012a).

Key findings from mapping the network

Actors connected to this network also have relationships which have not been detailed earlier. However, those which have been focused upon are the relationships and ties between organisations and groups which are of the most relevance for this research. That is to say, there has been a focus on organisations and groups taking action on land and anti-eviction issues and the relationships they have with other groups and organisations also working on the same issue. Through the localised focus of this research on the urban Western Cape and urban Gauteng, it can be seen that three main clusters of actors exist around the Poor People's Alliance, the Housing Assembly and SDI. It is also evident that at times these clusters have some overlap in terms of membership and links to other actors. Moreover, through mapping some of the relationships between groups and organisations which are not closely tied to these clusters, it is clear that there are in fact indirect relationships between all the clusters identified within the network beyond those ties which are easily observable within the localised case study.

Moving into the next part of the chapter and the chapters that follow, a greater focus is placed upon the Housing Assembly cluster of actors and the Poor People's Alliance cluster of actors. This is because these two clusters have a large amount of direct and indirect overlap. It has been established that there are links between these two clusters and the cluster of actors surrounding SDI. However, it is clear that SDI does not have a large number of, or close, relationships with actors outside of its own structures. This suggests that the scope for expanding, changing or improving the ways in which SDI works with other actors may be limited. Furthermore, the focus of SDI on schemes such as microcredit and savings schemes, plus the commitment to working with government wherever possible, contrasts somewhat with the positions put forward by many of the actors associated with both the Housing Assembly and the Poor People's Alliance. Indeed, in addition to the limited ties between the SDI-associated cluster of actors and other clusters within the network mentioned earlier, the approach of SDI limits the potential for greater collaboration with actors associated with the Housing Assembly or Poor People's Alliance. As an SDI press statement puts it, "SDI's experience, in every single country where it has a presence . . . have led it to dismiss the world view" attributed to Abahlali baseMjondolo "that regards the state and civil society as binary opposites" (SDI 2009). The statement goes on to say that

> SDI and AbM [Abahlali baseMjondolo] share the same point of departure. They both recognise that the power of those who control the world's resources depends on the systematic disempowerment of the global poor. This shared point of departure should be the basis for a broad-based alliance. This is the root of a real solidarity. Differences in strategies – between resistance and negotiating deals – create a healthy diversity within such an alliance.
>
> (SDI 2009)

However, as far as can be ascertained, this proposed alliance has not come to fruition (see, e.g., van Rensburg 2015). Moreover, given SDI's proclaimed dismissal of the worldview of actors affiliated to the Poor People's Alliance, it seems unlikely that a greater collaboration is feasible. Given this, and the analysis put forward in some of the literature of SDI as representing a form of nongovernmental co-option of poor people's struggles (see, e.g., Gibson 2011: 13), the discussion of potential improvement and increase of collaboration in the network in the rest of the book is concentrated largely on actors associated with clusters within the network other than SDI. At times, however, it is illuminating to discuss the praxis of SDI as shedding light upon that of other clusters through comparison.

Furthermore, it is clear that the case study network is not meaningfully transnational. It can be seen that whilst the actors associated with both the Housing Assembly and the Poor People's Alliance do have some international links, these are limited particularly with regard to the closeness of collaboration between actors. Consequently, the relationships analysed in the greatest detail in the rest of this chapter and in the chapters that follow are those between the groups and organisations operating in the localised case study areas of the urban Western

Cape and urban Gauteng. The subsequent analysis of the case study network also explicitly engages further with the assumptions put forward and the frameworks articulated in the largely transnational network-focused literature on advocacy networks.

What kinds of ties already exist?

With regard to the Housing Assembly and the Poor People's Alliance, there are two broad kinds of ties between network nodes which are of interest. There are ties between actors within these two clusters, and there are ties between actors linking the two clusters. Within these categories of relationship, ties vary with regard to their strength, duration and the degree of reciprocity. The reasons for these variations also differ.

The Housing Assembly

The strongest ties within the Housing Assembly appear to be between SAMWU and ILRIG. These organisations, especially ILRIG, act as hubs to which the other participants in the Housing Assembly are affixed. This is likely due in large part to the formal nature of and resources available to ILRIG and SAMWU. ILRIG is able to host meetings at which the members of the Housing Assembly can interact. Moreover, they have some capacity to provide funding to the social movement and community activist members of the Housing Assembly for travel to meetings and similar expenses. This facilitates the ties between the various members of the Housing Assembly.

SAMWU's resources are clearly also important for the functioning of the Housing Assembly. The Housing Assembly's written memorandum of demands to the City of Cape Town Council is produced on SAMWU-headed paper, listing SAMWU's Cape Metro Region office as the address (South African Municipal Workers' Union and Housing Assembly 2012). The Acting City Manager's response to the Housing Assembly was sent care of the SAMWU office (Marsden 2012). The importance of the fact that SAMWU can provide a reliable permanent address for correspondence translates into a strong tie between SAMWU and the rest of the Housing Assembly. However, this does not necessarily mean that SAMWU, as one of the hub nodes within the Housing Assembly, has strong ties with all of the individual Housing Assembly members.

Relationships between SAMWU and ILRIG as the hub of the Housing Assembly and the other members vary. Interviewees from social movements stated that even though ILRIG is in a position to reimburse expenses to activists travelling in order to attend workshops and meetings, the need to have or borrow money in order to initially pay for transport could be prohibitive. One research participant from ISIS commented that "we're unemployed, so with all the meetings we must borrow here travelling money, borrow there, and there's not always money so we can't" (Heunis and Hoedemaker 2012).[12] Interviewees from ILRIG also pointed to the difference between working with some social movements and community-based organisations in the Housing Assembly (Blake 2012). On the basis of the interview data, some groups such as ISIS seem to have had a closer and longer lasting relationship with the Housing Assembly than others. It was, for instance, suggested by an ILRIG worker that closer relationships are more difficult with the members of the Housing Assembly who are not already organised in some sort of structure. Consequently, there has been some attempt to assist communities in organising (Blake 2012).

The reasons behind the collaboration between the cluster of actors associated with the Housing Assembly vary. However, certain themes can be detected in analysing the rationales given by the various groups involved. First, from the point of view of the NGO ILRIG, pursuing relationships with social movements and community-based organisations as well as with trade unions fulfils the organisation's strategic aims (Xali 2012). According to their analysis, there is an imperative to provide assistance in struggles within the working class (Xali 2012). This includes struggles concerning employed workers represented by formal trade unions. Recognising the large constituency of unemployed people in South Africa, and their particular vulnerability to evictions and inadequate housing provision, necessitates also working with groups not covered by trade unions (Xali 2012). Furthermore, the literature evaluating the roles of trade unions and social movements post-apartheid supports the idea that there has been a shift in the focus of sites of struggle (see, e.g., Ballard et al. 2005; Beresford 2006). Trade unions do not hold as significant a position in calling for social change as they did during apartheid. The closeness of COSATU-affiliated unions to the ANC (discussed in relation to threats and opportunities ahead) provides one reason for the emergence of oppositional social movements (Ballard et al. 2005: 622–623). The centrality of unemployed people to many of these movements provides another (see, e.g., Beresford 2006: 53–54; see also Barrett 2015; McKinley 2015). In line with the literature on the subject, NGO representatives put forward the view that social movements require assistance in achieving their aims (Blake 2012; Ashley 2012; Ballard et al. 2005: 627). This is important for an analysis of the pursuit of transformative justice. In the next chapter this is explored in more detail with reference to the political responsibilities of network actors.

Second, ILRIG's analysis is in line with the positions put forward by research participants from trade unions and social movement activists associated with the Housing Assembly. Interviewees highlighted the long-standing tradition of social (as opposed to merely industrial) trade unionism in South Africa (Ashley 2012; Jacobs 2012). It is the aim of not only NGOs such as ILRIG to engage with both formally employed and trade union-represented workers and with community-based social movement activists, but also of SAMWU and, indeed, of COSATU to engage with social and political issues beyond those directly concerning industrial relations (Jacobs 2012; Louw 2012). Trade union representatives interviewed were keen to highlight that their aim is not to impose upon social movements in partnerships (Jacobs 2012; Louw 2012). Research participants from SAMWU and from COSATU reported that they would get involved in a relationship with groups such as housing rights social movements only if a "call for assistance" was made (Louw 2012; see also Jacobs 2012; Wa Mapena 2015). According to Mario Jacobs (2012), this is the manner in which SAMWU's relationship with the Housing Assembly came about. He commented that

> it is on that basis that we were approached by the Housing Assembly to say "SAMWU, we like what you are doing, we would want to get on board, we believe there are common issues at stake," and it serves the interests of both organisations if we rally our forces as one and not to a situation where we pursue the same issue via different organisations.
>
> (Jacobs 2012)

Third, the motivation for community-based and social movement organisations to participate in the Housing Assembly is multifaceted. Each facet relates to the aforementioned notion that social movements require assistance in order to achieve their aims. The educational and training workshops provided by ILRIG as part of the Housing Assembly activities is one instance of this. Some research participants from groups affiliated to the Housing Assembly stated that prior to becoming involved in housing activism, they "didn't know anything about politics" and that ILRIG's support had helped them in this regard (Heunis and Hoedemaker 2012).

The weight added to action taken by a larger group of actors is a factor motivating participation in the Housing Assembly. Activists interviewed expressed a desire to link up the activities of disparate groups with the same aims in order to increase effectiveness (Heunis and Hoedemaker 2012; Blake 2012). The need to demonstrate unity and strength in numbers was cited by interviewees from community-based and social movement organisations as a key motive for joining with the Housing Assembly (Heunis and Hoedemaker 2012).

The Poor People's Alliance

It has previously been mentioned that the links between the groups participating in the Poor People's Alliance in the Western Cape are strong. The Western Cape branch of Abahlali baseMjondolo grew out of the Western Cape Anti-Eviction Campaign, and research participants stated that the leadership of both groups are closely related. However, as mentioned earlier, not all of the groups that make up the Poor People's Alliance operate in the Western Cape (or urban areas of Gauteng). Moreover, it was suggested in interviews that several of the groups within the Poor People's Alliance are either in severe decline or have ceased to functionally exist. This includes those which operate in the Western Cape. Notwithstanding the possible collapse of some organisations involved (discussed in more detail ahead), the reasons given by interviewees for seeking to link up within the Poor People's Alliance were similar to those given by participants in the Housing Assembly. An interviewee from the Western Cape Anti-Eviction Campaign stated that the purpose of the Poor People's Alliance is to "table the issues of the community" (Twalo 2012). It was also suggested that the aim is for the Poor People's Alliance to "be the platform that every poor person in South Africa is going to make use of for the benefit of our own people" (Twalo 2012). The desire to link together disparate groups struggling around housing and related issues into a national platform was also expressed (Twalo 2012). As with the actors closely associated with the Housing Assembly, the research participants from community-based and social movement organisations which form the Poor People's Alliance reported the added campaigning strength as an important motivation for entering into relationships with other groups (Twalo 2012).

The attitude of the Poor People's Alliance's member organisations towards NGOs and other actors also partially explains the composition of the cluster and kinds of ties that exist within it. The theme of social movements requiring support to be effective in their action was evident in interviews with members of groups closely associated with both the Housing Assembly and the Poor People's Alliance. However, the degrees to which different organisations have been willing to seek support through partnerships with NGOs – such as ILRIG in the Housing Assembly – vary. A desire to access the training programmes and related support offered by ILRIG was given in interviews as one of the factors motivating groups to join the Housing Assembly. In contrast, the expressed desire to remain independent from NGOs seems to push the participants in the Poor People's Alliance towards close collaboration with each other rather than with initiatives such as the Housing Assembly. The comments of interviewees from social movement organisations in the Housing Assembly praising the support provided by ILRIG contrast somewhat with the view put forward by a representative of the Western Cape Anti-Eviction Campaign, who stated in relation to ILRIG that "we don't have smooth relationship with them" (Twalo 2012). When interviewed, the chairperson of the Western Cape Anti-Eviction Campaign emphasised the importance of affected communities to housing and related activism, several times stating that "without us there's nothing" (Twalo 2012). This sentiment was linked to both a critique of the AEC's perception of the role of NGOs in supporting social movement struggles and to the proposed manner in which the Poor People's Alliance's action ought to be organised and led. The threats to and opportunities for more effective collaboration between actors associated with these positions are explored in more detail ahead.

Ties between both clusters

There are both direct and indirect ties between the Housing Assembly and the Poor People's Alliance clusters of actors. These vary with regard to strength, duration and formality. Nevertheless, certain themes are recurrent in research participants' explanations of many of these relationships. With regard to the AEC's relationship with the Housing Assembly, Figures 3.1–3.3 indicate that individual AEC members and some groups affiliated to the AEC (such as the Mandela Park

Backyarders) participate in Housing Assembly events. Further to this, it is clear that the AEC's public position as critical of NGOs, including ILRIG specifically, does not translate into a universally held position within the organisation. As previously mentioned, the AEC's chairperson stated that the relationship with ILRIG had not been "smooth". Another AEC activist, however, commented that "some NGOs were quite supportive, I would say. Like ILRIG. They would support us" (Hendricks 2012).

Prior to the formation of the Housing Assembly, there had also been a relationship between SAMWU and the AEC which was supported by ILRIG.[13] Though it has declined and some of the union's support for the AEC has been withdrawn, interviewees reported that in some form this relationship is ongoing (Hendricks 2012). SAMWU also has a direct relationship with the AEC through activists taking part in both organisations (Jacobs 2012; Hendricks 2012). In the Western Cape, the AEC has also had a relationship with COSATU the trade union confederation (Louw 2012).[14] As with the relationship between SAMWU and the AEC, it would seem that the formal relationship between COSATU and the AEC has declined over time. However, interviewees reported that COSATU continues to work with activists from both the AEC and Abahlali baseMjondolo (Louw 2012).[15]

It was also reported by interviewees that Abahlali baseMjondolo, or at least some of its members, participate in Housing Assembly activities (Heunis and Hoedemaker 2012). The existence of these overlaps between the Housing Assembly cluster of actors and the Poor People's Alliance cluster of actors is consistent with the explanations of different groups' approaches put forward by research participants. The AEC chairperson commented that "we are a flexible kind of activist, or social movement activist, you know, because what is important at the end of the day is to convey the frustration, you know, and the homelessness and landlessness of our own people" (Twalo 2012). Similarly, another AEC member stated that the AEC "works with any organisation as long as it deals with the issues at hand – what the Anti-Eviction stands for. So if it's housing or related to housing then we work with any organisation" (Hendricks 2012). A SAMWU representative explained their approach by saying that "the union cannot simply only advance the interests and issues affecting workers. It must be broader than that". He went on to argue that "people are not going to come to you and say 'but we want to be part of your campaign' if they don't see you actively pursuing what your campaign is meant to achieve" (Jacobs 2012).

Furthermore, indirect links between the Housing Assembly and the Poor People's Alliance exist through the two clusters' interaction with COSATU. SAMWU is a COSATU affiliate. ILRIG works with COSATU. There is a perception put forward by some interviewees that COSATU has not been supportive of social movements. One interviewee commented that from COSATU "there's quite a lot of antithesis towards the social movements or popular things, they – these are 'unruly elements', 'undisciplined' et cetera, who, you know, are involved in these destructive service delivery riots and besides they're ultra-left, so that's that" (Ashley 2012). Another interviewee suggested that in contrast to SAMWU's actions, the COSATU federation had not been supportive towards social movements such as the AEC and that COSATU's position had at times been antagonistic due to the perception that social movements intend to challenge the ANC and Tripartite Alliance (Xali 2012). Despite this, research participants also posited that some elements within the COSATU leadership are keen to build broader alliances with community-based organisations (Ashley 2012).[16] Historic and ongoing links between COSATU and movements associated with the Poor People's Alliance were also highlighted. Mike Louw, an interviewee from COSATU's regional offices in Cape Town, commented that when it was first formed, the AEC "was a COSATU baby" (Louw 2012). He also emphasised that "the intention is, obviously, to try and work together as much as we can and to support one another wherever we can" (Louw 2012). Naming specific activists from Abahlali baseMjondolo and the AEC, Louw stated that "on an individual basis" COSATU and members of the Poor People's Alliance "can talk, we can advise one another, we can get involved in workshops and stuff like that" (Louw 2012). The rhetorical commitments of organisations closely associated with both the Poor People's Alliance and the Housing Assembly to working as much as possible with other groups which share similar aims appears to be borne out in reality to some extent. Though they are not all particularly strong or well-sustained relationships, it is evident that there are instances of collaboration and overlap between even some of the apparently most disparate nodes attached to the anti-eviction and housing rights network in South Africa, especially in the urban Western Cape.

What threats to and opportunities for more effective collaboration exist?

Having examined the kinds of relationships that exist within the case study network and explored a number of research participants' explanations of the motivation behind pursuing these, it is necessary to turn attention to issues affecting the relationships between actors and issues affecting the aims of the network. There are both threats to and opportunities for more effective collaboration between actors in the case study network. On the basis of the data collected in this research, there are some clear areas in which opportunities for more effective collaboration between network actors arise. However, certain actors' characteristics and approaches to practice necessarily come into conflict with each other. Nevertheless, there are some threats to effective collaboration which may also be understood as opportunities.

Specific characteristics of trade unions

One of the more obvious points of tension between the various actors involved in the case study network is that regarding the position and role of trade unions. The closeness of COSATU and its affiliated unions to the ANC is regularly cited in the literature and by those interviewed for this research as a problem for the building of alliances between trade unions and groups such as social movements (see, e.g., Ballard et al. 2005: 622; Beresford 2006; Ashley 2012; Louw 2012). Through participating in the Tripartite Alliance, COSATU and affiliated unions may be seen as unwilling or unable to criticise government policies and the effect these have on housing rights and for landless people. One interviewee stated that "COSATU has also become dominated by the politics of the ANC, which itself creates huge amounts of differences as tensions emerge within the ANC and so that preoccupies them to look within the Alliance" rather than building relationships with social movements and community-based organisations (Ashley 2012). The data collected in this research do not wholly support this interpretation. In interviews, representatives of COSATU and SAMWU (which is COSATU-affiliated) were at times critical of the ANC and its relationship to COSATU. Moreover, interviewees displayed a willingness to work with other groups including social movements critical of the ANC. In the Western Cape, specifically, it may be possible for this willingness to be translated into actual collaboration more effectively than in other parts of South Africa owing to the ANC's position as opposition party in both the City of Cape Town and Western Cape Province. It is easier for ANC-aligned groups to join with social movements in criticising or opposing Democratic Alliance (DA) policies than it is to criticise or oppose ANC policies. It remains to be seen how changes in the City of Johannesburg's government (where, following elections in 2016, the DA ousted the ANC to form a minority administration with support from smaller parties), and any future shifts in Gauteng's provincial government, might affect these dynamics (see, e.g., Macharia 2016).

The threat to effective collaboration which comes with COSATU's closeness to the ANC – and with it, to national government – is not likely to be entirely overcome, though. Social movement activists interviewed maintained criticism of the ANC and party politics more broadly. COSATU-linked research participants commented that the alliance with the ANC is likely to continue as long as the participating organisations view it as mutually beneficial, and that for the time being, those charged with decision making in this regard are likely to see the relationship as continuing to be of benefit (Jacobs 2012; Louw 2012). This is in line with some claims within the literature that COSATU trade unions are "trapped in corporatism" and thus face difficulties in forging links with social movement organisations (Beresford 2006). Mike Louw of COSATU stated, "if we were able to be independent we would then be able to draw a larger mass of people towards us to make sure that we can get them [the ANC] to change" (Louw 2012). However, he also commented that "there's always going to be these formal ties that the COSATU has, that causes others not to be friendly towards us" (Louw 2012).[17]

Furthermore, the fact that COSATU-affiliated trade unions tend to represent (relatively) securely employed, salaried (and, likely, disproportionately male) workers, whereas landless people and shack dwellers undertaking housing activism are more likely to be unemployed or in precarious or informal work (and more likely to be women), means that even if their interactions are not outright antagonistic, the overlap between trade unions' and social movements' constituencies and key priorities may not always heavily cross over (see, e.g., Barrett 2015; see also Mdlalose 2014; Beresford 2006).[18] Key to the development of partnerships and collaboration between the trade unions and the other actors (especially social movements) in the network will be a mutual willingness to engage in dialogue. On the part of those interviewed from SAMWU and COSATU, this appears to be present. Louw, for instance, suggested that COSATU is willing to try to overcome historical "stumbling blocks" preventing closer collaboration with the AEC and Abahlali baseMjondolo, but that this "seems to be a longer term project than what I thought it would be" (Louw 2012). The potential role of social movements in pursuing more effective relationships with unions (and other network actors) is detailed ahead.

SAMWU's status as a trade union is also important with regard to its role within the Housing Assembly. As a trade union, SAMWU has recognised expertise in negotiation. Moreover, the issues of service delivery and housing provision which come under the Housing Assembly's remit affect SAMWU members and may be affected by employers' (i.e. local governments') actions. This means it may be possible for the Housing Assembly's concerns to be reflected in collective bargaining and through SAMWU's contribution to South Africa's corporatist industrial relations mechanisms. Mario Jacobs of SAMWU stated that

> we are now at the point where we have declared a dispute against the municipality that will enable the union and its members supporting the local municipality to go on protected strike action in so far as that demands are concerned.
> (Jacobs 2012)

This kind of action has potential to facilitate opportunities for further collaboration with other network actors. The legally mandated and regulated process of an industrial dispute opens up a forum, which is accessible only to trade unions, in which concerns such as some of those of the Housing Assembly may be raised. Not all aspects of housing rights activism can be addressed in this way. However, the language, framing and formal legal processes through which industrial disputes take place might plausibly provide an opportunity for the common ground between the demands of the trade union and community-based organisations working on housing to be brought into focus (see, e.g., Jacobs 2012; Barrett 2015; see also Evans 2015). This in turn could produce an opportunity for deeper collaboration and, if the industrial relations approach to pursuing the network's goals proves fruitful, for further use of these modes of action. Indeed, the significance of anti-eviction work to the industrial role of farm workers' unions was highlighted by interviewees from the COSATU-affiliated Food and Allied Workers' Union (FAWU) and the independent Sikhula Sonke trade unions (Mbana 2012; Sikhula Sonke Official 2012). This area of commonality between the concerns of urban and rural workers and with (largely) unemployed landless people provides some potential for deeper collaboration between housing rights activists even beyond urban areas.

There are, however, factors that might prevent or limit wider collaboration between trade unions and other actors. The aforementioned barrier COSATU's ANC-affiliation can provide to close partnership between member unions and other actors is one. This is likely to be more of an issue for national organising as there is a higher likelihood of coming into conflict with ANC policies and ANC-controlled jurisdictions. Another factor is the question of the extent to which available resources provide these actors with the capacity to follow up on these opportunities. Indeed, referring to COSATU's commitments to engage with issues "beyond the factory gate", one research participant reported that "you have capacity of a union like COSATU at a national level to make important statements on corruption and so on, it doesn't filter through in terms of what its affiliates can do at a regional, local level" (Ashley 2012; see also Barrett 2015).

Capacity and resources of social movements and community-based organisations

Social movements and community-based organisations in the network are severely under-resourced. This is in terms of both financial and non-financial resources. An AEC representative reported that the Poor People's Alliance "is not being financed so that it can be effective" (Twalo 2012). Another AEC activist referred to the limiting effect of the group's lack of resources, stating, "we tried working outside the Western Cape but sometimes it's difficult because of the transport and so on" (Hendricks 2012). The same activist also commented that "financially we struggled" (Hendricks 2012). Similarly, an interviewee from the Johannesburg-based Inner City Resource Centre (ICRC) – a self-defined "community-based organisation" now registered as an NGO with its own office but which began much more informally – stated that funding was "a big challenge" and noted that "I dedicated my time and energy for eight years without any funding" (Sibanda 2015). In one sense, this lack of resources incentivises social movements and community-based organisations to pursue relationships with and support from other actors.[19] This can be the case even in instances where financial support is not provided. Referring to the AEC's relationships with NGOs and trade unions, a research participant from the AEC stated that

> sometimes you won't get financial – like – support, but you will get support in another way, like they would make, like, printing for us, all that type of thing. Like SAMWU would come on board; we can use their offices, their phones – that type of thing.
>
> (Hendricks 2012)

Similarly, a research participant from the ICRC argued that gaining access to office space and telephones through partnering with CALS was a key form of support prior to the organisation securing its own office space and (limited) funding (Sibanda 2015). Organisations such as NGOs and trade unions are likely to have resources such as office space and printing facilities. Social movements and community-based organisations frequently lack resources including of this sort. Within the case study network, interviewees from a number of organisations expressed a commitment to supporting social movements and community-based organisations in action on housing issues. Mike Louw's statement that COSATU intends to work with and support social movements on anti-eviction and housing rights issues "wherever we can" has already been mentioned (Louw 2012). When interviewed in 2012, Michael Blake of ILRIG described the organisation's position in relation to housing issues, positing that "what people are emphasising now is reaching out to all those affected by unfit housing conditions" (Blake 2012). Mthetho Xali, also of ILRIG, emphasised the organisation's position that it will work with both community-based struggles made up largely of unemployed people such as those involved in housing-related social movements and with organised labour represented through trade unions (Xali 2012). These commitments to support social movements coupled with the movements' needs to access resources available to NGOs and trade unions amounts to an opportunity for relationships between the community-based housing movements and the NGOs and trade unions to be developed.

The under-resourced nature of the community-based organisations and social movement organisations involved in housing-related activism in the case study network does not just highlight opportunities for collaboration. In itself, a lack of resources limits the scope of action taken by social movements. One interviewee from the AEC (quoted earlier) suggested that attempts to expand the group to include those outside of the Western Cape failed in part due to a lack of access to transport. Similarly, a representative of Sikhula Sonke reported that despite some previous collaboration and some platform sharing with the Western Cape Anti-Eviction Campaign, close and regular interaction is not possible due to both organisations' limited resources (Sikhula Sonke Official 2012).

The perception that NGOs and other actors possess resources which social movements and community-based organisations lack, and the consequences of this, can threaten successful collaboration. The chairperson of the AEC reported that

> We as social movement activists, we don't like our own community's issues to be – people to make us a laughing stock when it comes to our own issues. Because what we discovered from NGOs: they are getting funds elsewhere or in the country at the expense of social movements, you know, and they are not involved when it comes day by day problems of the community.
>
> (Twalo 2012)

An interviewee from AIDC, which has worked with groups affiliated to both the Housing Assembly and the Poor People's Alliance, and is involved in a campaign to create jobs oriented around halting climate change (see AIDC n.d.; One Million Climate Jobs Campaign n.d.), made reference to the problems these kinds of attitude can create for relationship-building from the point of view of NGOs. He stated that

> what makes it worse is when you put this in an NGO context where NGOs have lots of resources and it's understood "why can't you give us money for buses or this? You've got all this money," you look at – without understanding that NGOs [are] themselves accountable to donors. They receive money for building, let's say, a campaign on climate jobs; they can't give money for a housing conference or workshop or mobilisation et cetera. So there's these levels of distrust that have to be overcome and this has bedevilled a lot of initiatives post-apartheid.
>
> (Ashley 2012)

Related to the tensions over access to resources is the influence resources have upon power dynamics between network actors. The AEC chairperson commented on the AEC's relationship with AIDC by saying "we always complain to them that they dictate terms" (Twalo 2012). This exemplifies the distrust between apparently well-resourced NGOs and under-resourced social movements mentioned by Brian Ashley in the comments reproduced above. Referring to COSATU's approach to working with social movements such as the AEC, Louw argued that "we're not going to impose anything" (Louw 2012). However, in these relationships "sometimes when we would want to suggest or would want to argue in a particular direction others would want to suggest that we're trying to impose because of our size and this and that and the other" (Louw 2012). Consequently, the decision has sometimes been made to withdraw from pursuing close relationships with particular movements on particular issues (Louw 2012). Discussing the imbalance in access to resources between different groups and organisations involved in the Housing Assembly, Mario Jacobs similarly emphasised that SAMWU's position is that

> we're not prescriptive to say, and we can never begin to say, that we form this united front, the united front is informed by you bringing to the party *x* pounds or *x* number of South African Rands. The objective is to advance what is known as the common interests of the parties and not to say that that objective can only be achieved if we all plough in an equal number or an equal percentage of resources. It would be foolish to suggest any such approach to a united front tactic.
>
> (Jacobs 2012)

It is clear from the abovementioned comments from interviewees and from the existing literature that tensions over resources continue to threaten collaboration in certain areas. However, recognition of the resource imbalance in the network, such as that expressed by Jacobs, suggests the beginning of some scope for overcoming difficulties in these relationships. This is explored in greater detail in the next chapter with an analytical lens turned towards the political responsibilities of network actors.

Personalities, politics and organisational governance

Following on from the issues relating to the capacity and resources of social movements are threats to and opportunities for collaboration relating to the roles of individual personalities, and the politics and internal governance of different organisations. It has already been mentioned that COSATU representatives have found it possible to work with members of groups like Abahlali baseMjondolo and the AEC "on an individual basis" despite those groups' antipathy towards COSATU's ANC alignment.[20] This represents an important opportunity for developing more effective collaboration between different actors. Indeed, Patrick Bond argues that post-apartheid social movements have made most progress when they have built alliances with COSATU (though he warns that COSATU's ANC-affiliation has a limiting effect on such alliances) (Bond 2012). Similarly, the fact that Abahlali baseMjondolo members, individual AEC members and groups closely linked to the AEC have participated in the Housing Assembly (despite the organisational relationship between the AEC and ILRIG not always being "smooth")[21] represents an opportunity. Interviewees from a number of other organisations in the network also expressed the desire to unite community struggles over land and housing, to facilitate the capacity of communities to organise and to link these with specialist support in professionalised organisations (see, e.g., Makwela and Simelane 2015; Wa Mapena 2015). The ability of individuals to overcome organisational differences to the extent that it is possible for them to work with each other suggests there is enough common ground for further and deeper collaboration to be explored.

As well as representing opportunities for new or improved relationships, the influence of individual personalities can also threaten collaboration. This relates to issues of inter- and intra-organisational politics and to the internal governance of organisations. It is clear from the research carried out for this book that collaboration within and between, and the efficacy of, both the Poor People's Alliance cluster of actors and the Housing Assembly cluster of actors are affected by these issues. For instance, it has been questioned whether the AEC continues to exist in a meaningful sense. Interviewees reported variously that the AEC has significantly declined in recent years (Xali 2012), that it has split into more than one group (Heunis and Hoedemaker 2012) and that it no longer functionally exists (Blake 2012). One interviewee reported that "there is like an Anti-Eviction Campaign that is run by three or four, five people but accordingly to others there's no more Anti-Eviction Campaign" (Heunis and Hoedemaker 2012). Another interviewee added "there's two Anti-Eviction Campaigns. The old [name redacted] thing and the new elected committee" (Heunis and Hoedemaker 2012).

The negative impact of particular individuals dominating within social movement organisations was raised by several interviewees (see also Pointer 2004;

Legassick 2011; Mdlalose 2014). In particular, the lack of resources – especially financial resources – available to social movements was cited by research participants as a key factor motivating splits and internal divisions within organisations. An AEC activist explained,

> as time went on I would say people started to – individual people – started to think that they own the AEC, they own it. It's not anymore community-based organisation, it's not community. It's – they're thinking that they – it's like they want to run away with it, just get some sponsors, tell the sponsors this and that, get some money in and not actually ploughing it back to the community by pocketing it themselves.
>
> (Hendricks 2012)

She also reported that, despite successes for the organisation, "as the time went on people are getting big headed, you know. The AEC can't exist without them because they are the brains and all that and they don't need this one, they don't need that one" (Hendricks 2012). This tallies with the comments of an interviewee that, in relation to the internal governance of groups such as the AEC,

> it goes with a charismatic handful at the top, a militant style, you can bring on the people with a loudhailer et cetera but you actually miss out on who the people really are and their role is in building the organisation as opposed to the committee.
>
> (Blake 2012)

Another interviewee commented that social movements are made up of many people who

> become active who are unemployed. It then – people are on constantly on look-out of survivalist opportunities. So to get a, to get the, job if there's a job going with the Anti-Privatisation Forum or in the Anti-Eviction Campaign et cetera is critical in terms of altering life's circumstances et cetera.
>
> (Ashley 2012)

He went on to comment that this kind of situation "breeds a lot of, kind of, resentments and conflicts" and that in the past, social movements have been "torn apart" by issues relating to funding (Ashley 2012). Similarly, referring to the divisions within the AEC, an ISIS activist stated "there's always hassles and it's just money, money, money" (Heunis and Hoedemaker 2012).

As well as divisions sparked by conflict over financial resources, further issues relating to internal organisational governance affect collaboration within the network. Michael Blake referred to how, within groups participating in the Housing Assembly, there "have been all kinds of political divisions" and "all kinds of shenanigans" resulting in four separate organisations operating in the Delft area, some of which are also close to the AEC (Blake 2012). Despite these divisions, participation in the Housing Assembly is maintained. In interview, Blake summed up the existing dynamic, "hopefully through the Housing Assembly we can ensure that people come together and something gets sorted out but at the moment it's very messy" (Blake 2012). Reflecting this is the position of Abahlali baseMjondolo in the network. Whilst some interviewees reported that Abahlali baseMjondolo in the Western Cape is almost indistinguishable from the AEC, others differentiated between the two groups in their comments. While highlighting the perceived divisions within, and possible collapse of, the AEC, interviewees from ISIS contrasted this with reporting that Abahlali baseMjondolo members take part in the Housing Assembly and the perception that Abahlali baseMjondolo are "in real struggle" (as opposed to being engaged in opportunism or "hassles" over money) (Heunis and Hoedemaker 2012). However, it can also be seen that Abahlali baseMjondolo are not immune to the splits and divisions which have affected other groups in the network. In April 2012, it would appear that the previously existing leadership of Abahlali baseMjondolo's Western Cape branch was removed and replaced. This seems to have followed intervention from a delegation from Abahlali baseMjondolo in Durban in response to some form of complaint against the previous leadership (Abahlali baseMjondolo 2012a; Abahlali baseMjondolo 2012b). The exact details of these events remain largely mysterious to an outsider, and during the research for this book, it was not possible to successfully contact Abahlali baseMjondolo after these events occurred. These events would appear to lend credence to some of Heinrich Böhmke's concerns regarding the practice of Abahlali baseMjondolo and other social movements and may suggest that his hope that the Western Cape branch of Abahlali baseMjondolo would avoid the problems allegedly besetting the Durban branch has not been borne out (Böhmke 2010a; Böhmke 2010b; see also Mdlalose 2014; Steyn 2016).

The political positioning of different groups is also a key issue relating to collaboration within the network. It has already been noted that to some extent various organisations closely linked to the Poor People's Alliance cluster and the Housing Assembly cluster have managed to forge links. Commitments to work with other groups sharing overlapping interests are realised in reality in some cases, particularly through ties based on individuals participating in the activities of both the main clusters within the network. Conversely, threats to effective collaboration due to organisational politics are evident.[22] The perception some social movements, especially those affiliated to the Poor People's Alliance, have of NGOs is one such issue. The effect of the link between COSATU and the ANC (partly discussed above) is another.

Just as the AEC chairperson reported in interview that the AEC finds it difficult to have relationships with a number of NGOs due to the perception that they dictate terms, research participants from NGOs raised issues regarding the impact of this position. An interviewee from ILRIG stated

> there's been what I would regard as a very unhealthy approach on the part of the Anti-Eviction Campaign, when it still existed in some kind of form,

> where they've targeted the NGOs as virtually enemies and that – that divided some people.
>
> (Blake 2012)

Referring specifically to the influence of the AEC's politics on the functioning of the Housing Assembly the same research participant elaborated,

> so the Grassy Park people, they literally had to choose whether they were going to continue to have a relationship with the NGO [ILRIG] or they were going to continue to be part of the Anti-Eviction and they chose to be – come to training et cetera, et cetera.
>
> (Blake 2012)

In relation to the influence of social movements' political positioning on working with NGOs and trade unions, one interviewee posited that

> there's also a very problematic tradition of a sort of propagandistic leftist politics that comes out of the Trotskyist movement, which is extremely sectarian in South Africa in most, in most instances – not all – but in most instances, that shapes some of this politics, and because most people coming from these traditions are not going to be found in the trade union movement they attach themselves to some of these popular organisations.
>
> (Ashley 2012)

This sentiment was echoed in another interview in which the research participant stated that he "never understood the kind of politics, the political logic of, ja, demonising the NGOs basically. My own view on that is, ja, it's part of the politics itself. A sectarian, opportunist politics" (Blake 2012). Interviewees also contended that "it's personalities that get in the way" of more effective collaboration between groups (Louw 2012). One research participant commented that

> the only downfall, I suppose, is that at some point, because of personalities and because of – it's people – and then the criticism that flows to and fro may not necessarily just stick to the issues, it then goes to the personalities which causes maybe a lot more friction.
>
> (Louw 2012)

Additionally, the role of small political differences in major disagreements was highlighted by several research participants (Louw 2012; Ashley 2012; Blake 2012; Hendricks 2012; Xali 2012). Describing problems COSATU has encountered in pursuing relationships with others an interviewee reported,

> Sometimes the difficulties are really, you know, it could be of a very petty nature and other times it could be a principled difficulty but in most instances

> it's these very petty little things that cause these, these very good intentions to fall down, unfortunately.
>
> (Louw 2012)

Similarly, another interviewee commented that

> on the side of the popular movement, movements, organisations et cetera, there's a – just a dismissal of COSATU and the unions as being part of the ANC and therefore they are dismissed. Sometimes it's a little bit more sophisticated – argued that they represent a labour aristocracy, and so they are dismissed from that point of view.
>
> (Ashley 2012)

Another research participant commented that the political position pursued by some involved in shaping the actions of groups such as the AEC hampers collaboration because

> it's not based on any kind of seriousness. There's a populism, there's a mobilise – but very little in terms of thinking through what does it take to build serious organisations on the ground with a grassroots component and an accountable leadership and all that goes with it.
>
> (Blake 2012)

These issues may initially appear to indicate a significant threat to the improvement of relationships between network actors. However, this need not necessarily be the case. On the one hand, it is clear that these issues cause problems when organisations make attempts to collaborate. On the other hand, there are several indicators suggesting these problems might be circumvented or overcome. Many of the difficulties cited by research participants are recognised as relating to small issues. This suggests that the parties attempting to build a relationship substantively agree with one another. This in itself offers a starting point from which the development of a relationship may conceivably be built.

Shared rhetorical commitments

Despite the stated differences of opinion and political positioning, interviewees from a variety of different organisations (and organisations of different types) within the network expressed a desire to work with each other as much as possible. Interviewees from a variety of organisations closely linked to both the Poor People's Alliance and to the Housing Assembly expressed a desire to link up related struggles over evictions, housing and land. As well as the aforementioned comments from interviewees regarding COSATU's aim to work with others "as much as possible" (Louw 2012) and the AEC's aim to work "with any organisation" working on the same issues (Hendricks 2012), further points of rhetorical commonality between various network actors may be highlighted. The AEC chairperson, it has already been noted, stated that the Poor People's Alliance "must be the platform that every poor person in South Africa is going to make use of for the benefit of our own people" (Twalo 2012). Research participants from ISIS made a number of comments concerning a desire to unite related struggles. "What we decided at the Winter School was – and this is the thinking that the Housing Assembly had – that we cannot fight isolated in our own corners any-more" (Heunis and Hoedemaker 2012). "We decided at the Winter School was we want all the organisations from like locally, provincially, nationally and glob-ally, we want everybody to unite" (Heunis and Hoedemaker 2012).

> So all the comrades at the Winter School decided that it was a great plan to form a huge umbrella body where all the different organisations can be united and no more – no-one – fight in isolated in their own corners any more.
>
> (Heunis and Hoedemaker 2012)

"We're all fighting the same struggle so the more we are – like Lorraine said, we mustn't fight in isolation, we must group up with different, even provin-cially, out of the province. It will strengthen our struggles" (Heunis and Hoede-maker 2012). As previously highlighted, an interviewee from ILRIG commented that "hopefully through the Housing Assembly we can ensure that people come together and something gets sorted out" and "what people are emphasising now is reaching out to all those affected by unfit housing conditions" (Blake 2012).[23] The difference in rhetoric between the various organisations in the network appears to be not so much a substantive issue with regard to the most expedi-ent approach but more a question of whether the Poor People's Alliance or the Housing Assembly constitutes the correct or most appropriate umbrella body under which all affected communities might organise.

The congruence of various groups' stated aims provides an opportunity for those aims to be pursued and realised through more effective collaboration. Research participants were not, however, wholly uncritical in their discussions of the desire and potential for increased unity among actors. The threats to collabo-ration posed by the role of individuals, personalities and individual agendas have already been set out. Interviewees also made reference to the problems they faced in following up on the desire to collaborate with a broad range of actors. Some of these relate to previously outlined issues such as the lack of resources which may prevent community-based organisations assembling across a geographically wide area (Hendricks 2012). Others raise new questions. One interviewee raised the issue that since 1994, many apartheid-era activists

> have been able to move out of the townships, they have a house in the sub-urbs et cetera, so now you come and you want to organise around this issue and the social movements say "but, you know, you want to think for us and

> we must be your foot soldiers?" so to speak. So there's a lot of suspicion around people's, you know, different circumstances, particularly amongst, you know, the most marginalised sections in society.
>
> (Ashley 2012)

Shack dwellers, landless and homeless people involved in housing rights activism would fall into this "most marginalised" category (Ashley 2012). Another research participant warned that "organisations can have the best policy resolutions but those policy resolutions will mean nothing if they're not beginning to ensure that it's being implemented in the manner that it's designed" (Jacobs 2012; see also Barrett 2015; Wa Mapena 2015). Following up on having explained the aim of ISIS and the Housing Assembly to pursue unity with other groups taking action on the same issues, interviewees from ISIS emphasised that "we're still working on that" and that "we have a lot of work to do" (Heunis and Hoedemaker 2012). Elaborating on the specific risks attached to failing to collaborate, an interviewee from ISIS commented that "if you go as only ISIS and go and protest then government don't take any notice of you. It is almost as if we're just making a noise, that's all" (Heunis and Hoedemaker 2012). Furthermore, in relation to another group with whom ISIS has yet to successfully organise alongside,

> We had a protest march and they had a protest march but still the City didn't take us seriously. Whereas, we could've had one big march and brought the whole Southern Suburbs side to a standstill. That would've been great and I think then we would've achieved something and, as said previously, if we can be united much more can be achieved.
>
> (Heunis and Hoedemaker 2012)

It appears that there is a widespread commitment, at least in rhetoric, to overcome the reportedly small differences, which research participants said currently hamper collaboration. Furthermore, many of the impediments to more effective collaboration between network actors cited by research participants relate to the influence of individuals. There is no doubt that individuals can have an important, potentially negative, effect on organisations' practice. Nevertheless, organisations are not individuals and individuals are not organisations. It might be possible for existing ties based on cooperation between individuals to be developed into deeper organisational relationships. It might also be possible to pursue organisational relationships if ties can be facilitated other than through individuals who might hamper collaboration.

Conclusion

Several conclusions can be drawn from the research put forward in this chapter. The first, broad, conclusion which comes out of this exploration is that many of the opportunities that exist for improving collaboration in the network are double-edged, operating also as threats. The same can also be said of many threats to collaboration which can simultaneously be interpreted as offering opportunities for more effective collaboration. The main instances of this phenomenon are as follows. The status of trade unions provides on the one hand, an opportunity for greater collaboration and the utilisation of industrial relations processes in order to further housing rights aims (see also Evans 2015). On the other hand, closeness to the ANC and the perception of size and resources being used to impose upon network partners presents a threat. There is evidence to suggest that both (COSATU-affiliated) trade unions and other actors (such as social movements) benefit through linking up their campaigning activities (Friedman 2012; Bond 2012). Similarly, the resources available to NGOs can offer both an incentive and means to carry out closer collaboration between actors, and can serve to create or reinforce a power dynamic perceived by some as disempowering and threatening relationships with grassroots actors. The role of individual personalities in the network is also double-edged. New and closer relationships may be built through developing ties between actors on the basis of individual links. However, the potential for individuals to exert disproportionate influence over organisations' actions and the possibility for personal disagreements to overshadow broader interests can threaten effective collaboration.

A second, related, conclusion surrounds the centrality of resources and access to resources for network building and action. Resources or a lack thereof are strongly linked to the capacity of network actors and ultimately of the network as a whole. In the next chapter, this is explored in greater detail. Specifically, further attention is paid to the ways in which applying an analytical lens turned to the political responsibilities of network actors may be useful in overcoming the threats to, and maximising the opportunities for, effective collaboration between network actors. Building upon this, the next chapter also pays greater attention to the interaction between the action taken by the case study network and the pursuit of transformative justice. Important to this analysis is a recognition of the state of the network with regard to the kinds of ties that exist between the different actors, the motivations behind these and the current opportunities and threats to collaboration attached to this.

The third conclusion to be drawn from this analysis surrounds the stated aims and motivations for organisations and groups within the network pursuing relationships with one another. Different organisations within the network, including those closely associated with disparate clusters of actors, display a high degree of agreement when it comes to the desirability and utility of engaging in networked action. Moreover, despite differences and difficulties, collaboration does take place. As the analysis moves towards concentration upon the scope for transformative justice to be facilitated through developing the case study network, the apparent compatibility of diverse actors' understandings comes to the fore. Similarly, in proposing an analysis of the case study network based upon political responsibilities, the discernible aims and motivations of the affected actors are of particular importance.

Notes

1 See Tissington (2012a) SERI (n.d.-a); see also Clark (2013); SERI (n.d.-b, 2014a, 2014b, 2014c, 2014d); SERI and Centre for Urbanism and Built Environment Studies (n.d.); and Tissington et al. (2013).

2 The social movements and community-based organisations which participate in the Housing Assembly include the Gugulethu Backyard Dwellers, the Tafelsig Community Forum, Tafelsig Residents United, Blikkies for Hope, Blikkies-Delft Concerned Residents, the Symphony Way Pavement Dwellers, Informal Settlements In Struggle (ISIS), the Progressive Youth Movement, plus groups based in Vanguard Drive, Newfields and Maccassar (Blake 2012). The Symphony Way Pavement Dwellers are closely associated with the AEC (Symphony Way Pavement Dwellers 2011; Western Cape Anti-Eviction Campaign n.d.). Dale McKinley notes that in his study of labour-community alliances in South Africa, the Housing Assembly's relationship with SAMWU was one of only three such alliances found to be functioning (McKinley 2014: 3).

3 It is perhaps worth noting here that the establishment of the group ISIS (Informal Settlements In Struggle) and the interviews with its members cited in this book predate the international prominence of the Islamist armed group, terrorist network and self-declared caliphate known by various monikers including ISIS (Islamic State of Iraq and Syria), Daesh and Islamic State (see, for example, Tharoor 2014; Withnall 2014; Irshaid 2015). Excepting this note, all references to ISIS in the book denote Informal Settlements In Struggle, the Cape Town based housing activists, not the terrorist network.

4 Indeed, the degree to which some of the links claimed to exist between SDI and Abahlali baseMjondolo by some commentators are genuine is questionable (see, e.g., Böhmke 2010a; Majavu 2012a; Abahlali baseMjondolo 2010).

5 It is worth noting, in relation to this, that between the beginning of this research and its completion, a number of activists and staff members from groups in the network (including some who were interviewed) were (temporarily or permanently) suspended or removed from their positions (see, e.g., Abahlali baseMjondolo 2012b; Blake 2015; Barrett 2015; McKinley 2015). Within the scope of this research, it was not possible to discern in any instance the extent to which expulsions and other disciplinary processes reflect either genuine wrongdoing or (as sometimes alleged) the misuse of bureaucratic mechanisms to pursue personal or factional disagreements (see, e.g., Blake 2015; Mdlalose 2014; Steyn 2016).

6 See Abahlali baseMjondolo (2006, 2007, 2010, 2012a, 2012b, n.d.); AIDC (n.d.); Ashley (2012); Barrett (2015); Beresford (2006); Birkinshaw (2009); Blake (2012, 2015); Böhmke (2010a, 2010b, 2012); Brown-Luthango (2010); Chicago Anti-Eviction Campaign (n.d.); Development Action Group (2012a, 2012b); Fletcher (2013); Gibson (2011); International Labour Research and Information Group (n.d.); Hall (2010); Hendricks (2012); Heunis and Hoedemaker (2012); ISN Gauteng Provincial Leadership (2015); Jacobs (2012); La Via Campesina (n.d.-a, n.d.-b); Legal Resources Centre (n.d.-a, n.d.-b); Legassick (2003, 2010, 2011); Links (2011); Louw (2012); Majavu (2012a, 2012b); Makwela and Simelane (2015); Marsden (2012); Mbana (2012); Mchunu (2012); Ndabambi (2010); One Million Climate Jobs Campaign (n.d.); Pithouse (2006, 2011); Podlashuc (2011); Pointer (2004); Poni (2009, 2010); Poor People's Alliance (n.d.); Robins (2008); Samara (2010); South African Municipal Workers' Union and Housing Assembly (2012); SDI (2009, n.d.); SDI Programme Officer (2012); SERI (n.d.-a); Sibanda (2015); Sikhula Sonke Official (2012); Smit (2010); SPP Staff Member (2012); Symphony Way Pavement Dwellers (2011); Tissington (2012a, 2012b); Tolsi (2006); Twalo (2012);

van Rensburg (2015); Wa Mapena (2015); War on Want (n.d.-a, n.d.-b, n.d.-c, n.d.-d, n.d.-e, n.d.-f); Western Cape Anti-Eviction Campaign (n.d., 2006); Xali (2005, 2012); and Zikode (2009).

7 An interviewee from SDI explained:

> there's the Abahlali, that organisation, which is – they're also more militant around their actions, they also don't like the methodology of SDI but we meet them at meetings, the Human Rights Commission, where we do presentations and they've . . . made attempts to contact the leadership and said "let's talk and see . . . where we can collaborate" but we don't necessarily – I mean you'll find in one meeting [in] the Western Cape they're criticising us like there's no tomorrow and in Joburg the other day we were together at a function. So it depends on the context.
>
> (van Rensburg 2015)

8 DAG collaborates with at least twenty-five groups, which are plotted on the diagrams (Figures 3.1, 3.2 and 3.3) in this chapter. Of the groups DAG collaborates with, several also have ties to the major clusters of actors discussed earlier. The Zille-raine Heights community organises under the auspices of ISIS, which, it has already been noted, takes part in the Housing Assembly and has links to the AEC and Abahlali baseMjondolo from the Poor People's Alliance (Heunis and Hoedemaker 2012). Similarly, the Mandela Park Backyarders are closely linked to the AEC (Western Cape Anti-Eviction Campaign n.d.). Further, AEC representatives have taken part in DAG's programmes (Twalo 2012). Interviewees from the AEC have, however, criticised the extent to and manner in which DAG allows participation of community-based and social movement organisations (Twalo 2012).

9 In particular, the role of War on Want as a funder was highlighted in interview responses, as well as the role of the German trade union Ver.di in building relations with the AEC, including by hosting AEC visits to Europe (Twalo 2012). It is also evident that at least on an ad hoc basis, international organisations have provided funding and legal support to Abahlali baseMjondolo (Abahlali baseMjondolo n.d.). However, it does not appear that the branches operating in the urban Western Cape (or urban Gauteng) are well connected to international actors. Interviewees stated that the AEC finds it difficult to liaise with organisations outside of South Africa such as an AEC support group based in Chicago (Twalo 2012; Chicago Anti-Eviction Campaign n.d.).

10 SERI works with some organisations tied to each of the clusters of actors identified here, as well as with actors outside of these, such as the Built Environment Support Group and the Good Governance Learning Network, and Planact (Tissington 2012a). Consequently, the cluster of actors surrounding the Poor People's Alliance is indirectly linked to the cluster of actors surrounding SDI through both SERI's and SDI's relationships with Planact. DAG also works with Planact, sharing proposals and ideas (Development Action Group 2012b; Mchunu 2012). This provides another indirect link to other parts of the network.

11 An interviewee from Planact also suggested that one of their successes in working with grassroots community activists was in translating the stories of the communities they work with into "the language of the technocrats" in order to facilitate engagement with municipal government (Makwela and Simelane 2015).

12 Interviewees also highlighted the gendered impact of taking part in activism, particularly with regard to the second, household-level, struggle which can occur when women activists prioritise taking part in meetings or training over conforming to husbands' and partners' patriarchal expectations regarding household social reproduction activities, for example, spending money on transport and attending meetings rather than buying and preparing food (see, e.g., Heunis and Hoedemaker 2012).

13 This support took the form of SAMWU providing the AEC with office space and access to resources such as communication equipment (Hendricks 2012; Xali 2005).

14 Similarly, there are links between Stellenbosch-based farm workers' trade union Sikhula Sonke and the cluster of actors surrounding the Poor People's Alliance. In addition to these ties, Sikhula Sonke has relationships with other actors working on anti-eviction and land issues in the Western Cape. Though Sikhula Sonke is not COSATU-affiliated, COSATU and COSATU-affiliated unions such as the Food and Allied Workers' Union (FAWU) do work closely with Sikhula Sonke (Louw 2012; Mbana 2012; Sikhula Sonke Official 2012). Sikhula Sonke also works with the Surplus People's Project (SPP) (Sikhula Sonke Official 2012). SPP is an NGO which originally worked to oppose evictions in the urban Western Cape during the apartheid era. SPP's current focus is largely upon rural development and food sovereignty (SPP Staff Member 2012). However, particularly through relationships such as that with Sikhula Sonke, there continues to be a link between SPP's work and the area covered by this research. SPP has relationships with several further organisations and groups nationally and internationally which are of relevance to this research. Specifically, SPP has worked with the Legal Resources Centre (LRC) (SPP Staff Member 2012). LRC is an NGO providing legal support throughout South Africa and has worked on land and housing-related cases with DAG and with the groups linked to the Poor People's Alliance (Abahlali baseMjondolo n.d.; Legal Resources Centre n.d.-a, n.d.-b). SPP also has some ties to La Via Campesina and Brazil's MST (SPP Staff Member 2012). La Via Campesina is an international network of peasants' and landless people's movements (La Via Campesina n.d.-a). In South Africa, LPM is affiliated to La Via Campesina (La Via Campesina n.d.-b). Abahlali baseMjondolo have also had some contact with MST, providing another indirect tie between the Poor People's Alliance cluster of actors and SPP, though this does not appear to be a close or ongoing relationship (Poni 2009).

15 This is both through the relationships built by individuals and through COSATU working with the NGO AIDC (Louw 2012). AIDC works with Abahlali baseMjondolo as well as other social movement organisations taking action on land and housing issues (Ashley 2012). With regard to the relationship between COSATU and the AEC and Abahlali baseMjondolo, AIDC acts as something of an intermediary, providing a forum in which various actors can meet to facilitate collaboration (Louw 2012). However, effective, sustained and close collaboration has not always emerged from these opportunities for building relationships (Louw 2012).

16 How the expulsion of COSATU's general secretary (until 2015) Zwelinzima Vavi, and his installation at the head of the newly established, rival, SAFTU union federation (which claims to be committed to organising beyond the traditional base of industrial trade unionism) might affect these dynamics remains to be seen (see, e.g., Hunter 2015; Webster 2017).

17 It remains to be seen how the establishment of the new SAFTU union federation by unions critical of COSATU and the ANC will affect these dynamics (see Webster 2017).

18 For instance, whilst COSATU's Local Shop Stewards Councils (known as "Locals") have greater links to community-based campaigning on the ground than the more centralised union bureaucracy, housing and land-related issues only occasionally figure in Locals' key activities (see COSATU 2012: 44–55; see also Barrett 2015; Wa Mapena 2015).

19 Indeed, Shereza Sibanda from the ICRC suggested that it is necessary to have relationships with multiple legal NGOs and law firms – such as SERI and the Centre

for Applied Legal Studies (CALS) based at the University of the Witwatersrand – so that cases can be referred to different network partners on the basis of their capacity to take on the work at any given time (Sibanda 2015).
20 See Louw (2012).
21 See, for example, Twalo (2012).
22 Interviewees from the SDI-linked cluster of actors also highlighted the potential for political differences to hamper collaboration, with one NGO staff member indicating that the militancy and political affiliation of ISN activists could cause clashes with SDI's preferred mode of operation (van Rensburg 2015). For example, whilst the professionalised elements of the SDI cluster will support affiliated grassroots shack dweller activists in pursuing legal cases with organisations such as SERI, they do not encourage this or other more contentious tactics, instead preferring to emphasise and prioritise negotiation with government (van Rensburg 2015). On the other hand, ISN leaders suggested that being perceived as politically partisan (whilst viewing themselves as not politically affiliated) posed a challenge to building their organisation and its links to others (ISN Gauteng Provincial Leadership 2015).
23 Interviewees from Planact also made similar arguments, suggesting that Planact's role in networks is to provide "technical assistance" to communities with a view to bringing about "this united front of different organisations . . . able to speak with one voice" (Makwela and Simelane 2015).

References

Abahlali baseMjondolo. (2006) A Short History of Abahlali baseMjondolo, the Durban Shack Dwellers' Movement. *Abahlali baseMjondolo*, October. www.abahlali.org/node/16 [accessed October 10, 2011].

Abahlali baseMjondolo. (2007) A Brief Guide to the History and Praxis of Abahlali baseMjondolo for NGOs, Academics, Activists and Churches Seeking a Relationship with the Movement. *Abahlali baseMjondolo*, May. www.abahlali.org/node/1391 [accessed September 1, 2010].

Abahlali baseMjondolo. (2010) Once Again the Name of Our Movement Is Being Abused by the NGOs. Press Statement. *Abahlali baseMjondolo*, 14 May. http://abahlali.org/node/6702 [accessed June 14, 2013].

Abahlali baseMjondolo. (2012a) Collectivism vs. Individualism. Press Statement. *Abahlali baseMjondolo*, 19 April. http://abahlali.org/node/8726 [accessed January 29, 2013].

Abahlali baseMjondolo. (2012b) Election of an Interim Committee for AbM Western Cape, QQ Section, Khayelitsha, Cape Town, Sunday 22 April 2012. *Abahlali baseMjondolo*, 26 April. http://abahlali.org/node/8747 [accessed January 29, 2013].

Abahlali baseMjondolo. (n.d.) Supporting Abahlali baseMjondolo. *Abahlali baseMjondolo*. www.abahlali.org/node/269 [accessed November 25, 2012].

AIDC. (n.d.) About AIDC. www.aidc.org.za/index.php?option=com_content&view=article&id=47&Itemid=76 [accessed August 17, 2013].

Ashley, Brian. (2012) Personal interview, Cape Town, South Africa, 16 July.

Ballard, Richard, Habib, Adam, Valodia, Imraan and Zuern, Elke. (2005) Globalization, Marginalization and Contemporary Social Movements in South Africa. *African Affairs*, 104(417), 615–634.

Barrett, Jane. (2015) Personal interview, Johannesburg, South Africa, 20 October.

Beresford, Alexander. (2006) Trapped in Corporatism? Trade Union Linkages to the Abahlali baseMjondolo Movement in Durban. *Centre for Civil Society*. http://abahlali.org/files/Beresford.pdf [accessed January 29, 2013].

Birkinshaw, Matt. (2009) Abahlali baseMjondolo: "A Homemade Politics" – Rights, Democracy and Social Movements in South Africa. (Paper presented at "Alternative Futures and Popular Protest", Manchester Metropolitan University, Manchester, 15–17 March). http://libcom.org/library/abahlali-basemjondolo-%E2%80%98-homemade-politics%E2%80%99 [accessed December 14, 2012].

Blake, Michael. (2012) Personal interview, Cape Town, South Africa, 6 July.

Blake, Michael. (2015) Personal interview, Johannesburg, South Africa, 10 April.

Böhmke, Heinrich. (2010a) The Branding of Social Movements in South Africa. *Dispositions: A Journal*, 30 April. http://dispositionsjournal.blogspot.com/2010_04_01_archive.html [accessed November 25, 2012].

Böhmke, Heinrich. (2010b) The Shackdwellers and the Intellectuals: Don't Talk about Us Talking about the Poor. *PoliticsWeb*, 21 October. www.politicsweb.co.za/politicsweb/view/politicsweb/en/page71619?oid=206254&sn=Detail&pid=71616 [accessed December 14, 2012].

Böhmke, Heinrich. (2012) Ventriloquism, Fanon and the Social Movement Hustle. *Dispositions: A Journal*, 20 May. http://dispositionsjournal.blogspot.com/2012/05/social-movement-hustle_20.html [accessed December 14, 2012].

Bond, Patrick. (2012) South African People Power since the Mid-1980s: Two Steps Forward, One Back. *Third World Quarterly*, 33(2), 243–264.

Borgatti, Steve P. (2002) *NetDraw Network Visualization* (Harvard: Analytic Technologies).

Brown-Luthango, Mercy. (2010) Personal interview, Cape Town, South Africa, 10 August.

Chicago Anti-Eviction Campaign. (n.d.) Anti-Eviction Campaign: Cape Town; Chicago. http://chicagoantieviction.org/ [accessed November 25, 2012].

Clark, Michael. (2013) *Evictions and Alternative Accommodation in South Africa: An Analysis of the Jurisprudence and Implications for Local Government*. Research Report, November (Johannesburg: SERI).

COSATU. (2012) *Organisational Report to the 11th National Congress*. Unpublished document.

Development Action Group. (2012a) *Development Action Group in Partnership with 25 Citizen Groups*. Unpublished document.

Development Action Group. (2012b) *Written Response to Interview Questions*. Unpublished document.

Evans, Matthew. (2015) Trade Unions as Human Rights Organizations. *Journal of Human Rights Practice*, 7(3), 466–483.

Evans, Matthew. (2017) Contentious Politics and Contentious Scholarship: Challenges Researching Social Movements in South Africa. (Unpublished paper presented at "Activist Scholarship in Human Rights: New Challenges", School of Advanced Study, University of London, London, 28 June).

Fletcher, Nick. (2013) Bill Gates Buys £110m Stake in Security Group G4S. *The Guardian*, 10 June. www.guardian.co.uk/business/marketforceslive/2013/jun/10/bill-gates-stake-security-g4s?INTCMP=SRCH [accessed June 12, 2013].

Friedman, Steven. (2012) Beyond the Fringe? South African Social Movements and the Politics of Redistribution. *Review of African Political Economy*, 39(131), 85–100.

Gibson, Nigel C. (2011) *Fanonian Practices in South Africa: From Steve Biko to Abahlali baseMjondolo* (New York: Palgrave Macmillan).

Hall, Ruth. (2010) Personal interview, Cape Town, South Africa, 13 August.

Hendricks, Soraya. (2012) Personal interview, Cape Town, South Africa, 11 July.

Heunis, Lorraine and Hoedemaker, Eleanor. (2012) Personal interview, Cape Town, South Africa, 7 August.

Hunter, Qaanitah. (2015) Cosatu fires Zwelinzima Vavi. *Mail and Guardian*, 30 March. https://mg.co.za/article/2015-03-30-cosatu-fires-zwelinzima-vavi [accessed January 28, 2018].

International Labour Research and Information Group. (n.d.) What Is ILRIG? http://ilrig.org/index.php?option=com_content&view=article&id=3&Itemid=10 [accessed August 12, 2013].

Irshaid, Faisal. (2015) Isis, Isil, IS or Daesh? One Group, Many Names. *BBC Monitoring*, 2 December. www.bbc.co.uk/news/world-middle-east-27994277 [accessed December 12, 2017].

ISN Gauteng Provincial Leadership. (2015) Personal interview, Johannesburg, South Africa, 13 March.

Jacobs, Mario. (2012) Personal interview, Cape Town, South Africa, 30 July.

Keck, Margaret E. and Sikkink, Kathryn. (1998) *Activists beyond Borders: Advocacy Networks in International Politics* (Ithaca: Cornell University Press).

La Via Campesina. (n.d.-a) Organisation. http://viacampesina.org/en/index.php/organisation-mainmenu-44 [accessed November 25, 2012].

La Via Campesina. (n.d.-b) Our Members. http://viacampesina.org/en/index.php/organisation-mainmenu-44/our-members-mainmenu-71 [accessed November 25, 2012].

Legal Resources Centre. (n.d.-a) About Us. www.lrc.org.za/about-us [accessed November 25, 2012].

Legal Resources Centre. (n.d.-b) Housing & Planning. www.lrc.org.za/housing-planning [accessed November 25, 2012].

Legassick, Martin. (2003) Housing Battles in Post-Apartheid South Africa: The Case of Mandela Park, Khayelitsha. *South African Labour Bulletin*, 27(6).

Legassick, Martin. (2010) Personal interview, Cape Town, South Africa, 4 August.

Legassick, Martin. (2011) The State of the Left in South Africa. (Paper presented at "Politics in South Africa Today", Dialogue, Harold Wolpe Memorial Trust, Johannesburg, July). www.wolpetrust.org.za/dialogue2011/Microsoft%20Word%20-%20The%20state%20of%20the%20left%20in%20South%20Africa.pdf [accessed December 14, 2012].

Links. (2011) South Africa: Declaration of the Democratic Left Front; New Left Seeks Revamped SA. *Links*, 24 January. http://links.org.au/node/2117 [accessed April 16, 2013].

Louw, Mike. (2012) Personal interview, Cape Town, South Africa, 6 July.

Macharia, James. (2016) Herman Mashaba Elected Johannesburg Mayor, Marking the End of ANC Rule in the City. *Mail and Guardian*, 22 August. https://mg.co.za/article/2016-08-22-herman-mashaba-elected-johannesburg-mayor-marking-the-end-of-anc-rule-in-the-city [accessed January 8, 2018].

Majavu, Mandisi. (2012a) I Thus Caught That Colonial Mind-Set at Work: The Mis-Representation of Post-Apartheid Social Movements. *ZNet*, 9 April. www.

zcommunications.org/i-thus-caught-that-colonial-mind-set-at-work-the-mis-representation-of-post-apartheid-social-movements-by-mandisi-majavu [accessed December 14, 2012].

Majavu, Mandisi. (2012b) "White Talk" Reconstructs Whiteness as Victimised Personality. *Debate*, listserv message posted 16 April. http://lists.fahamu.org/pipermail/debate-list/2012-April/028527.html [accessed December 14, 2012].

Makwela, Mike and Simelane, Hloniphile. (2015) Personal interview, Johannesburg, South Africa, 13 May.

Marsden, Mike. (2012) Unpublished letter to Mario Jacobs and Mhlobo Gunguluzi, 17 July.

Mbana, Howard. (2012) Telephone interview, 16 July.

Mchunu, Nokukhanya. (2012) Personal interview, Cape Town, South Africa, 27 July.

McKinley, Dale T. (2014) *Labour and Community in Transition: Alliances for Public Services in South Africa*. Municipal Services Project Occasional Paper No. 24, June (Cape Town: University of the Western Cape).

McKinley, Dale T. (2015) Labor-Community Alliances in South Africa: Reclaiming (Some of) the Past, Inventing the Future? *The South Atlantic Quarterly*, 114(2), 457–466.

Mdlalose, Bandile. (2014) The Rise and Fall of Abahlali baseMjondolo, a South African Social Movement. *Politikon: South African Journal of Political Studies*, 41(3), 345–353.

Merry, Sally Engle. (2006) Transnational Human Rights and Local Activism: Mapping the Middle. *American Anthropologist*, 108(1), 38–51.

Ndabambi, Luthando. (2010) Personal interview, Cape Town, South Africa, 12 August.

One Million Climate Jobs Campaign. (n.d.) About. www.climatejobs.org.za/index.php/about [accessed August 17, 2013].

Pithouse, Richard. (2006) Solidarity, Co-option and Assimilation: The Necessity, Promises and Pitfalls of Global Linkages for South African Movements. In *Challenging Hegemony: Social Movements and the Quest for a New Humanism in Post-Apartheid South Africa*, edited by Nigel C. Gibson (Trenton: Africa World Press), 247–286.

Pithouse, Richard. (2011) Fidelity to Fanon. In *Living Fanon: Global Perspectives*, edited by Nigel C. Gibson (New York: Palgrave Macmillan), 225–248.

Podlashuc, Leopold. (2011) *The South African Homeless People's Federation: Interrogating the Myth of Participation*. Working Paper, African Centre for Citizenship and Democracy (Cape Town: University of the Western Cape).

Pointer, Rebecca. (2004) Questioning the Representation of South Africa's "New Social Movements": A Case Study of the Mandela Park Anti-Eviction Campaign. *Journal of Asian and African Studies*, 39(4), 271–294.

Poni, Mzonke. (2009) Another World Is Possible: Reflections and Criticisms on the World Social Forum, 2009, Belem, Brazil. *Abahlali baseMjondolo*. www.abahlali.org/node/4959 [accessed January 6, 2011].

Poni, Mzonke. (2010) Personal interview, Cape Town, South Africa, 12 August.

Poor People's Alliance. (n.d.) About the Alliance. http://sekwanele.wordpress.com/about/ [accessed September 1, 2010].

Risse, Thomas and Ropp, Stephen C. (2013) Introduction and Overview. In *The Persistent Power of Human Rights: From Commitment to Compliance*, edited by

Thomas Risse, Stephen C. Ropp and Kathryn Sikkink (New York: Cambridge University Press), 3–25.

Risse, Thomas and Sikkink, Kathryn. (1999) The Socialization of Human Rights Norms into Domestic Practices: Introduction. In *The Power of Human Rights: International Norms and Domestic Change*, edited by Thomas Risse, Stephen C. Ropp and Kathryn Sikkink (Cambridge: Cambridge University Press), 1–38.

Robins, Steven L. (2008) *From Revolution to Rights in South Africa: Social Movements, NGOs and Popular Politics after Apartheid* (Woodbridge: James Currey).

Samara, Tony Roshan. (2010) Order and Security in the City: Producing Race and Policing Neoliberal Spaces in South Africa. *Ethnic and Racial Studies*, 33(4), 637–655.

SDI. (2009) Slum Dwellers International Statement on the Attacks on Kennedy Road Settlement, Durban, South Africa. Press Statement, 1 October. http://abahlali.org/node/5826 [accessed April 18, 2012].

SDI. (2012) *Shack/Slum Dwellers International Annual Report 2012* (Cape Town: Shack/Slum Dwellers International).

SDI. (n.d.) Partners. www.sdinet.org/partners/ [accessed October 10, 2011].

SDI Programme Officer. (2012) Personal interview, Cape Town, South Africa, 3 August.

SERI. (2014a) *Makause: Resisting Relocation on the East Rand*. Community Practice Notes Informal Settlement Series 1 (Johannesburg: SERI).

SERI. (2014b) *Rooigrond: Community Struggle in the North West*. Community Practice Notes Informal Settlement Series 2 (Johannesburg: SERI).

SERI. (2014c) *Thembelihle: Engaging an Unresponsive State*. Community Practice Notes Informal Settlement Series 3 (Johannesburg: SERI).

SERI. (2014d) *Slovo Park: Twenty Years of Broken Promises*. Community Practice Notes Informal Settlement Series 4 (Johannesburg: SERI).

SERI. (n.d.-a) About Us. www.seri-sa.org/ [accessed November 25, 2012].

SERI. (n.d.-b) *Rental Housing in South Africa: Legislation, Regulations and Case Law – Rental Housing Act 50 of 1999; Gauteng Unfair Practices Regulations, 2001* (Johannesburg: SERI).

SERI and Centre for Urbanism and Built Environment Studies. (n.d.) *A Tenant's Guide to Rental Housing* (Johannesburg: SERI).

Sibanda, Shereza. (2015) Personal interview, Johannesburg, South Africa, 12 March.

Sikhula Sonke Official. (2012) Personal interview, Stellenbosch, South Africa, 17 July.

Smit, Warren. (2010) Personal interview, Cape Town, South Africa, 13 August.

South African Municipal Workers' Union and Housing Assembly. (2012) *Memorandum of Demands to the City of Cape Town Council in Respect of Service Delivery Demands and the City's Extended Public Works Programme (EPWP)*. Unpublished document, 5 July.

South African SDI Alliance. (2013) *Masikhase: Community Upgrading Finance Facility (CUFF)*. Project Report (Cape Town: Shack/Slum Dwellers International).

SPP Staff Member. (2012) Personal interview, Cape Town, South Africa, 20 July.

Steyn, Ibrahim. (2016) Intellectual Representations of Social Movements in Post-Apartheid South Africa: A Critical Reflection. *Politikon: South African Journal of Political Studies*, 43(2), 271–285.

Symphony Way Pavement Dwellers. (2011) *No Land! No House! No Vote!: Voices from Symphony Way* (Cape Town: Pambazuka Press).

Tharoor, Ishaan. (2014) ISIS or ISIL? The Debate over What to Call Iraq's Terror Group. *The Washington Post*, 18 June. www.washingtonpost.com/news/worldviews/wp/2014/06/18/isis-or-isil-the-debate-over-what-to-call-iraqs-terror-group/?utm_term=.424a37b4c34c [accessed December 12, 2017].

Tissington, Kate. (2012a) Telephone interview, 26 July.

Tissington, Kate. (2012b). "Tacticians in the Struggle for Change"? Exploring the Dynamics between Legal Organisations and Social Movements Engaged in Rights-Based Struggles in South Africa. In *Contesting Transformation: Popular Resistance in Twenty-First-Century South Africa*, edited by Marcelle C. Dawson and Luke Sinwell (London: Pluto Press), 201–221.

Tissington, Kate, Munshi, Naadira, Mirugi-Mukundi, Glady and Durojaye, Ebenezer. (2013) *"Jumping the Queue", Waiting Lists and Other Myths: Perceptions and Practice around Housing Demand and Allocation in South Africa*. Research Report, April (Johannesburg: SERI).

Tolsi, Niren. (2006) On the Far Side of Left. *Mail and Guardian*, 8 December. http://abahlali.org/node/454 [accessed June 15, 2013].

Twalo, Mncedisi. (2012) Personal interview, Cape Town, South Africa, 4 July.

van Rensburg, Sandra. (2015) Personal interview, Johannesburg, South Africa, 13 March.

Wa Mapena, Matserane. (2015) Personal interview, Johannesburg, South Africa, 2 November.

War on Want. (n.d.-a) No Land! No House! No Vote!. www.waronwant.org/component/content/article/16523 [accessed August 31, 2011].

War on Want. (n.d.-b) Shack Dwellers in South Africa. www.waronwant.org/overseas-work/informal-economy/shack-dwellers-in-south-africa [accessed December 9, 2010].

War on Want. (n.d.-c) Anti-Eviction in South Africa. www.waronwant.org/overseas-work/informal-economy/anti-eviction-in-south-africa [accessed December 9, 2010].

War on Want. (n.d.-d) Anti-Privatisation in South Africa. http://waronwant.org/overseas-work/informal-economy/anti-privatisation-in-south-africa [accessed April 16, 2013].

War on Want. (n.d.-e) Women Farm Workers in South Africa. http://waronwant.org/overseas-work/food-sovereignty/women-farm-workers-in-south-africa [accessed April 16, 2013].

War on Want. (n.d.-f) Landless in South Africa. www.waronwant.org/overseas-work/food-justice/landless-in-south-africa [accessed September 1, 2010].

Webster, Edward. (2017) South Africa Has a New Trade Union Federation: Can It Break the Mould? *The Conversation*, 25 April. https://theconversation.com/south-africa-has-a-new-trade-union-federation-can-it-break-the-mould-76609 [accessed May 11, 2017].

Western Cape Anti-Eviction Campaign. (2006) On the SMI, from the Anti-Eviction Campaign, 18 December. http://abahlali.org/node/462 [accessed June 15, 2013].

Western Cape Anti-Eviction Campaign. (n.d.) Contact List. *Western Cape Anti-Eviction Campaign*.http://antieviction.org.za/western-cape-anti-eviction-campaign-detailed-contact-list/ [accessed November 25, 2012].

Withnall, Adam. (2014) Iraq Crisis: Isis Declares Its Territories a New Islamic State with "Restoration of Caliphate" in Middle East. *The Independent*, 30 June. www.

independent.co.uk/news/world/middle-east/isis-declares-new-islamic-state-in-middle-east-with-abu-bakr-al-baghdadi-as-emir-removing-iraq-and-9571374.html [accessed December 12, 2017].

Xali, Mtetho. (2005) Seeking Trade Union and Community Organisation Linkages in the Cape Town Metropolitan Area: Possibilities for New Trade Unionism and New Social Movements. *Centre for Civil Society Research Reports*, 2(37), 167–207.

Xali, Mtetho. (2012) Personal interview, Cape Town, South Africa, 3 August.

Zikode, S'bu. (2009) Resist All Degradations and Divisions: S'bu Zikode in Interview with Richard Pithouse. *Interface*, 1(2), 22–47.

Chapter 4

Threats, limitations and political responsibilities in the network

Introduction

This chapter applies the concept of political responsibility to the case study network. This builds upon the previous chapter's analysis, which focused on the kinds of ties which exist between network actors as well as the threats to and opportunities for more effective collaboration. By focusing on political responsibility, this chapter moves towards an exploration of how threats to more effective collaboration might be overcome and opportunities for more effective collaboration may be brought to fruition. This analysis is ultimately central to the conclusions and recommendations put forward in the final section of the book. This chapter also synthesises the exploration of network actors' political responsibilities with a consideration of transformative justice. This sheds light on the aims of the network and how this can be understood in a broader context than the case study itself. Moreover, an understanding of the relationship between the network and transformative justice serves to reveal the particular political responsibilities of the actors concerned.

It is important throughout this chapter that some of the findings discussed earlier are highlighted. It was found that the case study network did not have a great many international links. This is central to developing a new synthesis building upon existing literature about the political responsibilities of networks. The existing literature, such as it is, presumes a transnational advocacy network as the unit of analysis. Particular emphasis is placed upon the status of Northern and Southern network partners within these discussions. As the case study network is not in a meaningful sense transnational, and Northern actors are almost entirely absent, the degree to which the existing literature – focusing on transnational networks – might be applied to the case study and similar networks is brought into question. Nevertheless, it is possible to adapt and apply the analytical approach of the existing literature to the case study. This adapted analytical approach is particularly useful in allowing evaluation of the relationships within the case study network and for assessing the network's contribution to processes of transformative justice.

As with the previous chapter, this chapter focuses in particular on an analysis of the network actors closely associated with the Housing Assembly cluster of actors and the Poor People's Alliance cluster of actors. However, this chapter also contains further analysis of the network relationships of other actors, including SDI and actors not closely linked to any cluster. This is because the exploration of political responsibilities lends itself usefully to explaining the form of the network including regarding the positions of actors not closely linked to the Housing Assembly or Poor People's Alliance.

This chapter first addresses the political responsibilities of actors associated with the Housing Assembly and the Poor People's Alliance in regard to the opportunities for and threats to effective collaboration identified in the previous chapter. After this, the chapter turns the political responsibilities lens of analysis on to actors outside these two clusters within the network. This attempts to explain why the network is formed in the way that it is, including shedding some light on the reasons behind different kinds of relationships within, between and outside of the main clusters identified.

Ultimately, this chapter draws conclusions in three areas. It is concluded that the political responsibilities framework can usefully be adapted to analyse the case study network, though the original conception of the framework is not wholly appropriate. Following this framework, the Housing Assembly and Poor People's Alliance clusters within the network are found to display higher levels of political responsibility than other areas of the network. However, shortcomings in these clusters' fulfilment of their political responsibilities are also highlighted. Finally, the chapter concludes that transformative justice and politically responsible networked action are synergistic processes. It is suggested that within the case study network, potential exists for the pursuit of a transformative agenda, principally through the facilitation of transformative justice as a process. This is chiefly the case through the praxis of the Housing Assembly and Poor People's Alliance clusters, especially if a greater realisation of political responsibilities is achieved and, particularly, in relation to the two clusters' relations with each other, rather than in relation to responsibilities within each cluster. Lessons may also be drawn from this for application to the Gauteng aspects of the case study, where there were few clearly identifiable clusters of actors within the network.

The Housing Assembly and the Poor People's Alliance

There are seven areas of political responsibility identified by Jordan and Van Tuijl (2000: 2054). These are "dividing political arenas", "agenda setting and strategy building", "raising and allocating financial resources", "information flow", "information frequency and format", "information translation into useful forms" and "the formalisation of relationships" (Jordan and Van Tuijl 2000: 2054). Making use of the analytical framework proposed in Chapter 1, these are the thematic areas through which the existing relationships, threats to and opportunities for more effective collaboration within the network are analysed. However, due to the degree to which they overlap, here the three areas of political responsibility relating to information are discussed together. The following discussion is consequently framed by five, rather than seven, elements of political responsibility.

Dividing political arenas

"Dividing political arenas" means "[r]ecognizing who has expertise and knowledge in which political arena and respecting the boundaries established by that expertise" (Jordan and Van Tuijl 2000: 2054). In relation to the Housing Assembly, three main political arenas can be seen. First, there is the grassroots politics of community mobilisation. Second, there is the arena in which political education and policy research takes place. Third, there is the arena of formal engagement and negotiation with government and related authorities. Each of these can feed into the others. However, these arenas are distinct from one another and understanding them as such makes the political responsibilities analysis clearer. It appears that within the cluster, the actors in the Housing Assembly largely meet their political responsibility in this area. For instance, SAMWU's role includes provision of resources (discussed in the previous chapter) such as the means to produce a memorandum of demands to the City of Cape Town and provide an address for related correspondence. SAMWU were also involved in pursuing some of the aims of the Housing Assembly via an industrial dispute. This particular arena is within SAMWU's remit and area of expertise but not that of other Housing Assembly members. Likewise, the role of ILRIG in the Housing Assembly focuses largely upon research and education activities. Housing Assembly action related to grassroots mobilisation of affected communities appears to be largely carried out by community-based organisations and social movements. The expertise and "long-term presence" (see Jordan and Van Tuijl 2000: 2054) of different actors within the Housing Assembly in different political arenas appears to be reflected in the division of activities in these arenas.

In some ways, the Poor People's Alliance contrasts with the Housing Assembly in relation to the dividing of political arenas. The actors which make up the Poor People's Alliance are all social movement organisations. It is difficult, therefore, to assess whether political arenas are divided responsibly. As the members of the Poor People's Alliance are broadly similar groups, it is not clear when or why one group would have greater expertise or established presence in a political arena than another. The cluster does have links to other organisations (and kinds of organisation) but in itself, the arenas in which the Poor People's Alliance has expertise and an established presence are more limited than the Housing Assembly. This limits the cluster's campaigning efficacy to some extent. Diverse links to different kinds of actors, containing different constituencies and possessing different expertise, can add value to social movement action (Friedman 2012). As some of the groups which make up the Poor People's Alliance do not operate in the Western Cape or urban parts of Gauteng, these largely fall outside of the scope of this case study. However, in one sense, this is a way in which political arenas are divided. For instance, KwaZulu-Natal–based groups do not ordinarily take action in the Western Cape where other groups have an established presence and vice versa. How this area of political responsibility plays out with regard to ties with actors outside of the cluster itself is explored in greater detail ahead.

Agenda setting and strategy building

The second area of political responsibility is "agenda setting and strategy building" (Jordan and Van Tuijl 2000: 2054). This is "closely related to the management of risks" (Jordan and Van Tuijl 2000: 2054). As such, this area of political responsibility maps closely onto the threats to collaboration identified in the preceding chapter. Jordan and Van Tuijl posit that politically responsible network actors must answer the questions "what are the substantive priorities; for whose benefit; using which time frame and with what level of antagonism are authorities or power holders approached in which political arena?" and that it is "essential to find a format to lay out explicitly what one's objectives are and to then develop a strategy with transparent goals" (Jordan and Van Tuijl 2000: 2055).

In the preceding chapter, it was noted that the actors associated with both the Housing Assembly and the Poor People's Alliance share many of the same goals. This is in regards to both the organisational aims surrounding securing housing rights and the strategic goals around linking the struggles of different affected communities (see, e.g., Blake 2012; Heunis and Hoedemaker 2012; Twalo 2012). There are, however, questions surrounding whether these actors meet all areas of this responsibility. The substantive priorities of the Housing Assembly and the Poor People's Alliance are broadly in line. Similarly, both clusters share a commitment to action being of benefit to the affected communities. This was emphasised by an interviewee from SAMWU, who noted that despite trade unions having a particular representative role regarding employed people, their action in the Housing Assembly should produce benefits more widely (Jacobs 2012).

Questions around whether the actors in each cluster meet their responsibilities regarding the time frame, level of antagonism and political arena in which to act are more difficult. On the basis of this research, the time frame question is almost impossible to answer. Interview responses collected for this book did not cover how the timing of action is decided, and this is not detailed by wider sources. It is the case that both the Housing Assembly cluster and the Poor People's Alliance cluster, plus many of the constituent actors within these, have established decision-making processes (see, e.g., Blake 2012; Jacobs 2012; Twalo 2012). However, it cannot be concluded decisively from this that time frame decisions are made responsibly. These decision-making processes may or may not work in practice (see, e.g., Mdlalose 2014).

With regard to choosing the political arena and level of antagonism, the evidence is clearer. Within the Housing Assembly, it seems that member social movements and community-based organisations have significant influence in deciding the political arenas and levels of antagonism employed. For instance, interviewees from ISIS made reference to a desire to make the City of Cape Town ungovernable (Heunis and Hoedemaker 2012). They also detailed a number of interactions with official representative government. Research responses indicate that ISIS have been supported by the other Housing Assembly members, including the NGO ILRIG in pursuing their chosen approach (Heunis and Hoedemaker 2012). This has included dialogue with Helen Zille in her role as Mayor of Cape Town, and subsequently as Premier of the Western Cape, and with Patricia de Lille, Zille's successor as mayor (Heunis and Hoedemaker 2012). According to the interviewees, these interactions have become more antagonistic over time as the organisation became increasingly dissatisfied with the results of the dialogue (Heunis and Hoedemaker 2012). Within the Poor People's Alliance, it is not entirely clear whether political responsibilities are met in this regard. On the one hand, the actors associated with the Poor People's Alliance have been able to engage in a variety of actions including both contentious, antagonistic protests and direct action aimed at defying government and less antagonistic legal challenges to evictions (see, e.g., Twalo 2012; Legassick 2010; Friedman 2012). Moreover, both Abahlali baseMjondolo and the AEC – the groups within the Poor People's Alliance operating in the Western Cape – are ostensibly under the control of their memberships (Twalo 2012). The scepticism of these actors towards NGOs and the fact that no NGOs participate directly in the Poor People's Alliance would suggest that decisions around political arenas approached and levels of antagonism are not imposed upon them (Twalo 2012; Abahlali baseMjondolo 2010). On the other hand, as previously outlined, there are questions surrounding the actual practice of decision making in these organisations (see, e.g., Hendricks 2012; Mdlalose 2014). The political responsibility of their actions in this sense can also be questioned.

Raising and allocating financial resources

There are questions regarding the extent to which the actors in the Housing Assembly and the Poor People's Alliance meet their political responsibilities in relation to the third aspect, the raising and allocation of financial resources. Jordan and Van Tuijl's original description of a scenario in which "the bulk of financial resources is in the hands of a relatively small group of NGOs in the North" (see Jordan and Van Tuijl 2000: 2055) does not directly apply. As previously mentioned, the case study network is not transnational in most of its activities. However, there are some transnational funding relationships between Northern actors and case study network members, including those associated with these two clusters. It is difficult for social movements and community-based organisations to obtain funding. This was highlighted in interviews with members of groups closely linked to both the Poor People's Alliance and the Housing Assembly (Heunis and Hoedemaker 2012; Twalo 2012).

The kind of action carried out by the Housing Assembly appears to have been divided for the most part in such a way as to not require significant expenditure of financial resources on the part of social movements and community-based organisations. Indeed, interviewees from some of the better financially resourced actors within the cluster noted that it would be necessary for them to contribute more financial resources than some of their partners (see, e.g., Jacobs 2012). It was evident from some interviews with social movements attached to the Housing Assembly that the financial resources of richer actors within the cluster were perceived as being used responsibly. However, interviewees' comments also suggested that the lack of further allocation of financial resources to poorer network partners inhibits action (Heunis and Hoedemaker 2012).

The raising and allocation of financial resources within the Poor People's Alliance cluster of actors brings up some of the same issues as within the Housing Assembly but also raises some new questions. Interviewees from both the AEC and Abahlali baseMjondolo indicated that these organisations have very limited financial resources (Poni 2010; Twalo 2012). Whilst this puts both these actors on a roughly equal footing with regard to the distribution of financial resources within the cluster, there are clear difficulties associated with this. First, and most obviously, lack of financial resources can limit the scope of possible action to be taken. Second, there is a risk that even if the finances are raised in a politically responsible manner, they may not be distributed and used responsibly. For instance, one of the few clear transnational relationships the Poor People's Alliance cluster has is a funding relationship with the UK-based NGO War on Want (Twalo 2012). War on Want emphasises its model of working with social movements as being partnerships, maintaining the autonomy of recipients of funding, and explicitly acknowledging the structural bases of and political aspects to this work (Miller 2012). This would appear to be consistent with Jordan and Van Tuijl's (2000) conception of politically responsible action by NGOs. However, there is a gap in the analyses of political responsibilities put forward by Jordan and Van Tuijl (2000) and by Hudson (2001). These analyses of political responsibilities in networks are focused upon the responsibilities of NGOs, particularly Northern NGOs (Hudson 2001; Jordan and Van Tuijl 2000). It has already been highlighted that the case study network does not operate transnationally for the most part. This draws the focus of a political responsibilities analysis of the network away from Northern actors. Furthermore, in taking an NGO-centric view of how political responsibilities in a network should be analysed, the kind of approach taken by Jordan and Van Tuijl and by Hudson would obscure scrutiny of clusters within the network in which no NGOs directly participate, such as the Poor People's Alliance. Interviewees commented on the alleged willingness of some individuals to tell funders "this and that" in order to obtain financial resources (Hendricks 2012). Respondents also reported that financial resources are not always transparently or appropriately distributed (Hendricks 2012). Another research participant stated that the individual circumstances of many social movement activists can lead to "survivalist" opportunism (Ashley 2012). Keeping this in mind, along with evidence put forward in the existing critical literature (e.g. Böhmke 2012; Pointer 2004; Mdlalose 2014), suggests that the politically responsible allocation of financial resources is an issue within the constituent movements of the Poor People's Alliance.

It may be that the responsible raising and allocation of financial resources is more important within groups such as the social movements which make up the Poor People's Alliance than it is between the Northern and Southern NGOs analysed by Jordan and Van Tuijl (2000) and by Hudson (2001). This is because the social movements in the Poor People's Alliance are more severely under-resourced even than the formal Southern NGOs Jordan and Van Tuijl (2000) and Hudson (2001) consider. This, coupled with the high degree of economic marginalisation and of unemployment amongst members of these movements, means that distribution of financial resources can have a much clearer impact upon individual movement members' well-being (Ashley 2012; Hendricks 2012; Twalo 2012; Heunis and Hoedemaker 2012; Friedman 2012). These factors exacerbate tensions over the use of resources and, consequently, draw attention to the importance of responsible allocation of financial resources.

Political responsibility in this area in a network such as the case study reflects that of transnational networks but is starker. Despite their relative lack of resources compared with Northern-based international NGOs, local Southern NGOs occupy a privileged position compared with social movements of the poor and marginalised. Within these movements, access to financial resources and the power to distribute these conveys a degree of privilege upon the power holding group or individual. The privileged position power over financial resources entails can be delimited by politically responsible allocation and distribution of these resources.

Information

Information flow (within and between these clusters), and information frequency, format and translation all impact upon the other areas of political responsibility as well as being considerations in themselves. In a highly politically responsible network, it would be expected that imbalances in resources would be recognised. Similarly, the activities and agendas of network members would be discussed. Network-level decisions would be shared and, through equitable exchange of information, campaigning areas in line with the transparent goals of the network would be decided. Each of these areas requires information to be responsibly handled within the network. Several of the instances of the Poor People's Alliance and Housing Assembly clusters of actors failing to fully meet their political responsibilities identified earlier relate to these information-related issues.

Transparency is a key theme which links political responsibilities relating to information together. Interviewees from groups closely associated with the Poor People's Alliance reported distrust of the motives of NGOs and suspicion over how resources are utilised (Twalo 2012). In relation to improving the relationship between the Housing Assembly (especially the hub NGO ILRIG) and the actors associated with the Poor People's Alliance, improved information flow and frequency may be necessary. Given the extent to which organisations in the Housing Assembly, including ILRIG, appear to meet their political responsibilities within the cluster, it can be suggested that these organisations fail to usefully translate information for use by actors in the Poor People's Alliance. It is not the case that no social movements or community-based organisations work with ILRIG in the Housing Assembly. Moreover, information sharing and effective translation appears to be present internally. There is not a fundamental difference in the kind of actor involved in the Poor People's Alliance as opposed to the Housing Assembly. The fact that research participants from ISIS indicated satisfaction with their relationship with ILRIG in the Housing Assembly serves to suggest that there is scope for Poor People's Alliance–affiliated groups such as the AEC to build a closer relationship with the Housing Assembly if information is more effectively managed between the two clusters.

Effective information exchange with the Poor People's Alliance is not, however, wholly the responsibility of the key actors within the Housing Assembly. Some of this political responsibility lies with the actors within the Poor People's Alliance. Information flow, frequency, format and translation are all two-way processes. A key disconnect between the understandings of the case study network put forward by actors closely involved in the Poor People's Alliance and the Housing Assembly lies in the extent to which key actors within each cluster are successful in conveying their positions. Given the previously outlined similarity between the aims of the groups closely tied to both clusters, and the declared willingness of interviewees from both clusters to work with those with whom they share aims, on the face of it one might be surprised that there is not more and closer collaboration between the two clusters. Consideration of the clusters' information-related political responsibilities provides some explanation.

There is a disconnect evident between the positions articulated by groups closely linked to the Poor People's Alliance and groups closely linked to the Housing Assembly and how these are perceived. On the one hand, some research participants from social movements in the Poor People's Alliance expressed suspicion of the motives and efficacy of NGOs, including those connected to the Housing Assembly. On the other hand, interviewees from Housing Assembly–connected NGOs stated that they do not understand the position put forward by groups such as the AEC in relation to NGOs (see, e.g., Blake 2012). An interviewee from the AEC referred to what he described as the hijacking of the Social Movements Indaba by NGOs including ILRIG (Twalo 2012). This event, in 2006, has been the source of much controversy and contestation (see, e.g., Tolsi 2006; Western Cape Anti-Eviction Campaign 2006). It is, however, evident that the concerns of the social movements (including the AEC and Abahlali baseMjondolo) are not well understood by those to whom they are directed. The political responsibility of effective information exchange is not well met. On the part of the Poor People's Alliance–linked social movements, there is an absence of effective explanation of the concerns and proposed means of mitigation to NGOs such as ILRIG. On the part of NGOs such as ILRIG, there is evidently a lack of successful communication of their position to groups attached to the Poor People's Alliance. This is especially the case with regards to articulation of their goals, activities and the constraints upon them. The shared rhetorical commitments evident in interview responses from both clusters indicates that compatible communication of information between the two clusters is possible and could be improved.

Formalisation of relationships

Within the Housing Assembly, relationships are formalised to varying degrees. Overall, the Housing Assembly has a chairperson, a formal relationship with SAMWU as providing a correspondence address and with ILRIG operating as a hub coordinating activities such as training for participants. Each participating organisation or individual outside of specific office holders, SAMWU and ILRIG is involved to a slightly less formal degree. Formal decision-making processes exist within the Housing Assembly.[1] However, interview responses indicate that the formalisation of the relationships within the Housing Assembly does not go as far as full organisational unity. Members of the Housing Assembly continue to act independently and, the research data suggest, there are few barriers to new organisations joining the Housing Assembly or current affiliates breaking their ties (Blake 2012; Blake 2015; Heunis and Hoedemaker 2012; South African Municipal Workers' Union and Housing Assembly 2012; Marsden 2012).

The Poor People's Alliance is a relatively formal structure. There is a clearly defined membership – the four constituent social movements (the AEC, Abahlali baseMjondolo, LPM and the Rural Network). However, each of these groups does take part in individual action, and the relationships the Poor People's Alliance have outside of its structures vary in their degree of formality. The degree to which the two clusters of the Housing Assembly and the Poor People's Alliance are formally associated within the network is more widely varied. As has been mentioned previously, groups closely linked to the Poor People's Alliance (such as the AEC-affiliated Symphony Way Pavement Dwellers), and members of groups including the AEC and Abahlali baseMjondolo, have taken part in Housing Assembly activities (Blake 2012; Heunis and Hoedemaker 2012). Direct and indirect ties between the two clusters are present but are not highly formalised.

Within the Poor People's Alliance cluster and the Housing Assembly cluster, relationships are formal and transparent. However, when the broader network is considered, including the links between these two clusters, there is less formalisation. Whilst the political responsibilities framework formulated by Jordan and Van Tuijl suggests that increased formalisation of relationships necessarily increases the political responsibility of a network (Jordan and Van Tuijl 2000), the reality of the case study network is more complicated than this. Some commentators praise the informal nature of relationships within some networks. Flexibility and the alleged circumvention of top-down and hierarchical structures are seen as advantageous (see, e.g., Graeber 2002; Klein 2001). As ever, the reality of the case study network is also more complicated than this.

The formalisation of relationships presents some risks which may in fact undermine the political responsibility of the network. A highly formalised cluster of actors which does not cooperate with, or actively excludes, other network actors would not be highly politically responsible. Conversely, informal relationships which facilitate decision making which is not transparent or the development of power structures and hierarchies which obstruct participation and reduce transparency would also reduce the network's political responsibility. The case study network displays both of these tendencies to varying degrees. It is possible that the formal relationship with ILRIG (which membership of the Housing Assembly entails) limits the scope for greater formalisation of relationships between actors in the Housing Assembly and those in the Poor People's Alliance. This is due to the close formal ties between the members of the Poor People's Alliance and the position of some of these actors as critical of NGOs including ILRIG. On the other hand, it is simultaneously possible that the relationships that do exist between the two clusters are facilitated in part by the fact that greater formalisation is not strongly pursued. It would not be politically responsible for the Housing Assembly and Poor People's Alliance to abandon the less formal relationships between the clusters in order to further formalise the relationships within the clusters.

Transformative justice and political responsibilities of the network

Applying the political responsibilities framework, as it has been adapted in this book, to the case study network sheds light on the potential for transformative justice in several ways. Those elements of the case study network which meet their political responsibilities to a high degree are engaged in praxis which contests the terrain upon which much of the transitional justice discourse is built. Politically responsible networked action requires better resourced, formalised and professionalised actors such as NGOs to engage with less formal grassroots activism, ideally with a high degree of cooperation between network actors and shared decision making. Consequently, politically responsible action in the case study network includes social movements and other actors whose approaches contrast with the elite-driven changes "at the top" which characterise transitional justice and the distorted mainstream approach to human rights (Daly 2002: 74; Stammers 2009: 8). Politically responsible action, therefore, allows space for more transformative approaches to be aired and attempted than is possible in networks which do not display a high degree of political responsibility. This is demonstrated through an analysis of the case study network's political responsibilities through the lens of transformative justice.

This section applies the abovementioned areas of political responsibility to an analysis of key actors within the case study network including those which are outside of the Housing Assembly and Poor People's Alliance clusters. Analysis of these actors serves in part as a comparison to the political responsibilities analysis of the Poor People's Alliance and the Housing Assembly above. In part, this section also serves to explain why the Poor People's Alliance and Housing Assembly clusters within the network are of particular interest for this research.

Dividing political arenas

Throughout the network as a whole, the division of political arenas between actors varies widely. In addition to the political responsibility of the Housing Assembly and Poor People's Alliance clusters in this area, discussed earlier, several other relationships within the network are worthy of consideration. It is particularly worthwhile to highlight the division of political arenas within the SDI-associated cluster of actors. Here, familiar areas of action can be discerned. There is grassroots community mobilisation, policy and research work and formal engagement and negotiation with government and related authorities. The formal structures of the SDI-associated cluster (the secretariat, local federations of shack dwellers and local partner NGOs) define the roles of each element of the cluster relatively clearly. Within the cluster at least, there is a transparency and clarity over the arenas in which each node acts (SDI Programme Officer 2012; South African SDI Alliance 2013; van Rensburg 2015; ISN Gauteng Provincial Leadership 2015). There is, however, some tension with regard to how the SDI-associated cluster's actions within these political arenas relate to the actions of other network nodes (such as those associated with the Housing Assembly and/or Poor People's Alliance) in the same political arenas.

It has already been noted that the cluster of actors associated with SDI does not have a great many, or strong, ties to other nodes in the network. In one respect, this means that political responsibility is not well met. Jordan and Van Tuijl argue that "[r]ecognizing who has expertise and knowledge in which political arena and respecting the boundaries established by that expertise is the first necessary act of accountability in a joint NGO advocacy effort" (Jordan and Van Tuijl 2000: 2054). This is even more important when the network is not only made up of NGOs. In a network, such as the case study, containing grassroots and non-professionalised actors as well as NGOs it is particularly important that the political responsibility to recognise expertise and knowledge of particular political arenas, and to respect the boundaries of action this implies, is fulfilled. It is not clear that the SDI-associated cluster of actors fulfills this responsibility as fully as might be possible, or indeed as fully as the Poor People's Alliance and Housing Assembly–linked clusters discussed earlier. On the one hand, SDI argues for bottom-up practice, with the shack dwellers' federations taking a lead role in shaping the activities of the cluster (SDI Programme Officer 2012; SDI 2012; see also van Rensburg 2015). On the other hand, SDI has been criticised as promoting a top-down model of activism (Gibson 2011: 13). Leopold Podlashuc, who worked for SDI between 2003 and 2008 (see Podlashuc 2011: 34), for instance, argues that

> it appears that SDI's success relied on tight control over the tactics of the grassroots locally, achieved through the disbursement of money to key

> leaders, who would then "look up" toward the coordinators, instead of "looking down" toward their constituency.
>
> (Podlashuc 2011: 21)

These tensions also affect other political responsibilities. With regard to the division of political arenas, however, the lack of agreement over whether and how actors associated with SDI operate in the same political arenas as other network nodes suggests that this political responsibility is not fully met.

Some analysis of the role of DAG in the network with regard to dividing political arenas also has relevance here. Similarly to SDI, DAG does not have a large number of strong ties with the rest of the case study network. However, DAG's work within its own arena of expertise and with academic and government-based planners is balanced to some degree by their partnerships with community-based organisations (Mchunu 2012; Development Action Group 2012). There is recognition of the different political arenas in which different actors operate. Though there has been some criticism of the nature of DAG's partnerships with community-based organisations, this impacts more upon other areas of political responsibility than on the division of political arenas (see, e.g., Twalo 2012).

There are lessons for transformative justice which emerge from consideration of the division of political arenas in the case study network. Most significantly, the network includes action taken by network members in both elite spaces such as government and academia and at the grassroots. The extent to which this is coordinated varies across the network. Nevertheless, a transformative justice agenda requires change throughout society. Through network members' recognition of the importance of grassroots activism, and through this action (largely) being undertaken by those groups and organisations recognised within the network as having a long-term presence in the arena, at least one of the necessary conditions for the pursuit of transformative justice is met (Chapter 2 discusses the necessary conditions for transformative justice in more detail).

Agenda setting and strategy building

Agenda setting and strategy building cross over to some degree with the division of political arenas. Throughout the network, it is the nodes with the strongest relationships with one another for which the political responsibilities regarding agenda setting and strategy building are most clearly met. It is also between strong ties that this responsibility might most obviously be unfulfilled, particularly with regard to the need to manage risks. Those actors within the network which do not have many links to others are less likely to be in a position where it would be possible for them to put others at risk. However, a lack of involvement and influence over agendas by affected communities and grassroots actors would also indicate a failure to fully meet this responsibility.

DAG, for instance, operates largely according to its own agenda and does not maintain significant long-term relationships with affected communities. Whilst this does mean that community participation in DAG's programmes does not entail a great deal of organisational or individual risk for participants, it is also the case that these communities do not have a decisive role in setting DAG's agenda or deciding its strategic approach (Twalo 2012). Whilst DAG's goals are relatively transparent and there may well be opportunity for DAG's partners to discuss the strategy being pursued, the space for strategies to be reviewed in accordance with the priorities of actors other than DAG itself do not seem to be present. In contrast, as discussed earlier, this research indicates that there is greater scope for strategies to be shaped by affected communities through the clusters of actors associated with the Poor People's Alliance and the Housing Assembly.

Analysing the political responsibility of agenda setting and strategy building in the cluster of actors within the case study network associated with SDI is difficult. On the one hand, the narrative from official SDI sources would suggest that affected communities have significant influence over decision making and that the professionalised NGO elements of the cluster support the strategies put forward by shack dwellers themselves (SDI Programme Officer 2012; SDI 2012; South African SDI Alliance 2013; van Rensburg 2015; see also Robins 2008: 77–99). On the other hand, critics of SDI tend to argue almost the opposite. It is suggested in these narratives that SDI's strategies are not open for discussion or review by the affected communities and that shack dwellers are recruited to provide legitimacy for a pre-existing agenda imposed from the top down, from international donors, government and intergovernmental partners, to affected communities (Gibson 2011: 13; Pithouse 2011: 232; Podlashuc 2011). Gibson argues that

> SDI is not a democratic organisation of shack dwellers but an elite organisation that works as a gate keeper with other NGOs and academic institutions (such as the Sustainability Institute at Stellenbosch University). Echoing World Bank "boot-strap" programmes for the poor, and the currently fashionable micro-financing programmes, their major initiative is to encourage micro-saving and credit schemes, which often pathologise the poor for their "inability" to save.
>
> (Gibson 2011: 272)

What is uncontested is that SDI as an organisation is present in many countries and promotes a particular philosophy with regard to the roles of savings schemes and microcredit in facilitating development for shack dweller communities (see, e.g., SDI 2012; South African SDI Alliance 2013; see also Robins 2008: 77–99). It is not then implausible to imagine that the structures present in the cluster of actors associated with SDI in the case study network might not be open to the pursuit of alternative strategies. Indeed, some existing research records significant organisational problems being caused within SDI's structures in Cape Town when shack dweller communities (organised in the South African Homeless People's Federation) did not conform to the NGO's desired model of organisation (and ultimately disaffiliated from SDI) (Robins 2008: 77–99; Podlashuc

2011). According to Podlashuc, "[a]ll the SDI's axioms of savings, exchange, social capital, transparency, and co-production came to nought in the free-for-all that erupted when the homeless savers realised the limitations of the system to which they had been contributing" (Podlashuc 2011: 25). Moreover, he argues that during the period of this internal conflict

> repeated claims by the SDI Alliance of building community-driven actions for addressing need, giving women a primary role in community-based structures and creating space for the poor to control their own development, did not allow them to be financially independent. The refrain of the Alliance that they were giving finances and resources directly to the poor was not true; absolute financial autonomy, of the type of an independent not-for-profit company, would have meant the loss of strategic control over the movement. The autonomy that the Alliance spoke of should be seen as mere lip service to donors, who wanted to hear the narrative of social entrepreneurship.
>
> (Podlashuc 2011: 25)

An interviewee from SDI in Gauteng also noted that militancy on the part of affiliated shack dwellers and the pursuit of more contentious approaches to engagement with government are not encouraged by the NGO (van Rensburg 2015). Indeed, the same interviewee noted that part of the dynamics between the NGO and grassroots elements of the SDI Alliance surrounds managing the expectations of shack dweller activists who expect, or demand, wide-reaching change and full realisation of the promises of South Africa's constitution in a short period of time (van Rensburg 2015). She noted that even a successful application of SDI's methods to secure land and housing for a group of savers was "a long process", giving an example beginning in 2002 when a savers group first secured land, where building started only in 2015 (van Rensburg 2015). The interviewee also recounted an early 1990s visit to South Africa by a delegation from SDI's structures in India, noting that in India,

> they were at that time fifty or sixty years in a democracy, and they were still sleeping on the pavements and they were still shitting in the streets, and, so, "guys, don't think that you can have a democracy and everything is going to be the land of milk and honey – it's not going to happen".
>
> (van Rensburg 2015)

It has also been suggested that elsewhere in South Africa government insistence that organised shack dwellers must affiliate to SDI's structures in order to be considered legitimate led to the arrest and torture of Abahlali baseMjondolo members upon their refusal to comply with this demand (Pithouse 2011: 232). Indeed, a rare point of agreement between the analyses of Richard Pithouse and Heinrich Böhmke is the shared view that SDI's approach is a bad one (Pithouse 2011: 232; Böhmke 2010).

Applying an analytical lens turned to transformative justice reveals several considerations around the setting of agendas and building of strategies within the case study network. In the pursuit of a transformative agenda, it is necessary for affected communities to be involved in decision making. Indeed, given the prioritisation given by many victims of conflict and authoritarian regimes to socioeconomic concerns such as those relating to land and housing, there is an imperative from a transformative justice perspective to take account of these views in the building of strategies and setting of agendas in networked action. Taking this into consideration, there is increased transformative potential in networked action which allows affected communities to contest the structures which facilitate and maintain their socioeconomic conditions.

As well as the achievement of successful outcomes, the provision of processes by which these structures are contested is important for the pursuit of socioeconomic rights (see, e.g., Aberese Ako, Anyidoho and Crawford 2013). Some of the most obvious achievements of actors within the case study network (particularly social movements associated with the Poor People's Alliance and the Housing Assembly) may be in addressing the immediate needs of their constituents, for example, through the successful prevention of evictions (Legassick 2010). However, there are also wider achievements. According to Dale McKinley (2012: 40), these kinds of actors contribute to "placing mass struggles back onto the political and organisational 'agenda' of the left" and to

> providing critical opposition to both the ideas and practice of the neoliberal policies of the ANC government and contributing to a deepening of the class and ideological divisions with the ANC-led Alliance; and helping to create a renewed social, political, and moral consciousness and solidarity around the most basic needs of life, both domestically and internationally.
>
> (McKinley 2012: 40)

Referring to Abahlali baseMjondolo's grassroots mobilisation and to the movement's engagement with law through partnering with NGOs such as SERI, Kate Tissington makes a similar point. She argues that "[c]hallenging the state's approach to development, highlighting the inequalities in South Africa's land and housing distribution, and mobilising for something different is an important step towards challenging the status quo and the current economic system" (Tissington 2012: 214–215). As such, these processes are also important to the pursuit of transformative justice. Following this line of reasoning, it can be seen that the strategies of SDI within the case study network (and, indeed, those of DAG) have less of a role to play in promoting transformative justice than other elements of the network, particularly the Housing Assembly and Poor People's Alliance clusters.

Whether the cluster of actors associated with SDI in the case study network is characterised by bottom-up agenda setting, its strategies are inherently untransformative. Regardless of whether savings schemes and microcredit assist affected shack dweller communities, they do not constitute, or meaningfully contribute towards, the radical change throughout society which transformative justice seeks (Podlashuc 2011; Daly 2002; Gready et al. 2010). It is not the case that this approach or working with the state, for instance, necessarily precludes the pursuit of transformative justice.[2] However, these strategies take place within the existing framework set out by transitional elite bargains. Prioritising working with the state does preclude the pursuit of transformative justice when (as is often the case in contemporary South Africa) this requires working within a paradigm which is untransformative.[3] For instance, interviewees from the Poor People's Alliance cluster were critical of the government's housing subsidy and house building programmes. This was due to both the scope of the programmes (i.e. the number of houses made available) and the quality of the housing (see, e.g., Legassick 2010; Twalo 2012; Hendricks 2012). Moreover, interviewees did not suggest that the transitional justice mechanisms put in place after the end of apartheid had effectively addressed the housing and land rights issues with which they are concerned. Indeed, one interviewee (from the AEC) commented that the label of "previously disadvantaged people" is not helpful and that instead the poor and marginalised in his community, and involved with the Poor People's Alliance, should be referred to as "currently disadvantaged" (Twalo 2012). Working closely with the state requires a degree of acceptance of policies which many actors within the network view as inadequate. If the state were to actively pursue a transformative agenda (of the sort discussed in Chapter 2), then working closely with the state might contribute to transformative justice. Strategies such as savings schemes and microcredit, on the other hand, cannot in themselves be used to contest an untransformative paradigm.

Raising and allocating financial resources

The severe lack of some network members' financial resources and the implications of this have already been discussed. This is worth re-emphasising in light of the following considerations. First, there is tension evident between the refusal of financial support from NGOs and donor agencies perceived as seeking to buy influence by some social movements (such as those affiliated with the Poor People's Alliance), and the need to access resources in order to take effective action. This refusal of funding which is perceived as being tied to attempts to co-opt movements is on one level politically responsible. However, as previously outlined, the lack of resources itself (partly precipitated by refusals of funding) can indirectly lead to the undermining of political responsibilities. Second, there is a challenge to politically responsible action associated with the raising of financial resources from sources such as international philanthropic foundations. Jordan and Van Tuijl's (2000) conception of political responsibilities includes the need for financial resources to be separated from decision-making power within networks. This can reasonably be extended further. For instance, SDI is funded by a variety of international donors, including the Bill and Melinda Gates

Foundation (SDI n.d.; SDI 2012: 44–45). Some criticism of SDI's approach has focused upon these sources of funding in relation to the comparative influence of resource-rich donors over strategies affecting poor shack dwellers (Gibson 2011: 271; Pithouse 2011: 232). Even if the raising of financial resources from these sources is genuinely divorced from decision-making power, there are challenges to politically responsible action. The Gates Foundation recently invested in G4S (Fletcher 2013), the very private security company which has been implicated in repression of and violence against shack dweller communities and actors involved in the case study network (Samara 2010: 642–643). This is problematic.

From the point of view of transformative justice, there are more questions raised than answers provided by this research with regard to the political responsibilities of the network over the raising and allocation of financial resources. In order to facilitate the primacy of affected communities in the setting of agendas and in the politically responsible division of action by network members between political arenas, there is a need, from a transformative justice position, to separate decision-making power from financial resources. If this political responsibility is not met, then the exclusivity and elite nature of the transitions at the top which transformative justice seeks to go beyond are likely to be reproduced. Conversely, financial and other resources are a necessity for taking action. If the sources of funding which might be perceived as politically irresponsible are to be eschewed, it is not always clear what the responsible alternative might be.

Information

Earlier chapters highlighted the fact that ties within and between the Housing Assembly and Poor People's Alliance clusters of actors are the most common, strong and enduring links within the case study network. The previous discussion indicates the importance of information-related political responsibilities to these clusters, particularly with regard to the impact of responsibilities in this area upon meeting political responsibilities in other areas. Outside of the actors closely associated with these clusters, use of information varies. It is, for instance, possible that within the SDI-associated cluster of actors, internal information exchange is frequent and is articulated into useful forms. However, as the above-mentioned debate over whether SDI is undemocratic and elite-oriented indicates, it is questionable whether there is equality and multi-directionality in the flow of information in the cluster. Moreover, the unresolved confusion which abounds with regard to the extent of Abahlali baseMjondolo's participation or non-participation in SDI's structures is indicative of a failure of the cluster to provide the transparency in information sharing which maximal political responsibility would require (see, e.g., Abahlali baseMjondolo 2010). Many of the other actors in the case study network have relationships with other network nodes based on short-term or narrow cooperation. For example, participants in DAG's workshops or the relationship the Legal Resources Centre has in providing legal support to other network members. As such, Jordan and Van Tuijl's (2000) model of political responsibilities surrounding information is not as easily applied to these actors as some of the other elements of political responsibility. As discussed in greater detail ahead, Jordan and Van Tuijl's (2000) formulation of these political responsibilities is based upon the assumption of a formalised, or at least relatively long-term and campaign-based, network. Elements of the case study network fit this description, particularly the main clusters of actors which are explored in this chapter and elsewhere in the book. However, outside these, it is much more difficult to meaningfully explore the political responsibilities relating to information. In shorter term or more narrowly defined network relationships, it is not necessarily the case that the absence of the modes and frequency of communication highlighted by Jordan and Van Tuijl would be an indication of failure to meet political responsibility.

In relation to transformative justice, political responsibilities of network members regarding information are of most relevance when considering the appropriate format and translation of, and equality of access to, information. The elite practices associated with the standard toolkit of transitional justice can be challenged through transformative justice only if this is open and accessible to non-elite actors. In the case study network this is evident to varying degrees. Responsibilities in this area are met and potentially underpin moves towards transformative justice in instances where affected communities and grassroots actors have access to and influence over network-relevant and network-produced information. For instance, the responses of research participants indicate that this is the case within the Housing Assembly cluster, though may be to a lesser extent between the Housing Assembly cluster and the Poor People's Alliance cluster (Heunis and Hoedemaker 2012; Hendricks 2012; Twalo 2012). Whereas, if the criticisms of the SDI model of organising are accepted, the responsibility is not as well met – and potential for pursuing transformative approaches are reduced – in this cluster.

Formalisation of relationships

Outside of the Housing Assembly and Poor People's Alliance clusters, the degree of formalisation of relationships between network nodes varies. As mentioned earlier, the model of political responsibilities proposed by Jordan and Van Tuijl (2000), with formalised relationships seen as inherently more responsible, is not wholly adequate. Transparency may be more important than formalisation itself. Moreover, formalisation of some relationships may undermine and preclude the development of politically responsible ties in other areas. For instance, the high degree of formalisation and apparent rigidity in the relationships between the SDI-associated actors in the network serves in part to close down opportunities for new or stronger partnerships to be built between these actors and others within the case study network (see, e.g., Abahlali baseMjondolo 2010).

From the point of view of transformative justice, the political responsibilities of the network relating to the formalisation of relationships need to be considered in light of the foci of transformative justice on inequalities and on holistic societal, rather than elite-oriented, change. This requires making some assessment with regard to whether relationships (formal or not) reflect transformative aims. Consequently, formalised relationships (and, indeed, less formal ties) are politically responsible only if they facilitate access to the mechanisms of change for affected communities and those at the grassroots and if they present a challenge to unequal outcomes and processes. Whilst this may be seen to be fulfilled to a greater extent within the Housing Assembly and Poor People's Alliance than in the interaction between these two clusters, it is less evident in the SDI-associated cluster. As discussed earlier, the formal partnership of the Housing Assembly provides means by which affected communities can articulate themselves and has undertaken activity contesting the dominance of established political elites (Heunis and Hoedemaker 2012). Similarly, research participants indicated that the Poor People's Alliance and its formally constituent organisations provide a platform for affected communities' concerns to be raised and have had some success in challenging existing power (Twalo 2012). Conversely, the cluster of actors associated with SDI has been criticised due to the perception in some quarters that its formalised relationships exclude the possibility of wider grassroots participation, particularly due to the commitment of SDI to working with government and other elite actors. Arguably, this takes place at the expense of transformative potential.

Conclusion

There are three main areas in which conclusions can be drawn on the basis of the analysis discussed in this chapter. First, there are conclusions to do with the ways in which the framework of political responsibilities can usefully be developed and adapted in order for the framework to be applied to the case study network in particular and networks which do not conform to Jordan and Van Tuijl's assumptions in general. Second, there are conclusions made with regard to the extent to which the case study network displays political responsibility, drawing upon the adaption of the political responsibilities framework put forward in the chapter. Third, conclusions are put forward regarding the synthesis of political responsibilities with transformative justice and, in particular, with regard to the role and potential for the case study network in the pursuit of a transformative agenda.

In relation to the political responsibilities framework, it may be concluded that Jordan and Van Tuijl's approach contains important elements which are transferable to the analysis of the case study network, whilst also necessitating some adaption in order for this to be most useful. Specifically, it can be seen that whilst the political responsibilities framework in its original formulation is focused very much upon North-South networks consisting of NGOs, the same issues are also present in the Southern, domestic network of social movements, trade unions and NGOs analysed in the case study. The importance placed in the framework on an analysis of the power dynamics present in networks due to inequalities in resources and access to information are particularly relevant, and may even be more significant in networks (such as the case study) where there are both well-resourced (or at least better resourced) professionalised actors and voluntary or informal grassroots actors present. On the other hand, some elements of the political responsibilities framework require development in order to be usefully applied to the case study network. In particular, the suggestion in the original formulation of the political responsibilities framework that increased formalisation of relationships in networks necessarily increases political responsibility may be questioned. From the analysis put forward in this chapter, it is evident that the formalisation of relationships such as within the SDI-associated cluster of actors can undermine political responsibility. Instead, it is concluded that transparency in relationships and the ability of network participants to access information and resources, and to operate in appropriate political arenas, are more important factors to be measured when considering the political responsibilities of networks such as the case study.

Having applied the abovementioned developed version of Jordan and Van Tuijl's political responsibilities framework to the case study network, several specific conclusions about the network can be drawn. The degree of political responsibility in the case study network varies between the various clusters of actors within the network and between the various other relationships evident in the network. It is clear that no relationships within the case study network meet the ideal type benchmark of maximally politically responsible action. Nevertheless, there are areas within the network where a high degree of political responsibility is evident. In particular, in the areas of political responsibility that it was possible to investigate in this research project, the Housing Assembly displays a high degree of political responsibility, especially within the cluster. The Poor People's Alliance cluster also displayed a higher degree of political responsibility than several of the other relationships present in the network. The main shortcoming in regard to the political responsibilities of these two clusters was in relation to the ties between the clusters, particularly in relation to information exchange. There may, however, be scope for this to be improved. Conversely, lower degrees of political responsibility are evident in other parts of the network. Given the status of the SDI-associated cluster of actors within the network as accounting for multiple links between several actors, and in some respects meeting elements of Jordan and Van Tuijl's (2000) conception of political responsibility, particular attention was paid to analysis of this cluster. It can be concluded that the SDI-linked cluster of actors does not display as high a level of political responsibility as the Poor People's Alliance or the Housing Assembly clusters. Principally, this is because of the problematic nature of the raising and allocation of financial resources and the setting of agendas within the cluster. Furthermore, as has already been discussed, the degree to which relationships within the SDI-linked cluster are formalised serves in some ways to undermine political responsibility, despite Jordan and Van Tuijl's (2000) original suggestion that formalisation of relationships necessarily improves political responsibility.

Building upon the above conclusion regarding the relatively high degree of political responsibility evident in the Housing Assembly and Poor People's Alliance clusters of actors, further conclusions may be made with regard to the potential for the advancement of transformative justice. This chapter highlights the potential synergy between politically responsible networked action and action which promotes transformative justice. This is especially the case in relation to the need for transformative approaches to integrate grassroots actors and perspectives outside of elite transitional spaces. As such, the actions of the Housing Assembly and Poor People's Alliance clusters of actors in particular are highlighted in the network as contributing to and having the potential to further transformative justice, at least in terms of processes. This is as the more politically responsible action present in these clusters provides a means by which diverse actors, especially communities affected by socioeconomic inequalities and structural violence, express themselves politically. These clusters within the network particularly contribute to a potentially transformative agenda in ways which other parts of the network – such as the SDI-associated cluster – do not, due to their contestation of the terrain upon which conditions are built. For transformative justice to be effectively implemented, wide-reaching change throughout much of society (not just the top) is necessary. The grassroots elements of the case study network, particularly within the two major clusters highlighted earlier, call for wide-reaching change. Through networked action which displays a comparatively high degree of political responsibility, there is space for these calls to be articulated into practice within the network. In less politically responsible networked action, there is not the space for these transformative calls to be expressed as easily and, moreover, there is not space for transformative action to be pursued in contravention of the agenda set by powerful or elite network partners. There are, however, areas in which the political responsibilities of the Poor People's Alliance and Housing Assembly clusters of actors might be improved, and as a consequence, there is scope for the pursuit of transformative justice to be improved within the case study network. The next chapter and the final conclusions of the book engage with lessons to be learned by and from the case study network as well as on recommendations drawn from this research.

Notes

1 Indeed, a constitution and statement of what the Housing Assembly stands for have been agreed and formally adopted (Blake 2015).

2 Sandra van Rensburg, from SDI, emphasised in interview that whilst many academics view SDI as "too much up government's backside", that SDI's approach is "about striking the deals, partnering and chipping away at this massive mountain", arguing that "it's not you're up government but as government use communities, we're using them, whether they know it or not", adding "they're not doing us any favours, they're just supposed to be doing their work" (van Rensburg 2015).

3 Indeed, van Rensburg (2015) noted that one of the difficulties of SDI's approach is that "you make a lot of enemies in the process", meaning that "you've got to pull back and let the diplomatic team take over".

References

Abahlali baseMjondolo. (2010) Once Again the Name of Our Movement Is Being Abused by the NGOs. Press Statement. *Abahlali baseMjondolo*, 14 May. http://abahlali.org/node/6702 [accessed June 14, 2013].

Aberese Ako, Matilda, Anyidoho, Nana Akua and Crawford, Gordon. (2013) NGOs, Rights-Based Approaches and the Potential for Progressive Development in Local Contexts: Constraints and Challenges in Northern Ghana. *Journal of Human Rights Practice*, 5(1), 46–74.

Ashley, Brian. (2012) Personal interview, Cape Town, South Africa, 16 July.

Blake, Michael. (2012) Personal interview, Cape Town, South Africa, 6 July.

Blake, Michael. (2015) Personal interview, Johannesburg, South Africa, 10 April.

Böhmke, Heinrich. (2010) The Branding of Social Movements in South Africa. *Dispositions: A Journal*, 30 April. http://dispositionsjournal.blogspot.com/2010_04_01_archive.html [accessed November 25, 2012].

Böhmke, Heinrich. (2012) Ventriloquism, Fanon and the Social Movement Hustle. *Dispositions: A Journal*, 20 May. http://dispositionsjournal.blogspot.com/2012/05/social-movement-hustle_20.html [accessed December 14, 2012].

Daly, Erin. (2002) Transformative Justice: Charting a Path to Reconciliation. *International Legal Perspectives*, 12(1/2), 73–183.

Development Action Group. (2012) *Written Response to Interview Questions*. Unpublished document.

Fletcher, Nick. (2013) Bill Gates Buys £110m Stake in Security Group G4S. *The Guardian*, 10 June. www.guardian.co.uk/business/marketforceslive/2013/jun/10/bill-gates-stake-security-g4s?INTCMP=SRCH [accessed June 12, 2013].

Friedman, Steven. (2012) Beyond the Fringe? South African Social Movements and the Politics of Redistribution. *Review of African Political Economy*, 39(131), 85–100.

Gibson, Nigel C. (2011) *Fanonian Practices in South Africa: From Steve Biko to Abahlali baseMjondolo* (New York: Palgrave Macmillan).

Graeber, David. (2002) The New Anarchists. *New Left Review*, 13, 61–73.

Gready, Paul, Boesten, Jelke, Crawford, Gordon and Wilding, Polly. (2010) Transformative Justice: A Concept Note. Draft Concept Note Developed by the Worldwide Universities Network Transformative Justice Group, October.

Hendricks, Soraya. (2012) Personal interview, Cape Town, South Africa, 11 July.

Heunis, Lorraine and Hoedemaker, Eleanor. (2012) Personal interview, Cape Town, South Africa, 7 August.

Hudson, Alan. (2001) NGOs' Transnational Advocacy Networks: From "Legitimacy" to "Political Responsibility"? *Global Networks*, 1(4), 331–352.

ISN Gauteng Provincial Leadership. (2015) Personal interview, Johannesburg, South Africa, 13 March.

Jacobs, Mario. (2012) Personal interview, Cape Town, South Africa, 30 July.

Jordan, Lisa and Van Tuijl, Peter. (2000) Political Responsibility in Transnational NGO Advocacy. *World Development*, 28(12), 2051–2065.

Klein, Naomi. (2001) Reclaiming the Commons. *New Left Review*, 9, 81–89.

Legassick, Martin. (2010) Personal interview, Cape Town, South Africa, 4 August.

Marsden, Mike. (2012) Unpublished letter to Mario Jacobs and Mhlobo Gunguluzi, 17 July.

Mchunu, Nokukhanya. (2012) Personal interview, Cape Town, South Africa, 27 July.

McKinley, Dale T. (2012) The Crisis of the Left in Contemporary South Africa. In *Contesting Transformation: Popular Resistance in Twenty-First-Century South Africa*, edited by Marcelle C. Dawson and Luke Sinwell (London: Pluto Press), 23–43.
Mdlalose, Bandile. (2014) The Rise and Fall of Abahlali baseMjondolo, a South African Social Movement. *Politikon: South African Journal of Political Studies*, 41(3), 345–353.
Miller, Hannah. (2012) A Change in Charity Law for England and Wales: Examining War on Want's Foremost Adoption of the New Human Rights Charitable Purpose. *International Journal of Human Rights*, 16(7), 1003–1022.
Pithouse, Richard. (2011) Fidelity to Fanon. In *Living Fanon: Global Perspectives*, edited by Nigel C. Gibson (New York: Palgrave Macmillan), 225–248.
Podlashuc, Leopold. (2011) *The South African Homeless People's Federation: Interrogating the Myth of Participation*. Working Paper, African Centre for Citizenship and Democracy (Cape Town: University of the Western Cape).
Pointer, Rebecca. (2004) Questioning the Representation of South Africa's "New Social Movements": A Case Study of the Mandela Park Anti-Eviction Campaign. *Journal of Asian and African Studies*, 39(4), 271–294.
Poni, Mzonke. (2010) Personal interview, Cape Town, South Africa, 12 August.
Robins, Steven L. (2008) *From Revolution to Rights in South Africa: Social Movements, NGOs and Popular Politics after Apartheid* (Woodbridge: James Currey).
Samara, Tony Roshan. (2010) Order and Security in the City: Producing Race and Policing Neoliberal Spaces in South Africa. *Ethnic and Racial Studies*, 33(4), 637–655.
SDI. (2012) *Shack/Slum Dwellers International Annual Report 2012* (Cape Town: Shack/Slum Dwellers International).
SDI. (n.d.) Partners. www.sdinet.org/partners/ [accessed October 10, 2011].
SDI Programme Officer. (2012) Personal interview, Cape Town, South Africa, 3 August.
South African Municipal Workers' Union and Housing Assembly. (2012) *Memorandum of Demands to the City of Cape Town Council in Respect of Service Delivery Demands and the City's Extended Public Works Programme (EPWP)*. Unpublished document, 5 July.
South African SDI Alliance. (2013) *Masikhase: Community Upgrading Finance Facility (CUFF)*. Project Report (Cape Town: Shack/Slum Dwellers International).
Stammers, Neil. (2009) *Human Rights and Social Movements* (London: Pluto Press).
Tissington, Kate. (2012) "Tacticians in the Struggle for Change"? Exploring the Dynamics between Legal Organisations and Social Movements Engaged in Rights-Based Struggles in South Africa. In *Contesting Transformation: Popular Resistance in Twenty-First-Century South Africa*, edited by Marcelle C. Dawson and Luke Sinwell (London: Pluto Press), 201–221.
Tolsi, Niren. (2006) On the Far Side of Left. *Mail and Guardian*, 8 December. http://abahlali.org/node/454 [accessed June 15, 2013].
Twalo, Mncedisi. (2012) Personal interview, Cape Town, South Africa, 4 July.
van Rensburg, Sandra. (2015) Personal interview, Johannesburg, South Africa, 13 March.
Western Cape Anti-Eviction Campaign. (2006) On the SMI, from the Anti-Eviction Campaign, 18 December. http://abahlali.org/node/462 [accessed June 15, 2013].

Chapter 5

Transformative justice processes, policies and practice

Introduction

This chapter builds on Chapters 3 and 4, asking, on the basis of the case study, whether and to what extent networks can contribute to transformative justice processes, policies and practice. It considers the conditions for effective network relationships with regard to the effective pursuit of transformative justice in South Africa and discusses how these lessons might apply to other contexts. In particular, the chapter highlights the importance of financial and non-financial resources to effective network action.

First, this chapter discusses what is meant by transformative justice policies, processes and practice as well as the scope for their implementation in South Africa. In particular, questions raised by scholars such as Pádraig McAuliffe (2017) regarding the degree to which post-conflict states are malleable to transformative justice are addressed. Next, the chapter focuses in on findings from the case study, exploring the degree of political responsibility evident in the case study network and highlighting the importance of processes. Finally, the chapter concludes by offering some observations regarding the transferable lessons which might be applied to contexts other than South Africa with regard to the pursuit of transformative justice processes, policies and practices. The key areas in which these conclusions are drawn are related to the processes of transformative justice (what these are and how they might be facilitated), the importance of access to resources in affecting potentially transformative outcomes and the convergence of politically responsible action with the promotion of transformative justice.

The scope for transformative justice policies, practices and processes in South Africa

For the purposes of this book, transformative justice policies, practices and processes are intended to refer to action taken (whether by governmental or nongovernmental actors) which has the effect (and the intent) of overcoming the legacies of past injustices (resulting from conflict and authoritarianism – particularly apartheid in the South African case) beyond the scope of transitional justice, and of furthering the achievement of the necessary conditions for transformative justice in post-conflict and post-authoritarian contexts (identified in Chapter 2). This means policies, practices and processes which contribute towards the realisation of socioeconomic rights and the addressing of structural violence, not just the realisation of civil and political rights or addressing direct interpersonal violence. In keeping with the understanding of transformative justice – and its necessary conditions – put forward in this book (especially Chapter 2), and with the findings which come out of exploration of the case study of land and housing activism (see Chapters 3 and 4, particularly), transformative justice processes and practices are those which facilitate the central involvement of affected communities in articulating their needs and which maintain political responsibility in relationships within and between groups and organisations seeking to contest untransformative structures and policies. Transformative justice policies are those which are shaped by affected communities and which address their concerns with regard to socioeconomic rights issues and the overcoming of structural violence. In relation to the case study, this would include policies which move towards a more redistributive paradigm of land reform and the linking of this to the provision of adequate, well-located housing, secure tenure and the prevention of evictions (see Chapters 2, 3 and 4 for greater discussion of structural violence and socioeconomic rights in relation to transformative justice and for detailed discussion of the case study).

In South Africa, as well as in other contexts, these kinds of processes, practices and policies require mobilisation and social and political action of various forms in order to take advantage of opportunities to challenge and shift the status quo, and to resist or avoid the possibility of transformative agendas being undermined through co-option, repression or a lack of political momentum. It is argued here that in South Africa steps towards transformative justice can be made and that lessons can be drawn from this for other contexts with regard to when maximally transformative outcomes might be possible and what kinds of policies, practices and processes would be necessary to achieve these.

Pádraig McAuliffe has argued that post-conflict states may not be as malleable to transformative change as some advocates of transformative justice suggest (McAuliffe 2017). It is not entirely clear whether contemporary South Africa comes under McAuliffe's definition of a post-conflict state. McAuliffe defines post-conflict as "generally . . . the situation pertaining when an armed conflict comes to an end" (McAuliffe 2017: 5). He also notes that "[t]here are no fixed boundaries between conflict and post-conflict", that "there is a psychological element to it insofar as a consensus exists among antagonists, society at large and peacebuilders that there is peace, or at least that a new non-violent political dispensation prevails" (McAuliffe 2017: 5). South Africa is mentioned only rarely throughout McAuliffe's (2017) book *Transformative Transitional Justice and the Malleability of Post-Conflict States*. Certainly, it is possible to question whether post-apartheid and post-conflict ought to be considered as synonymous. Nevertheless, important issues are raised by McAuliffe in the overview and evaluation he presents of the literature on what he variously terms "transformative justice", "transformative transitional justice", the "transformative turn" in transitional justice and "fourth generation transitional justice" (see, e.g., McAuliffe 2017: vii–x, 20–25). Key to McAuliffe's argument is that much of the critical transitional justice literature which calls for transformative change in post-conflict societies severely overestimates the extent to which post-conflict states are malleable to different potential outcomes, and overestimates the extent to which "external" and "local" iterations of transitional justice mechanisms are practically able to facilitate transformative change (McAuliffe 2017). Certainly, McAuliffe is correct to emphasise the importance of context to the viability of any given transformative justice process or policy. Material conditions matter. Interests, orientations and actions of conflict parties and potential spoilers have an impact regardless of the normative case for any given policy or process aiming at facilitating transformation (McAuliffe 2017). It is important – necessary, even – to take account of what is as well as what ought to be.

Nevertheless, it is argued here that transformative justice is a useful concept and that it can add value to consideration of policies, processes and practices which might contribute to addressing structural violence in post-apartheid South Africa, as well as in other contexts. For this to be the case, it is important to re-emphasise the position taken in this book that transformative justice is best conceived as separate to – though overlapping with – transitional justice (see, especially, Chapter 2). To this end, McAuliffe's (2017) critique of the extent to which transitional justice mechanisms can realistically be expected to contribute to transformative justice ought to be taken on board. Transformative justice is not likely to be achieved – certainly not maximally – through transitional justice alone (see, e.g., Waldorf 2012; McAuliffe 2017). Moreover, with regard to South Africa in particular (and with relevance to a number of other contexts), it is worth thinking of transformative justice as a much less time-bound notion than transitional justice (see Chapter 2; see also Gready et al. 2010; Gready and Robins 2014).

In South Africa, it would not be unreasonable to suggest that the transition period is over. Some of the literature on critical transitional justice and transformative justice might present this as the closing of key opportunities for change as the (alleged) malleability present during transition ends (for an overview of this literature, see McAuliffe 2017). However, an alternative view is presented here. Constraints that exist during transitions do not necessarily remain post-transition (see, e.g., Collins 2010). Moreover, social and economic change is not only a matter of concern during or immediately following periods of conflict. For all that specific periods of conflict, instances of direct violence or periods of oppressive and authoritarian rule produce and exacerbate inequality, structural violence and human rights violations, these need not be inextricably linked in the ways in which they are responded to. Indeed, the emphasis (at times) placed on the politics of exception in transitional justice ought to be questioned (see, e.g., Gissel 2017).

Transitional, post-conflict settlements need not be permanent and absolute in defining the limits of social change or contestation of current conditions. It may even be the case that greater malleability exists in the period after transitions than during immediate post-conflict transitions. In South Africa, for instance, key axes of contestation are no longer drawn on (quite) the same lines as during the apartheid period. The National Party no longer exists (with its rump successor New National Party having first joined with the Democratic Party to form the Democratic Alliance then later joined the ANC and dissolved) (see, e.g., South African History Online 2011). The apartheid military and security regime is no longer in place. The ANC is in power, and social movement challenges to the government now manifest more directly as challenges to the ANC as liberation movement turned government than as challenges to apartheid structures and political supporters of these (see, e.g., Pithouse 2016). Indeed, one interviewee argued that South Africa is in a Weimar Republic–type period (adding, "I don't know who Hitler is") (Blake 2015). Changing patterns of power in the ruling party, and differing dynamics of contention across the parliamentary and extra-parliamentary opposition, manifest as potential for transformative change as well as potential regression (see, e.g., Ashman, Levenson and Ngwane 2017; Guardian 2017; Mail and Guardian 2017; Pithouse 2016; Beresford 2016).

Responding to the imperative to address structural violence and realise socio-economic rights in post-apartheid South Africa, processes, policies and practices could be overtly framed as intending to promote transformative justice, could be implicitly shaped by a transformative justice agenda or could be analysed and evaluated according to the extent to which they promote transformative justice regardless of how they are framed or conceived by those designing or implementing them (see, e.g., Evans 2014; see also Gready 2014). Necessary conditions for transformative justice have already been elaborated (in Chapter 2) as comprising the inclusion of affected communities in shaping agendas, a focus on addressing economic conditions, emphasis on long-term societal changes and attention to the historical and structural roots of injustices. These may be used as the starting point for evaluating the extent to which processes, policies and practices promote transformative justice. Following this evaluation, it is possible to articulate further recommendations for increasing the extent to which transformative justice is pursued. This kind of evaluation and any recommendations do need to take account of the kinds of issues raised by McAuliffe (2017). Wholly idealistic recommendations which do not take account of actually existing conditions, including limitations on the scope of action by particular actors, will not be useful. This does not mean that no practices, policies or processes which promote transformative justice are ever possible.

Sharlene Swartz's (2016) concept of social restitution may also be usefully applied here. Swartz's focus is not primarily on the state, but instead on the possibilities which exist for undoing (or at least mitigating) the effects of apartheid through everyday social practices (Swartz 2016). In particular, Swartz argues for the establishment of "10–10–10 restitution dialogues" where "ten people, who are different to each other, [meet] together over ten weeks (or a few more), and hav[e] ten conversations" focused on themed tasks Swartz views as necessary steps for social restitution (Swartz 2016: 279).[1] Both the extent to which the voluntary practices of restitution advocated by Swartz are taken up and the content of government policy positions can be influenced by the mobilisation of groups such as social movements, NGOs and trade unions. Transformative justice is, at least in part, about discourse. Shifting understanding of the present towards recognition of the ways in which current conditions are shaped by past injustice is one step towards transformative justice. Seeking ways in which these enduring injustices might be overcome is another. There is potentially a role for the voluntarism Swartz advocates here (see Swartz 2016). There is also potentially a role for the state. Indeed, one of the potential shortcomings of Swartz's proposals is the very fact that they would be voluntary (even whilst she argues they may form a moral – or religious – obligation), and therefore are not likely to be taken up by all relevant persons (especially those politically opposed to Swartz's desired outcomes) (Swartz 2016). The authority – or, at least, the power – of the state to implement policies without relying upon voluntary participation distinguishes its potential from that of Swartz's proposals (though, of course, new shortcomings may manifest).

Plainly, the state is a powerful and important actor. It cannot be ignored. Moreover, the state must be understood as multifaceted and dynamic. Local, provincial and national government all have different characteristics and suggest different possibilities for the pursuit of transformative justice policies and practices. Indeed, interviews conducted for this research project indicated a high degree of variation in the characteristics of relationships with, and degree of support from government representatives and departments for the positions taken by groups and organisations in the network, including those advocating a more transformative approach to land and housing (see, e.g., Heunis and Hoedemaker 2012; Makwela and Simelane 2015; Wa Mapena 2015; ISN Gauteng Provincial Leadership 2015; Sibanda 2015). The ruling party is not monolithic (nor, indeed, are opposition parties). Different currents, factions and groupings within the ANC – and outside it – cause shifts in priorities and in policy agenda (see, e.g., Beresford 2009; Beresford 2016; Ashman, Levenson and Ngwane 2017).

Moreover, a focus on transformative justice as only the preserve of either established transitional justice mechanisms or of voluntary action outside the purview of the state could be problematic. Inasmuch as South Africa and other post-conflict and post-authoritarian states exist within a world of states, the primary duty-bearer in the promotion and fulfilment of human rights will often be the state. Too great a focus on the roles of non-state actors or on voluntarism could lead to states being absolved of their responsibility to act in the interest of human rights, including with regard to pursuing what can be framed as transformative justice policies and practices (see, e.g., Evans and Wilkins 2017).

Transformative justice requires looking beyond transitional justice tools and mechanisms, and looking beyond a short-term transition period (see Chapter 2, especially, in this regard). Transformative justice also requires taking account of actually existing conditions in the present rather than only the conditions present at the time of transition or an ideal end result. Conditions and circumstances in contemporary post-transition South Africa are not the same as during the transition period. There are opportunities in this as well as threats. McAuliffe is rightly critical of the tendency towards over-optimistic claims which some advocates of more transformative versions of transitional justice fall into (McAuliffe 2017). Perhaps, he suggests, outcomes and processes which are far from ideal are nevertheless the best that can be achieved in the lived reality of post-conflict transitions (McAuliffe 2017).[2] Even if this is the case, however, it is possible for circumstances to change, for power dynamics and interests to shift, and for post-conflict justice to be revisited. Post-transitional justice is one way in which this might occur (see, e.g., Collins 2010). Transformative justice, as conceived in this book, is another. Earlier chapters have shown the ways in which NGOs, trade unions and social movements can – and, importantly, do – contest the terrain upon which an untransformative political paradigm is built (see Chapter 4, especially). The following section sets out lessons from the case study for understanding the potential for transformative justice policies, processes and practices to be enacted in South Africa and, especially, how these lessons might apply beyond South Africa.

Lessons for understanding the potential for transformative justice policies and practices

A key aim of this book can be summed up as seeking to address the overarching question: can transformative justice be advanced through networks of trade unions, social movements and NGOs in the global South? Addressing this main question raises several further questions: how do NGOs, trade unions and social movements currently engage with each other in networks? Which actors participate in networks? How do these actors' approaches to networks differ? What can be learned from the approaches of NGOs, trade unions and social movements in networks? What risks and opportunities do these approaches present? The book puts forward answers to each of these questions inasmuch as they apply to the case study. The potential for future research is discussed later, particularly in the conclusion to the book (Chapter 6). However, particularly in relation to the exploration of the case study network put forward in the preceding chapters, the objectives can be said to be as follows: to map participation in the network, analyse relationships within the case study network, evaluate the political responsibility of the case study network, synthesise conclusions addressing the overarching and secondary research questions (identified above) and create recommendations for research and practice. These objectives are addressed ahead (in this section and in the chapter's conclusion) in terms of their contributions to providing lessons for understanding the potential for transformative justice policies and practices. These are subsequently taken forward for further elaboration (especially in relation to recommendations for research and practice) in the conclusion of the book (Chapter 6).

Mapping participation in the case study network

In mapping participation in the case study network, several findings were made (see Chapter 3 for diagrammatic mapping of the network and discussion of key network nodes and clusters). Social movements, trade unions and NGOs do interact both directly and indirectly in the network. Particular clusters of actors within the network are also identifiable, particularly around the Housing Assembly, Poor People's Alliance and SDI. More importantly, however, it is evident from the mapping process that the case study network is not in a meaningful sense a transnational advocacy network. This brings some of the literature on networks and collective action into question. As identified earlier in the book, much of the literature focuses on networks which are transnational. Mindful of this, this study, in part, sought to explore the degree to which analysis of transnational networks can be adapted and applied to domestic networks. This research suggests that this is partially possible. However, there are features of transnational networks discussed at length in the existing literature which cannot be identified in the case study network. The boomerang effect and spiral process, for instance, are not present in the network. Transnational links are necessary for these processes to occur in the manner described in the literature (see, e.g., Keck and Sikkink 1998: 12–13; Risse and Sikkink 1999: 18–20; Risse and Ropp 2013: 5–9).

The tools put forward for the analysis of networks in the existing literature (focused on transnational advocacy networks) are not wholly adequate. There is reason to believe that in at least some key ways, domestic networks (particularly those based in the global South) behave differently and should be considered distinctly from transnational networks. Given the inadequacy of the existing analytical tools for use on domestic networks, evaluation of and recommendations for the practice of domestic networks also need to be distinct. In considering how this might be applied as a lesson for transformative justice in other contexts, it is worth emphasising the degree to which participation of affected communities and diverse constituencies of actors (including, for instance community-based organisations and social movements as well as NGOs) in politically responsible collective action is central to the pursuit of transformative justice (see Chapters 1 and 2). Moreover, the importance of access to resources (including, but not limited to, financial resources) for collective action of this sort to take place, and the degree to which many actors in the case study network lack these resources is worth emphasising. The fact that these actors are under-resourced links in some ways to the very reasons why (as, often, members of poor and marginalised communities) these actors ought to be involved in shaping the agenda of transformative change. This is not peculiar to the case study network or to South Africa. Other contexts where transformative justice might be pursued will (by definition) be affected by structural violence. Those most affected by structural violence in post-conflict and post-authoritarian contexts other than South Africa are likely to face similar difficulties to those involved in the case study network in accessing the resources required for maximally effective collective action. Advocates of transformative justice and, especially, better resourced actors who might pursue relationships with affected communities at the grassroots ought to keep this in mind, as well as the ways in which political responsibility might be maintained (and negative impacts of differential power dynamics mitigated) in such relationships.

Relationships within the case study network

The relationships within the case study network display a variety of characteristics. Elements of the network involve highly formalised ties between nodes. For instance, the cluster of actors associated with SDI has a clear structure and format (see, e.g., van Rensburg 2015), and the Housing Assembly is based at its core on a formal structure and a formalised relationship between SAMWU, ILRIG and other participants (see, e.g., Blake 2012; Blake 2015). Other elements of the network involve much less formal interaction. Moreover, relationships between the network nodes vary in the extent to which they are long lasting, based on organisational or individual ties and with regard to whether there are direct relationships. One of the key findings of the research presented in previous chapters (particularly Chapters 3 and 4) is that increased formalisation of relationships in networks may not always be desirable. It was found that there are opportunities associated with relationships which are not highly formalised. Transparency of relationships was found to be more important. Findings relating to this are discussed further ahead.

Another key finding centres on the importance of informal relationships and ties based on individual (rather than organisational) relationships to strengthening networks. Informal relationships present opportunities for a network as a whole to be strengthened where highly formalised relationships in some instances close down the scope for increased collaboration and wide participation in network action.

Evaluating political responsibility of the case study network

The analysis of the relationships present in the case study network leads directly on to the evaluation of the political responsibility of the network. Findings in this area are threefold. First, the research brought to the forefront the utility of a political responsibilities analysis as a means of analysing the potential for transformative justice in networks. This is because the aspects of transformative justice this research is primarily concerned with are those relating to the process of action. It is possible to synthesise the political responsibilities analysis with consideration of the processes which contribute to transformative justice (see Chapter 1). This is particularly the case when attention is paid to the scope for grassroots participation in action involving affected communities and the space (or absence of space) for elite practices and dominant policy paradigms to be contested, challenged or altered. More politically responsible action provides more transformative potential. An analysis of political responsibilities can usefully be applied to actors working in contexts where transformative justice might be pursued. This analysis can illuminate the potential for and limits of transformative processes in particular and may underpin analysis of the scope for successful transformative outcomes and how these might be pursued.

Second, it is important that this research found that it is necessary to adapt the political responsibility framework in order for it to meaningfully be applied to networks, such as the case study, which include trade unions and social movements rather than just NGOs. The political responsibility framework was, for instance, adapted to place greater emphasis on the transparency of network relationships as an indicator of responsibility rather than on formalisation. This was instrumental in producing findings regarding the varying degrees of responsibility displayed in the relationships within and between the clusters and nodes which make up the network. This is important as a nuanced view of politically responsible network relationships opens up a wider range of possibilities for action than an application of the original framework without adaptation would imply. It is not simply the case that formal relationships are better. Recognition of this by actors pursuing network relationships (and those who study them) allows greater attention to be paid to analysing what is in practice good or bad about an existing or proposed relationship.

Third, taking the adaptation of the political responsibility framework into account, it was found that throughout the network, varying degrees of political responsibility are present. The most politically responsible relationships in the network were those between clusters of actors which maintained a degree of flexibility in the relationships they engaged in. Not all the relationships within (and between) these clusters were highly formalised. However, the degree of transparency as well as other factors such as the extent to which grassroots actors can access the clusters indicated that these were more politically responsible than other elements of the network. This leads to the wider transferable lesson for actors engaging in networks that reflection upon the nature of their ties to other actors and a willingness to pursue different characters of links with different partners can be fruitful. Indeed, as previously mentioned, a higher degree of formalisation of relationships (such as that evident in the SDI-associated cluster within the case study network) can at times lead to less politically responsible relationships (see Chapter 4 for further discussion). The nature of formal relationships can limit the extent to which narratives alternative to those endorsed by dominant network actors are able to be articulated and can prevent the broadening of participation in the network by excluding involvement of groups which are unwilling or unable to commit to working in relatively narrowly defined, formal structures.

Conclusion

In addressing conditions for effective network relationships in pursuing transformative justice, several specific conclusions can be made on the basis of this research. The overarching research question asked whether transformative justice can be advanced through networks of trade unions, social movements and NGOs in the global South. On the basis of the case study presented in this book, broadly, the answer to the main research question is that networks including trade unions, social movements and NGOs can advance transformative justice. The specific conclusions in relation to this overarching question and the secondary questions concerning transformative justice processes, policies and practices are addressed next.

Processes of transformative justice

Transformative justice is concerned with both processes and outcomes. However, with regard to the contribution that could be made by networks of trade unions, social movements and NGOs, this chapter (and the book more broadly) makes specific conclusions mainly in relation to the processes of transformative justice. These largely come out of consideration of the political responsibilities of actors within the case study network and the identification of the opportunities these network relationships present. In particular, processes of transformative justice to which networks can contribute are those relating to contesting the social, economic and political status quo and those relating to facilitating the involvement of affected communities.

Importantly, transformative justice is concerned (in part) with remedying structural violence. Transformative justice also necessitates the involvement of affected communities and grassroots actors. In both these areas, it can be concluded from the case study research that networks of trade unions, social movements and NGOs in the global South contribute to the pursuit of transformative justice. Elements of the case study network explicitly challenge the structures which facilitate unequal access to land and housing and which lead to evictions. Challenges of this sort are necessary for a transformative approach. Indeed, it is arguable that more generally for "rights-based approaches . . . to be progressive, then a vigorous opposition to prevailing neoliberal ideology is required" (Aberese Ako, Anyidoho and Crawford 2013: 69). The research did, however, also find that the extent to which this structural violence is challenged (and consequently the extent to which transformative justice is pursued) varied within the case study network. Some parts of the network do not significantly challenge the existing paradigms which facilitate structural violence. These actors contribute less to transformative justice than those which enable overarching conditions and the root causes of these to be questioned and challenged.

The above conclusion leads on to several related further conclusions which also shed light on the research questions. These are particularly in relation to the research questions asking how NGOs, trade unions and social movements currently engage with each other and asking what can be learned from the approaches of NGOs, trade unions and social movements in networks. First, as already highlighted, the positioning of the actors concerned with regard to opposing or maintaining the structural status quo matters. The processes through which actors within the case study network challenge evictions and advocate housing rights impact upon the relationships they have with other network members and upon the scope for transformative outcomes to be achieved. The willingness to engage in contentious politics and overt criticism of the state varied in the case study network. In regard to pursuing transformative justice, network actors which provide a platform for the concerns of affected communities to be addressed – which may include by more contentious tactics – contribute more to transformative processes. There is a need for decision-making processes and campaigning strategies to be open to the grassroots, particularly affected communities and network members who are otherwise less well-resourced or less powerful on the face of it. Consequently, a degree of openness to the preferred approaches of affected communities is indicative of a network relationship with greater potential for contributing to transformative justice. Opening up of decision-making processes supports the challenging of structures and established practices which facilitate structural violence. Network relationships built around action which opposes the status quo in regard to (in this case study) the implementation of land and housing rights encourage further ties with and wider participation of affected communities disadvantaged by the existing paradigm. In networks, processes which advance transformative justice are mutually reinforcing.

Outcomes and resources

It is difficult to overemphasise the extent to which social movements and community-based organisations (and, to some extent, the NGOs and trade unions) in the case study network are under-resourced. Moreover, this is not a unique state of affairs (see, e.g., Aberese Ako, Anyidoho and Crawford 2013: 54–55). This has a severe impact on the action a network can take. The limit on action entailed by a severe lack of resources available to a network impacts upon the extent to which the network contributes to transformative justice outcomes in and of itself. Moreover, the case study shows that the lack of resources available to grassroots actors can also be partially reproduced in the more professionalised sections of a network. This is especially the case when financial resources available to NGOs (particularly local Southern NGOs) but tied to specific uses are also considered. Conflicts over use of resources, especially financial resources, also represent one of the most significant threats to the effective continuation of relationships in networks.

With regard to enacting transformative outcomes, resources are extremely important. This is both in terms of the range of actions available to be pursued which may contribute to transformative outcomes and in terms of the processes by which distribution and use of resources within a network can contribute to transformative outcomes. In relation to the former, it can be concluded that access to resources influences a network's ability to take action across a wide geographic area and in particular political arenas. For instance, the lack of international links in the case study network is in part due to the lack of resources available for network members to build and sustain these links. This means that strategies of the sort highlighted in much of the literature on transnational advocacy networks do not apply. The boomerang effect is not possible. The spiral process is not available. Change at the levels of global governments and intergovernmental organisations are not available. In relation to the processes of distribution and use of resources it can be concluded that where control of resources is dominated by a small part of a network without access and meaningful oversight from other network participants the potential for transformative outcomes is reduced. This is for two principal reasons. Conflicts over resource use and distribution can lead to the breaking up of network relationships. Control of resources by actors pursuing less transformative goals can lead to the exclusion of other options from the realm of possible courses of action.

Despite the severe lack of resources in the case study network and the limiting effect this has on enacting transformative outcomes, there is good reason for believing that the case study network achieves a degree of success. The sustained presence of the case study network and its constituent actors over a significant period of time allows the abovementioned processes of transformative justice to take place with regard to articulating the concerns of affected communities. This is in itself a success. The actors associated with the case study network may not, for instance, be an effective opposition to ANC domination when it comes to the likelihood of a change in government. However, even the successful articulation of rhetorical opposition to dominant narratives is an important step. Moreover, individual, (on the face of it) isolated and piecemeal achievements by the case study network and actors within it, such as preventing specific evictions, mobilising protest action, successful legal cases (especially the defeat of the Slums Act in a case brought by Abahlali baseMjondolo in Durban) and direct negotiation with politicians, each contribute towards transformative outcomes, even if only in a small way (Legassick 2010; Heunis and Hoedemaker 2012; Jacobs 2012; Tissington 2012). In themselves, these successful outcomes do not constitute the outright achievement of transformative justice. They may, however, contribute towards it. Taking these achievements together, and in the context of other networks contesting the same terrain and achieving similar piecemeal successes, leads to the conclusion that, despite not being ideal, action taken by the network works (see Alexander and Pfaffe 2014; see also Zuern 2011). It is likely that if the actors which make up the case study network had access to greater resources, including the strategies which become available through close partnerships with powerful or better resourced international actors, that there would be more scope for the achievement of transformative outcomes. Nevertheless, these outcomes are not entirely precluded by the reality of the network's circumstances. This suggests that, in contrast with more pessimistic readings of McAuliffe's (2017) arguments, there is at least some malleability and scope for transformative justice in contexts such as South Africa.

Political responsibility and transformative justice

It has already been noted that elements within networks which display a high degree of political responsibility are better able to contribute to transformative justice. The crucial influence of access to resources on action taken by networks is impacted upon by the extent to which network relationships are politically responsible. Regardless of the amount of resources available, the separation of financial resources from decision-making power is one of the fundamental aspects of politically responsible networked action. Elements within the case study network where the allocation of financial resources and decision-making processes are transparent demonstrate greater scope for the pursuit of transformative justice. Where it is not clear that resources are used responsibly and, relatedly, when it is not evident that decision-making processes are accessible to individual network members and affected communities, the potential for transformative justice is undermined.

In addition to the responsible distribution of financial resources and the transparency of decision-making processes, the degree to which networks meet political responsibilities relating to information and communication impact upon how the research questions are answered. The extent to which affected communities are able to articulate their views and engage meaningfully in action is at times limited in the case study network by a lack of successful communication between network nodes. It is possible for there to be a high degree of commonality in the analyses of two or more actors but strong ties between them to be hampered by difficulties the actors face in making themselves fully understood by their counterparts. On the basis of the case study, it is possible to conclude that improved communications and access to information within the network would allow for more effective collaboration. More significantly, it was evident that there is a degree of payoff which comes with perseverance in seeking common ground and means of effective communication between disparate actors. More effective collaboration between network clusters facilitates the transformative justice processes discussed previously. Actors in networks are able to engage in more and better collaboration through developing and nurturing links as they emerge. The case study highlighted the importance of some ties between network nodes being based upon relationships between individuals. This provides one way by which organisational barriers to collaboration in networks can be overcome and communication between actors can be facilitated. The case study suggests that actors which are more insular, and do not persevere in building links (even if these are initially fragile), display less political responsibility and contribute less to transformative justice.

In the next chapter, overarching conclusions are drawn and recommendations for research and practice are made. These build upon the analysis put forward in this chapter, as well as on the preceding chapters. In particular, in the next chapter, attention is refocused upon how networks such as those explored in the case study, but also those in other contexts which share similar characteristics, may fulfil their political responsibilities and pursue transformative justice as effectively as possible.

Notes

1 These themed tasks are to "Establish a diverse group and have a conversation"; "Discuss how you see South Africa"; "Talk about the effects of past injustice on the present"; "Discuss the meaning of restitution and its potential"; "Discuss the difference between charity and restitution"; "Locate all participants in the conversation about injustice"; "Discuss ideas for action to restore our damaged humanity"; "Make a plan for implementing and evaluating your ideas"; "Discuss attitudes needed for restitution and obstacles that might arise"; "Make plans for an ongoing project" (Swartz 2016: 279–281).

2 As do others, such as Lars Waldorf (see, e.g., Waldorf 2012).

References

Aberese Ako, Matilda, Anyidoho, Nana Akua and Crawford, Gordon. (2013) NGOs, Rights-Based Approaches and the Potential for Progressive Development in Local Contexts: Constraints and Challenges in Northern Ghana. *Journal of Human Rights Practice*, 5(1), 46–74.

Alexander, Peter and Pfaffe, Peter. (2014) Social Relationships to the Means and Ends of Protest in South Africa's Ongoing Rebellion of the Poor: The Balfour Insurrections. *Social Movement Studies*, 13(2), 204–221.

Ashman, Sam, Levenson, Zachary and Ngwane, Trevor. (2017) South Africa's ANC: The Beginning of the End? *Catalyst*, 1(2), 75–106.

Beresford, Alexander. (2009) Comrades "Back on Track"? The Durability of the Tripartite Alliance in South Africa. *African Affairs*, 108(432), 391–412.

Beresford, Alexander. (2016) *South Africa's Political Crisis: Unfinished Liberation and Fractured Class Struggles* (Basingstoke: Palgrave Macmillan).

Blake, Michael. (2012) Personal interview, Cape Town, South Africa, 6 July.

Blake, Michael. (2015) Personal interview, Johannesburg, South Africa, 10 April.

Collins, Cath. (2010) *Post-Transitional Justice: Human Rights Trials in Chile and El Salvador* (University Park: Pennsylvania State University Press).

Evans, Matthew. (2014) Addressing Historical Wrongs in Post-Transition South Africa: What Role for Transformative Justice? (Unpublished paper presented at "South Africa's Democracy at 20: Diagnosis and Prognosis", South African Association of Political Studies National Biennial Conference, University of South Africa, Pretoria, 11 September).

Evans, Matthew and Wilkins, David. (2017) Transformative Justice, Reparations and Transatlantic Slavery. *Social and Legal Studies*. DOI: 10.1177/0964663917746490.

Gissel, Line Engbo. (2017) Contemporary Transitional Justice: Normalising a Politics of Exception. *Global Society*, 31(3), 353–369.

Gready, Paul. (2014) Transformation without Transition in Egypt? *Transformative Justice in Egypt and Tunisia*, 19 July. www.transformativejustice.co.uk/transformation-without-transition-egypt/ [accessed March 6, 2015].

Gready, Paul, Boesten, Jelke, Crawford, Gordon and Wilding, Polly. (2010) Transformative Justice: A Concept Note. Draft Concept Note Developed by the Worldwide Universities Network Transformative Justice Group, October.

Gready, Paul and Robins, Simon. (2014) From Transitional to Transformative Justice: A New Agenda for Practice. *International Journal of Transitional Justice*, 8(3), 339–361.

Guardian. (2017) The Guardian View on the ANC's New Leader: A Fresh Start. *The Guardian*, 18 December. www.theguardian.com/commentisfree/2017/dec/18/the-guardian-view-on-the-ancs-new-leader-a-fresh-start [accessed December 21, 2017].

Heunis, Lorraine and Hoedemaker, Eleanor. (2012) Personal interview, Cape Town, South Africa, 7 August.

ISN Gauteng Provincial Leadership. (2015) Personal interview, Johannesburg, South Africa, 13 March.

Jacobs, Mario. (2012) Personal interview, Cape Town, South Africa, 30 July.

Keck, Margaret E. and Sikkink, Kathryn. (1998) *Activists beyond Borders: Advocacy Networks in International Politics* (Ithaca: Cornell University Press).

Legassick, Martin. (2010) Personal interview, Cape Town, South Africa, 4 August.

Mail and Guardian. (2017) Slates Dashed in Top-Six Election. *Mail and Guardian*, 18 December. https://mg.co.za/article/2017-12-18-slates-dashed-in-top-six-election [accessed December 21, 2017].

Makwela, Mike and Simelane, Hloniphile. (2015) Personal interview, Johannesburg, South Africa, 13 May.

McAuliffe, Pádraig. (2017) *Transformative Transitional Justice and the Malleability of Post-Conflict States* (Cheltenham: Edward Elgar).

Pithouse, Richard. (2016) *Writing the Decline: On the Struggle for South Africa's Democracy* (Johannesburg: Jacana Media).

Risse, Thomas and Ropp, Stephen C. (2013) Introduction and Overview. In *The Persistent Power of Human Rights: From Commitment to Compliance*, edited by Thomas Risse, Stephen C. Ropp and Kathryn Sikkink (New York: Cambridge University Press), 3–25.

Risse, Thomas and Sikkink, Kathryn. (1999) The Socialization of Human Rights Norms into Domestic Practices: Introduction. In *The Power of Human Rights: International Norms and Domestic Change*, edited by Thomas Risse, Stephen C. Ropp and Kathryn Sikkink (Cambridge: Cambridge University Press), 1–38.

Sibanda, Shereza. (2015) Personal interview, Johannesburg, South Africa, 12 March.

South African History Online. (2011) National Party (NP). *South African History Online*, 30 March. www.sahistory.org.za/topic/national-party-np [accessed September 7, 2017].

Swartz, Sharlene. (2016) *Another Country: Everyday Social Restitution* (Cape Town: BestRed).

Tissington, Kate. (2012) "Tacticians in the Struggle for Change"? Exploring the Dynamics between Legal Organisations and Social Movements Engaged in Rights-Based Struggles in South Africa. In *Contesting Transformation: Popular Resistance in Twenty-First-Century South Africa*, edited by Marcelle C. Dawson and Luke Sinwell (London: Pluto Press), 201–221.

van Rensburg, Sandra. (2015) Personal interview, Johannesburg, South Africa, 13 March.

Waldorf, Lars. (2012) Anticipating the Past: Transitional Justice and Socio-Economic Wrongs. *Social and Legal Studies*, 21(2), 171–186.

Wa Mapena, Matserane. (2015) Personal interview, Johannesburg, South Africa, 2 November.

Zuern, Elke. (2011) *The Politics of Necessity: Community Organizing and Democracy in South Africa* (Madison: University of Wisconsin Press).

Chapter 6

Conclusion

Introduction

Based upon an exploration of the case study network, this book has sought to address the following overarching question: can transformative justice be advanced through networks of trade unions, social movements and NGOs in the global South? This question is important for several reasons.

First, there are gaps in the existing literature with regard to investigation of advocacy and activist networks based primarily or solely in the global South. Second, there are few existing studies focused on discussion of networks which are made up of actors other than NGOs. This is particularly the case with regard to discussion of networks which could be defined as human rights networks. Within the existing literature, it is often the case that any discussion there is of diverse actors in advocacy networks (such as trade unions and social movements) frames these as part of labour networks or other framings which do not explicitly overlap with human rights and/ or are discussed from the perspective of NGOs engaging with other actors in the human rights and transitional justice-oriented networks which much of the literature concentrates upon. This book takes a broader view of human rights and consequently a broader view of the networks which may be analysed in reference to human rights.

Related to this, the main research question arises from the lack of a significant body of existing literature on transformative justice. In particular, transformative justice provides a framework through which it is possible to coherently analyse the networks identified as falling outside the focus of the existing literature due to their diverse composition, Southern location and issue focus on socioeconomic concerns and other human rights and human rights-overlapping issues. However, the lack of existing literature on the subject leads to the necessity in this research of asking what role the abovementioned actors might play in advancing the theory and practice of transformative justice.

The importance of power and of political responsibilities

The previous chapter highlighted the relationships between processes of transformative justice and outcomes, between outcomes and actors' (financial and non-financial) resources, and between the pursuit of political responsibility and transformative justice. Here, these are taken further, with a particular emphasis on the ways in which the findings from the case study can shed light on broader questions or be applied to other case studies. The theme of power is discussed next. Following this, the importance of political responsibilities and their interaction with transformative justice is emphasised.

Both the strengths and the weaknesses of the case study network and action taken by its components indicate the importance of power to the pursuit of transformative justice. Power takes many forms and does not simply exist in the formal sphere, though this is important. In thinking through how transformative justice might be pursued, including with regard to land distribution and housing provision, it is necessary to confront the possibilities and limitations produced through the balances of power which actually exist.

The degree to which actors in the case study network are constrained by access to financial and non-financial resources gives an indication of the importance of access to – and control over – resources in producing power dynamics which are either more or less problematic from the perspective of pursuing transformative justice. Access to resources is a form of power which is most clearly held by the larger, more formal elements of the case study network – and, indeed, in analogous networks elsewhere. In order to prevent imbalances in resources from translating into significant and problematic imbalances in power which are likely to undermine transformative justice (e.g. by reducing the possibility of affected communities shaping the agenda of policy and practice), politically responsible action is required in networks such as the case study.

As emphasised throughout the book, political responsibility and transformative justice are (or at least ought to be) synergistic processes. Participation by affected communities in shaping the agenda of policy and practice is necessary for transformative justice. For this to be most effectively (and responsibly) facilitated it is necessary for actors (whether informal and grassroots or professionalised and well-resourced) to take account of, and implement, the kinds of processes called for in a political responsibilities framework, particularly as adapted in this book. The lessons for research and practice which are highlighted in this chapter are concerned especially with this area, with a focus on areas identified in the case study where action might be taken to improve political responsibilities, and the wider application these might have to actors in contexts other than the case study.

Lessons for research and practice

Participants in networks should take steps to develop and improve communication and the dissemination of information amongst those with whom they have existing relationships and those with whom relationships may be sought in the future. In particular, efforts should be made to explain appropriately and in detail the reasons behind strategic decisions and to explain structural and other limitations on action. It was identified earlier in the book that in the case study network the Housing Assembly cluster of actors and the Poor People's Alliance cluster of actors share many of the same goals and rhetorical commitments. There appears, however, to at times be a state of confusion with regard to the actors which make up these clusters understanding each other's positions. Confusions such as this limit the extent to which actors with similar aims and commitments (such as the two clusters highlighted in the case study) are able to forge links with each other and, as a consequence, limits the extent to which networks in which they participate are effective as a whole.

In practice, this means that more professionalised and comparatively well-resourced network members such as NGOs and trade unions should be clear in their interactions with grassroots organisations and non-professional social movements what their approach is and why, and about what the legal, financial or other constraints there are on the action they take. This means explaining when and why funds can be used for specific purposes only. It also means engaging in open discussion with partners and potential partners about proposed strategies and putting forward detailed defences of these.

This has particular implications for actors such as grassroots community-based organisations and non-professional social movements in networks. These groups and organisations should on the one hand be prepared to actively discuss their own analyses and proposed strategies, providing explanation for the courses of action preferred and defences of the positions taken. On the other hand, these groups and organisations should also be prepared to listen and receive communication. For communication and information sharing to be improved, there has to be a multifaceted dialogue.

Both professionalised organisations and grassroots actors should be prepared to engage in discussion with one another with a view to gaining better understanding of the convergences and tensions in their positions. In the case study network for instance, if communication was improved between the social movements which make up the Poor People's Alliance and the various groups and organisations which make up the Housing Assembly, the case study network would be strengthened. A stronger and more unified network is better able to take action.

It was noted earlier in the book that one of the key opportunities for strengthening the case study network comes from an exploration of the relationships which tie network nodes at an individual rather than an organisational level. It was also noted that the influence of individuals can lead to the breaking down of network relationships and the failure to fully live up to political responsibilities. In order to reduce this risk as much as possible, and in order to maximise the opportunities individual relationships represent, networks (and the actors which make them up) should recognise and actively reflect on the importance of individuals to establishing (or destabilising) relationships. Groups and organisations within networks, or seeking to establish networks, should develop their existing ties with individuals associated with organisations which they are not already formally partnered with. This is not an outright replacement for organisational relationships. However, particularly in the event of organisational scepticism of a mooted relationship on behalf of one party, links to individuals and the development of these offers a means by which some form of collaboration may still be pursued. Indeed, it may be possible to establish better communication channels and shared understandings in this manner. Moreover, if successful, individual relationships can contribute to the establishment of closer organisational relationships which otherwise it might not be possible to establish.

In building these relationships, emphasis should be placed upon exploring the common ground which exists between actors. Moreover, the possibility of coming to mutually acceptable positions regarding analysis and strategy should be explored as a priority in building relationships. Similarly, any scope for developing greater links in formal – or at least transparent – organisational relationships should be discussed and explored with any individuals with whom it is possible to build relationships between formally disparate actors. Indeed, it is worth noting that the research for this book did reveal collaboration between apparently disparate actors in the case study network, that this collaboration can be positive in terms of the politically responsible pursuit of transformative justice and that it could be built upon. Specifically, the discussion in Chapters 3 and 4 highlights the relationships which exist between the Poor People's Alliance and Housing Assembly clusters. These include relationships between social movements such as the (Poor People's Alliance–affiliated) AEC (which have at times expressed antagonism towards NGOs and COSATU-affiliated unions) and Housing Assembly–linked actors such as the NGO ILRIG and the (COSATU-affiliated) trade union SAMWU.

The book earlier emphasised that transparency in relationships may be a more useful measure of a network's political responsibility than formalisation of relationships. The importance for transformative justice processes of clear means by which affected communities can articulate their concerns and interrogate or contest established approaches is also highlighted throughout the book. With this lesson in mind, it is recommended that members of networks strive to increase and maintain transparency in their relationships and actions.

Increasing transparency has several aspects. With regard to network relationships, important areas where transparency could usefully be increased on the basis of the case study findings are in relation to the extent and scope of partnerships. In practice, this particularly relates to the ways in which network nodes frame their commitments to one another in terms of time, resources and the limits of action. Some relationships within the case study network, such as those between social movements and organisations which provide legal support, are clearly limited in their scope. Other relationships appear broader. However, critical risks are apparent in cases where relationships fail to live up to one or more of the parties' expectations and understandings of the partnership. Groups and organisations in networks need to be clear about what it is they are able to offer each other. This means that network participants should take steps to ensure they are open in identifying the ways in which it is possible to work together and should identify limits to this work. For instance, areas where it is not possible to work together due to commitments to other partners, limits placed upon the use of financial resources or due to a lack of resources should be identified and discussed inasmuch as it is possible to do so.

With regard to processes of network action, key areas where transparency could usefully be increased in the case study network relate to decision making, resource distribution and accountability. Major criticisms of both the professionalised actors and grassroots movements involved in the case study network revolve around the perceptions of some that decision making by these actors is not accountable to those affected or that the distribution of resources (especially financial resources) is arbitrary, unfair or on some level corrupt. Increasing and maintaining transparency in these processes would address this problem to some extent. In particular, those criticisms which stem from the abovementioned lack of effective communication and information sharing between network members might also be addressed in part through increased transparency in the processes of taking action. On this basis, a key transferable lesson is that network participants should endeavour to ensure that decision-making processes and the reasoning behind strategic decisions and distribution of resources are clear to other network participants and open to scrutiny by those affected. In instances where this exists already in a network to some degree, care should be taken to maintain and to promote transparency. Where it is absent, steps should be taken by individual network nodes and their partners to develop transparency further.

Key contributions of the book

This book makes contributions to theory, methodology and practice. Whilst there are limitations to the research, important developments are made by this study. Principally these relate to the theorising of transformative justice, to the application of a range of methods and analytical frameworks to the case study and to the practical implications of the findings.

Transformative justice is, as noted earlier, a relatively young concept and is under-theorised. This study synthesised and applied a concept of transformative justice which significantly develops the existing literature in the area. This book argues that transformative justice ought to be considered as separate from transitional justice. It is argued that whilst transitional justice and transformative justice may overlap at times (e.g. if transitional justice mechanisms are able to contribute to transformative outcomes), that it is necessary for transformative justice to take a different focus than that of transitional justice and make use of a separate toolkit from transitional justice. The book proposes a number of areas upon which transformative justice should be focused and in doing so also begins to develop elements of a possible transformative justice toolkit. In particular, the book has highlighted the importance of processes to the pursuit of transformative justice, rather than focusing only upon outcomes. This definition, focus and proposed elements of a transformative justice toolkit lead to implications for how future research on – and practice aiming to further – transformative justice might be carried out and regarding the areas in which future transformative justice research might be fruitfully concentrated, and the ways in which this might be pursued.

Methodologically, research for this book builds upon and combines existing approaches. Importantly, the book makes use of tools adapted from social network analysis and applies these to the advocacy network which makes up the case study. This is a new contribution in the sense that sociological methods typically applied to individual social relationships are applied to organisational networks typically analysed from the perspective of comparative politics or international relations. Furthermore, the book adapts and applies a political responsibilities analysis. This builds upon the existing framework for analysing advocacy networks but contributes new insight by developing the analytical tools so that they can more appropriately be applied to the kind of network (domestic, not just made up of NGOs) explored in the case study. In these two ways, the study presented in the book adds to the range of methods used to investigate and analyse advocacy and activist networks.

In terms of the implications this might have for future research on transformative justice, it is worth considering both the ways in which transformative justice research is necessarily interdisciplinary and the ways in which relationships between social and political actors are fundamental to transformative justice. Transformative justice research draws on politics, law and sociology at least, with likely overlap with other disciplines such as anthropology and development studies (and perhaps, psychology – and more) (see, e.g., Gready et al. 2010; Gready and Robins 2014; Lambourne 2014). Isolating a single discipline and focusing upon its particular set of established methods and foci alone is likely to lead to an incomplete, partial account of what transformative justice is and could be, or the ways in which different actors might contribute to its realisation. Of course, no single study can do everything. There is, therefore, a need for future research on transformative justice to be mindful of the limits present in the approach of any given study as well as a need to be open to the possibilities thinking and acting across disciplinary divides might bring. In particular, a consideration of the ways in which a narrow legal focus in (some) transitional justice research has led to (some of) the very shortcomings in transitional justice which have been identified as needing to be addressed in transformative justice ought to spur researchers on to consider what (inter)disciplinary methods, techniques and lenses of analysis could reveal beyond established boundaries of mainstream transitional justice research (or of development, or other intersecting disciplines) (see, e.g., Gready et al. 2010; see also McAuliffe 2017; Bell 2009).

Furthermore, as this book argues, relationships between diverse actors are fundamental to transformative justice. This is particularly the case with regard to the imperative to include affected communities in the shaping of agendas claiming to address their needs or facilitate the realisation of their human rights. In pursuing this imperative, questions are raised about how one might go about interrogating the extent to which scope for the participation of affected communities exists in networks advocating transformative justice – or at least advocating positions which might compose elements of transformative justice. To this end, the methodological approach adopted in this book represents one way in which network relationships can be analysed and knowledge produced which addresses key elements of what transformative justice might be and how it might be pursued. Similar methods could be applied to future studies addressing other networks and potential sites of transformative justice.

Practical contributions of this study mostly come out of the recommendations for practice detailed earlier. In particular, attention should be drawn to the importance of transparency (not necessarily formalisation) of network relationships. This adds nuance to the existing literature on networks, which often proposes formal relationships as inherently more desirable than less formal ties (see, e.g., Jordan and Van Tuijl 2000). The study also produces knowledge with practical implications in relation to the findings that groups within the case study network which at times appear antagonistic towards one another share many of the same aims and rhetorical commitments, and in relation to the suggestion that those ties between these elements of the network which do exist (largely based on relationships with individuals) should be developed. If lessons such as these are heeded in the case study or other analogous networks, there would be an impact upon the practice of individual actors and on networks as a whole. Moreover, with regard to transformative justice in practice, these contributions are important in revealing ways in which the participation of affected communities, and the pursuit of transformative agendas, can concretely be developed in networks.

Beyond the case study, there are further, related, implications. For example, the lesson that relationships between groups and organisations can be initiated and developed through relationships between individuals can be applied to other networks. Similarly, an assessment of the degree to which shared rhetorical commitments of different – and perhaps, on the face of it, antagonistic – groups might translate into opportunities for greater or more effective collaboration could also be applied to networks other than the case study presented in this book. Moreover, the analytical tools used in this book, and the areas of priority for the pursuit of transformative justice (and the necessary, contributing, conditions for this) highlighted in the book have the potential to be applied beyond the case study (by researchers, practitioners or those at the nexus of the two).

What this book does not do

There are many things this book does not do. There are also limitations on what the study does achieve. Limitations are principally in relation to the overall scope of the research project, the methodological approach and gaps in the data collected. Limitations are a necessary consequence of carrying out a discrete research project. As these are outlined ahead, they should, on the one hand, be taken as a provocation to undertake further research with a view to addressing the gaps identified, and on the other hand, they should serve as a reminder that the end of the research process is to some degree artificial and that all research exposes limitations and gaps, raising new questions, even as it reveals new knowledge.

This study set out to explore the relationships between and approaches of NGOs, trade unions and social movements in the case study network and apply this to the research questions. Consequently, the book largely concentrates upon the ways in which different organisations and groups work together or do not work together, rather than on questions about the effectiveness or impact of their work. Issues such as the extent to which the state is influenced by actors in the case study network are largely outside the scope of this study. Questions surrounding the extent to which material outcomes are influenced by the action of the case study network also fall outside the remit of this study for the most part. For these reasons, it is not possible to draw as many wide-reaching conclusions or to make as many recommendations about the ways in which land and housing rights should be implemented or about the extent to which the network contributes to transformative outcomes than it is to, for example, identify ways in which politically responsible relationships might be pursued with a view to facilitating processes of transformative justice. These areas would be better explored through separate research projects designed specifically for the purpose. In part, this is because the nature of transformative justice requires taking a longer term view than transitional justice. There is not a clear time-bound start and end point after which transformative justice is over and the degree of transformation can be measured. Processes and outcomes are linked, but the kinds of outcomes which a study such as this can illuminate compose only part of the overall range of potential transformative outcomes which might be observed over a longer period of time, using additional and alternative methods of study.

A defence of case study research in general and a justification of the specific case study selection are provided in the introductory chapter of the book. Nevertheless, there are things that cannot be learned from the case study. It is not, for instance, possible to gain insight into the particularities of groups and organisations involved in action outside of the relatively narrow case study network. The focus of the study on actors in the urban Western Cape and urban Gauteng excludes the possibility of gaining significant knowledge of other actors such as those engaged in similar action in other areas of South Africa or internationally. The case study does demonstrate some important transferable lessons, and it is possible to generalise in some ways from this (see, e.g., Flyvbjerg 2006). For example, it is useful to observe that domestic advocacy networks of this sort exist, and it is not unreasonable to suggest that some of the challenges encountered by this network and some of the means of overcoming these challenges might also be applicable to other networks. In the specific detail, however, it is not possible to know with any certainty exactly what the character of relationships in other networks is or exactly what practical issues might emerge. This is one reason why the political responsibilities analytical framework is of use. The same framework may be applied to different case studies in order to produce an analysis based on the same points of reference and, in this sense, may be used to propose means of overcoming challenges which are framed in consistent terms.

There are necessarily some gaps in the data, especially primary data collected through interviews in the field. This kind of data collection is always limited by practical concerns. In this case, constraints included limits on the available time in which to conduct fieldwork and the problem of reliably making contact with potential research participants (given the nature of the research in terms of shifting and developing political situations and organisational changes, as well as the impact of the broader social and economic context in which the groups and organisations focused upon operate). In addition (and somewhat related) to this, there are, necessarily, gaps in the data due to the emergence of some themes and points of interest in the research after substantive data collection had taken place, or after key research participants had been interviewed and without the available option of conducting multiple interviews in all cases, and due to some interview responses lacking detail in areas which might have been useful for the research project.[1]

The study relies upon interviews with key informants conducted between 2010 and 2015. These informants were largely leaders, practitioners, activists or staff members at groups and organisations involved in the case study network. As such, these interviewees were well placed to discuss their organisations' ties to other groups, their strategies and their analytical positions. Furthermore, rich data on the key areas discussed in the book were successfully collected through this research processes. Data saturation was reached relatively early on in the data collection process (see Baker and Edwards 2012). On the one hand, some areas, which are focused upon in the book, were revealed with relative ease by the research. On the other hand, areas about which there are gaps in the data collected represent issues which are more difficult to illuminate through the research process used. The presence of these gaps points to both the potential for future research to address these and to the possible scope for other methods to be used in order to augment those applied here and, perhaps, shed light on the areas where gaps currently exist.

Concluding remarks

In a sense, both the more robust findings and the necessary limitations of the research put forward in this book imply areas where future research could be concentrated. Broadly, two main areas where conclusions can be drawn, and where further research ought to be pursued, emerge. These are the theory and practice of transformative justice (for future research, particularly in relation to tools for promoting transformative outcomes), and the action and composition of networks (for future research, particularly comparative study of domestic networks).

This book concentrates on theorising transformative justice and on the processes of transformative justice. In particular, the study focused upon the action taken by NGOs, social movements and trade unions with regard to the right to housing (and related areas) in post-apartheid South Africa. With regard to the contributions these actors make (or can make) to transformative justice, particular attention should be drawn to the role of these kinds of groups and organisations (and the networks which link them together) in facilitating the participation of affected communities in expressing their concerns and shaping political agendas in such a way that untransformative paradigms (and the persistence of structural violence) may be challenged and more transformative positions may be articulated and pursued. This is important and further research could be carried out exploring means by which affected communities' contestation and challenging of structural violence might be facilitated. However, given this book does not significantly investigate the specifics of how transformative justice outcomes might be promoted (especially at the level of state action), this may be a more crucial area into which further research may be needed.

An important question raised by this research is regarding the tools which could be used to promote transformative justice. If transformative justice is separate from transitional justice (as this book argues), then there is a need to develop a separate toolkit for promoting transformative justice. Future research in this area might concern itself with asking what policies, programmes and methods in the governmental, nongovernmental or intergovernmental spheres might be created or adapted to promote transformative outcomes. Chapter 5 of this book goes some way to beginning this discussion. Nevertheless, particularly with regard to exploring transformative justice policies and practices in contexts other than South Africa, it will be necessary to go beyond what this book provides. Indeed, keeping in mind the aim of transformative justice to avoid overly prescriptive top-down interventions, a book such as this ought not to attempt to provide a recipe or formula for universal application. Instead, each different context should be treated as distinct. This does not, however, mean that no transferable lessons can be learned from the specifics of the particular context explored in this book. Indeed, one lesson concerns the need for transformative justice to respond to the actually existing conditions present in any given context, rather than relying upon prefabricated solutions. Further lessons also emerge from this research. For instance, the importance of considering transitional justice to be separate from, and longer term than (even while – potentially – concurrent to) transitional justice leads to consideration of tools and mechanisms outside the ordinary remit, and time-bound scope, of transitional justice.

On the basis of the analysis of the existing literature on advocacy networks put forward in this book, it is clear there is a gap with regard to discussion of domestic networks. This book contributes towards filling this gap. However, further questions are raised which could form the basis of further research building upon this study. There is for instance, a question raised by this study about the political responsibilities of network members. This is particularly in relation to how responsibilities may be improved and, especially in the context of pursuing transformative justice, whether there is a means by which the appropriateness or otherwise of network members' relationships with the state, state-aligned actors or the interests of powerful actors separate to the grassroots and affected communities might be assessed. The study concluded that networks of trade unions, NGOs and social movements can contribute to advancing transformative justice. Future research could focus in greater detail on the barriers to advancing transformative justice, including within networks. It would be worthwhile conducting research into instances where network action of this sort does not contribute to transformative justice. Similarly, comparative study of other networks would further shed light on the ways in which networks (especially domestic networks) operate and whether it might be possible to improve their praxis to further contribute to transformative justice.

By way of final, concluding, remarks, the following should be emphasised. This book puts forward original contributions to the study of transformative justice, of human rights more broadly, of advocacy networks and of post-apartheid South Africa. In doing so, the book significantly develops the existing scholarship in these areas, particularly with regard to the theorisation of transformative justice. It will be necessary for future research in these areas, especially research which reflects upon practice, to relate to the ideas and concepts set out in this book, as well as the small (but increasing) body of transformative justice research. Through this ongoing, dialectical, conversation the gaps between scholarly ambition and empirical reality in transformative justice, and the gaps between research and practice, might be bridged to a greater extent than has so far been achieved. This book serves to begin this process.

Note

1 It was not, for example, possible to gain a full picture of all the political responsibilities of the case study network due to some areas not having been discussed in any detail by research participants.

References

Baker, Sarah Elsie and Edwards, Rosalind. (2012) *How Many Qualitative Interviews Is Enough? Expert Voices and Early Career Reflections on Sampling and Cases in Qualitative Research*. Review Paper, National Centre for Research Methods (Southampton: Economic and Social Research Council).

Bell, Christine. (2009) Transitional Justice, Interdisciplinarity and the State of the "Field" or "Non-Field". *International Journal of Transitional Justice*, 3(1), 5–27.

Flyvbjerg, Bent. (2006) Five Misunderstandings about Case-Study Research. *Qualitative Inquiry*, 12(2), 219–220.

Gready, Paul, Boesten, Jelke, Crawford, Gordon and Wilding, Polly. (2010) Transformative Justice: A Concept Note. Draft Concept Note Developed by the Worldwide Universities Network Transformative Justice Group, October.

Gready, Paul and Robins, Simon. (2014) From Transitional to Transformative Justice: A New Agenda for Practice. *International Journal of Transitional Justice*, 8(3), 339–361.

Jordan, Lisa and Van Tuijl, Peter. (2000) Political Responsibility in Transnational NGO Advocacy. *World Development*, 28(12), 2051–2065.

Lambourne, Wendy. (2014) Transformative Justice, Reconciliation and Peacebuilding. In *Transitional Justice Theories*, edited by Susanne Buckley-Zistel, Teresa Koloma Beck, Christian Braun and Friederike Mieth (Abingdon: Routledge), 19–39.

McAuliffe, Pádraig. (2017) *Transformative Transitional Justice and the Malleability of Post-Conflict States* (Cheltenham: Edward Elgar).

Index

Note: *Italicized* page numbers indicate a figure on the corresponding page. Page numbers in **bold** indicate a table on the corresponding page.

For Product Safety Concerns and Information please contact our
EU representative GPSR@taylorandfrancis.com Taylor & Francis
Verlag GmbH, Kaufingerstraße 24, 80331 München, Germany